A Publication of
The Institute of Irish Studies
Queen's University, Belfast

THE EARLY ENGLISH AND CELTIC LYRIC

THE EARLY ENGLISH
AND CELTIC LYRIC

BY

P. L. HENRY

B.A., M.Econ.Sc., D. Phil.
Reader in Celtic, Queen's University
Belfast

LONDON: GEORGE ALLEN & UNWIN LTD.
NEW YORK: BARNES & NOBLE INC.

PRINTED IN GREAT BRITAIN

TO MY MOTHER

FOREWORD

It is a pleasant duty to express my obligation to all those who have helped in the production of the present study, among whom I would wish to include my predecessors in the field.

I have to thank my colleague Professor H. Wagner for many constructive observations in the course of the work, and for his views on the completed manuscript. I am also indebted to Professor Proinsias Mac Cana for reading the MS and for several critical comments on the Irish and Welsh sections of it. To Professor Gearóid Mac Eoin I owe some improvements in the reading and interpretation of the two Irish poems edited in Chapter III. I have also to thank members of the R.I.A. dictionary staff who enabled me to consult unpublished material, and the editors of *Die Sprache* and of ZCP for permission to reprint *The Opening Of The Finnsburg Fragment* (Chapter XIII), and matter in Appendix IIa, respectively.

I owe a special debt to The Institute Of Irish Studies of Queen's University for their gracious acceptance of this work to initiate their series.

CONTENTS

ABBREVIATIONS

(Established abbreviations of *English* source-titles are adopted; others
are intended to be transparent, and radical contractions are avoided.
Titles of *Edda* poems are occasionally contracted to their initial syllable.
For Irish cf. further *Contributions to a Dictionary of the Irish Language,*
Royal Irish Academy, Dublin)

ACL	*Archiv für celtische Lexikographie* III, edd. W. Stokes, K. Meyer, Halle, 1907
A.L.	A. Owen, *Ancient Laws and Institutes of Wales,* 1841
BB	Facs. of *Book of Ballymote* (1887)
BBC	*The Black Book of Carmarthen* (ed. G. Evans, Pwllheli, 1907)
BBCS	*The Bulletin of the Board of Celtic Studies.* Cardiff 1921–
B.T.	J. Bosworth and T. N. Toller, *An Anglo-Saxon Dictionary,* 1882 (Suppl. 1921)
CLlH	*Canu Llywarch Hen,* ed. Ifor Williams. Caerdydd, 1935
ECNP	K. Jackson, *Studies in Early Celtic Nature Poetry,* Cambridge, 1935
EIL	G. Murphy, *Early Irish Lyrics,* Oxford, 1956
EWGP	K. Jackson, *Early Welsh Gnomic Poems,* Caerdydd, 1935
Four Songs	K. Meyer, *Four Old Irish Songs of Summer and Winter,* London, 1903
H.E.	Bede's *Historia Ecclesiastica*
Heldensage	R. Thurneysen, *Die irische Helden- und Königsage bis zum siebzehnten Jahrhundert,* Halle, 1921
ITS	Irish Texts Society
KZ	*Kuhns Zeitschrift*
JEGP	*Journal of English and Germanic Philology*
LEWP	I. Williams, *Lectures on Early Welsh Poetry,* Dublin, 1954
LL	*The Book of Leinster*
LU	*Lebor na hUidre*
Med. Aev.	*Medium Aevum*
MLR	*Modern Language Review*

ABBREVIATIONS—*continued*

OE	Old English
ON	Old Norse
PBB	*Paul und Braunes Beiträge*
RC	*Revue Celtique*
RES	*Review of English Studies*
R.I.A.	Royal Irish Academy
W.	Welsh
W.B.	*The White Book of Rhydderch*
YBL	*Yellow Book of Lecan*
ZCP	*Zeitschrift für celtische Philologie*

A hedge of trees o'erhangs my head,
A blackbird sings a lay to me;
Above my booklet lined for words
The woodland birds trill out in glee.

A clear-voiced cuckoo calls to me
In mantle grey from heights of bough.
God keeps me well! for here I write
A scripture bright in great woods now.

*(From the Old Irish; cf. EIL,
p. 4, and R. Flower, The Irish Tradition, p. 43, who adds:)*

This is the poetry of the *ankerholds* in the woods so charmingly
described in the life of St Déglán of the Déisi (Plummer, VSH ii 58):

For he was in his own dear cell which he had built, himself for
himself. It is between wood and water in a strait and secret spot
on the sea's brink, and a clear stream flows by it from the wood to
the sea, and trees gird it beautifully round about . . .

INTRODUCTION

THE OLD ENGLISH LYRIC: *GENRE*, ORIGIN;
PENITENTIAL AND OUTCAST POETRY;
WELSH AND IRISH SOURCES; COURSE OF THE INVESTIGATION

In the course of his inquiry into the justification for speaking of the Old English elegy as a separate *genre* of poetry, B. J. Timmer came to the conclusion that only two of the nine O E lyrics, The *Wife's Lament* and *Wulf and Eadwacer*, contained the ingredients proper to the elegy[1]: lament over misery, separation from the loved one, banishment, change of luck, comparison with former happiness and a longing for love expressed in a lamenting tone. The remaining seven poems he would exclude from the elegiac genre on account of their different atmosphere and tone and because of the religious purpose of some of them. From the elegiac genre Heusler following Imelmann had already excluded the *Ruin*, the *Riming Poem* and the *Penitent's Prayer* as religious-didactic pieces.[2] Timmer further excludes *Wanderer* and *Seafarer* on the same grounds; the *Riming Poem* and the *Penitent's Prayer* as religious poems related to these; and the *Husband's Message* as completely lacking the elegiac tone. *The Ruin*, a descriptive poem, he would exclude on account of its lack of personal involvement, and *Deor* as a heroic lyric with too restricted an elegiac element to qualify for the *genre*. As a result of his findings Timmer sensibly suggests that we should avoid the name 'elegy' in the wider application, as it properly applies only to the two poems mentioned and to the laments in *Beowulf* 2247 ff., 2444 ff.; the appropriate and essential term 'elegiac mood' can be applied widely afield.

Timmer's classification is based on theme and tone and does not include formal criteria. The form of the poems varies from the sequence of alliterative long lines to embryonic verse-structure with refrain and other repetitive means.[3]

Prior to Timmer the Chadwicks had utilized for their vast comparative undertaking a broad frame based on rather heteroclite and sometimes overlapping criteria (*The Growth of Lit.* I, 28, 42). Cp. particularly their types B and E which happen to be most relevant for

---

[1] *The Elegiac Mood in Old English Poetry*, English Studies 24 (1942), 33–44.
[2] *Die Altergermanische Dichtung²*, Potsdam 1941, p. 146.
[3] Chronology: their time of composition is doubtful: *Deor*, c. 900, perhaps; *Penitent's Prayer*, late ninth, or tenth, century; the others may be eighth century; cp. p. 133, f.n. 1.

our present purposes. They assign our lyrics to Type B: Poems dealing with situation or emotion, and consisting wholly or mainly of speeches, and consider them under the heading 'Poetry and Saga relating to unspecified Individuals' (Chapter 14). This disposition is of course a far cry from *genre* analysis, and Type B accommodates much else besides the lyrics we are concerned with.

Not only the classification but also the antecedents of these poems is problematical. Heusler (op. cit., p. 150) was of the opinion that they owed little to the Germanic tradition of Klage— and Erblied and that their finer sentiment and feeling for nature indicated an outside source, possibly Celtic, in which he thinks of Welsh and Irish.

Welsh sources had already been touched upon by E. Sieper in his influential book *Die altenglische Elegie* (Strassburg, 1915). His distance from the subject (Die keltische Poesie . . . ist unendlich primitiv, p. 66) did not prevent Sieper from identifying certain common motifs and structural peculiarities in Old English and in poems of the Llywarch Hen and other Welsh cycles (p. 60 ff.). Indeed his Chapter III (Keltische Einflüsse) though obviously written at second hand and dated remains the fullest and most suggestive confrontation with relevant Welsh material. The title 'Keltische Einflüsse' not only marks Sieper's allegiance to the historical approach in the narrower genealogical sense (Germanic-Old English); it symbolizes also his neglect of the synchronic side: the elegy is an *a priori* Gattung or *genre* which does not require further analysis; it has its genealogy on the one hand; on the other it is disturbed by contiguous cultures which do not belong to the family tree.

In Part 2, Ch. 2 of his basic *Studies in Early Celtic Nature Poetry* (Cambridge, 1935) K. Jackson treats 'Elegy and Fenian Poetry' in a broad Celtic–English framework (as he does Gnomic Poetry in Ch. 3) and writes *inter alia* of contact areas between hermit and exile (or Wild Man) poetry. His tendency to draw sharp distinctions of type here (pp. 121–23) lead him to conclusions different from ours. Professor Jackson has made other notable contributions to the study of Irish and of Welsh literature.

In the course of her Introduction to her edition of *Seafarer* (Methuen, 1960) Mrs I. L. Gordon follows Sieper in sketching similarities between the O E 'elegies' and the Llywarch Hen poems. She discounts the probability of direct influence and points out that the 'over-all result is quite different in form and spirit'. But they derive she thinks from a common Celtic background; or in the words of N. K. Chadwick the OE lyric elegies are of 'Celtic inspiration'.

H. Pilch seeks a definitive solution for this problem in rather short compass. His interesting paper *The Elegiac Genre in Old English and Early Welsh Poetry*[1] seems however to be based on material evidence too slender and restricted for such a weighty theme. Omitted are references to Timmer and to Irish literature; also a discussion of the Welsh elegiac genre proper. Pilch sets out to establish an OE elegiac genre with the aid of the Chadwick frame. He then places the *Leper of Abercuawg* in the centre of a comparative treatment. Finally the Welsh poem is made to represent a *genre* in imitation of which the 'elegiac *genre* in Old English' was created. A further independent development of the two '*genres*' is posed on the basis of 'new themes such as the wife separated from her husband and lover'. (But such a separation is central to the Irish story of Suibhne Geilt and to the Suibhne-Eorann poem which we place beside the *Wife's Lament*, p. 27 below).

In her *Studien Zu Den Angelsächsischen Elegien* (Marburg, 1948), important for its comprehensive treatment, close analysis, and identification of leading key-words, E. D. Grubl uses the term 'elegy' in the older sense[2]. Particularly relevant is her study of the semantic fields of *cearu* and *sorg* (pp. 180 ff.), which for full interpretative purposes require the addition of the *longung* (*longaþ*) complex. On pp. 77 ff. she compares the figure in Bede H. E. II, 13 of human life in terms of a sparrow flying in through one door and out through another with the central themes of *Wanderer*, *Seafarer*, and *Riming Poem*: the transitoriness of this life and the quest of that which is eternal. Here she overlooks the point that the source of the sparrow simile is to be found in Psalms 10.2 and 123.7 (anima nostra sicut passer . . .). In fact many of the seeming obscurities of penitential poetry such as the *Penitent's Prayer* tend to dissolve when motifs from the Penitential Psalms are brought to bear upon them (cf. p. 179).

It is not possible to do justice here to the achievement of Mrs N. K. Chadwick in her wide-ranging investigations of Early English, Celtic and Early Norse literature and culture and of comparative literature in general—if only because they are continuing. Her treatment of

[1] ZCP 29 (1964), pp. 209–24 (basic text often only lightly paraphrased; cf. further p. 67, f.n. 2 *infra*).
[2] Cf. pp. 21–22. She deals with *Wanderer* and *Seafarer* under the heading *Vergänglichkeitsklagen*.

individual themes, as of *Geilt* (*Sc. Gaelic Studies* V (1942) 106 ff.) is perceptive and basic; inevitably one will make reservations on certain details of association and interpretation. Apart from literary analyses she offers—more characteristically perhaps—an analysis of institutions which provides a natural background for studies such as ours.

The present investigation owes its origin primarily to two independent observations of a comparative and interpretative kind on the *Seafarer*: lines 37–38 which speak of seeking the land of *peregrini* far away and 58–66a on the bird-soul ranging over the sea and returning later to the body. Both of these concepts so richly attested in Early Irish literature were immediately acceptable from a Celtic point of view and they proved on closer inspection to be on record elsewhere in Old English Poetry. When later we found that other scholars invoking Irish historical and literary connections had reached similar conclusions[1] we were encouraged to think that further analytic and comparative studies might help to clear a way through an area still largely uncharted: it has yet to be convincingly shown to what *genre* even the better-known poems such as *Wanderer* and *Seafarer* belong. That is to say, their place in the civilization and culture of their time is still obscure. We need to be clear not only about the theme and subject of the OE lyric but also about what underlies the selective process and motivates the treatment. Meanwhile the closely cognate aspects of Celtic literature which we originally thought to convey here as 'background' have had to be treated much more independently and fully so that a picture of the systems might emerge in which the detail functions.

The literary *genre* today is rarely more than a ready-made portmanteau term like *lyric, elegy, novel* serving for greater convenience in description.[2] As such its functional value is strictly limited. On the other hand the *genre* may be an object of investigation, an end-product ascertained by empiric examination of related individual poems. Each of these taken separately is thoroughly and comprehensively investigated on the basis of criteria extracted from itself. All aspects and levels of meaning have to be followed as far as they will lead us, naturally. Vital cruces have to be wrung of their secrets if possible so that

[1] Cf. D. Whitelock, The Interpretation of *The Seafarer*, in *The Early Cultures of North-West Europe*, edd. Fox-Dickins, Cambridge 1950, p. 261 ff. on *peregrinatio*; cf. p. 35 below; and V. Salmon, ' "The Wanderer" and "The Seafarer" and the Old English Conception of The Soul', MLR 55 (1960), pp. 1 ff.

[2] Cf. R. Wellek, A. Warren, *Theory of Literature*, Chapters 9, 17 (Peregrine Books Y 28, 1963).

one may penetrate through them to background revelations social cultural or institutional to which poems of a category can be intimately related. Cf. our section on *elþeodigra eard* below, p. 195 ff. For poetry as enigmatic—not to say mystifying—as much Early English and Welsh poetry is, this seems the only safe method.

The main result of our work on this level has been to establish an Old English *genre* of *penitential poetry* with *Seafarer* and *Penitent's Prayer* as chief exponents, flanked by the corresponding genres in Early Irish and Welsh. A test of the progress this may imply is the functional value accruing to the new term (*penitential*) in relation to individual poem, category and socio-cultural nexus as against the older one (*elegiac*). Moreover the residual Old English lyrics can be treated in the light of their relationship to this *genre*. In the compass of the present work it has not been possible to cover both tasks fully. Faced with a choice we have thought it advisable to consolidate our main finding and to leave the detailed treatment of the residual lyrics over.

The relation between these and the penitential lyric is intriguing and crucial. In Early Celtic and English, the penitential lyric is part of a wider context or framework of *outcast* poetry which in Welsh may be symbolized by the homeless wandering figures of Llywarch Hen and Heledd both of them fallen from high estate. A Welsh triad[1] presents them together with the unknown Llemenic in the following terms: *Tri trwydedawc llys arthur. a thri anuodawc. llywarch hen. a llemenic a heled* 'the three privileged guests at Arthur's Court and the three homeless wanderers Llywarch Hen, Llemennig, and Heledd'. The improbable association with Arthur evokes the earlier and happier period of attachment and the *comitatus* mirrored in *Finnsburg* and the *Gododdin*, when the retainer attached to his lord paid with his life if needs must for his mead.[2] Indeed the great Welsh poem is built around this theme of repayment. The Llywarch and Heledd[3] of later Welsh poetry and the period of dislocation represent the type of the misfortunate one marked out from the beginning by fate, the *improbus*, *direid nef a daear* 'outcast (wretch) of heaven and earth' (BBC 70) who contributes to his downfall with his tongue: pride goes before a fall. Cp.

---

[1] Cf. I. Williams, *The Poems of Llywarch Hên*, p. 34 (Sir John Rhŷs Memorial Lecture 1932), R. Bromwich, *Trioedd Ynys Prydein*, Cardiff 1961, p. 172.
[2] Cf. KZ 77, p. 140 ff., Göttingen, 1961.
[3] Chronology: their two cycles are referred by I. Williams to *c.* AD 850 (CLlH p. lxxiii).

the portrayal of the proud and the humble man in *Vainglory*, Ex. Book 147 ff.

The antithesis which Welsh poetry suggests on the vertical plane between the *retainer who belongs* and the *friendless forlorn one* it develops too on the synchronic: so in st. 31 of the *Leper of Abercuawg* (CLlH, p. 23 ff; p. 74 *infra*) the outcast for whom God's clemency is invoked is described as former page (*mackwy*) and bold warrior (*goewin gynran*) in a royal household.—Its final stanza depicts the wretched one praying in an oratory and suggests modes of transition to penitential poetry. In the *Old Man's Lament* (ibid., p. 8 ff.) Llywarch is adroitly made to address his plaint of decline from an honourable place to his sole remaining support, his stick. The *Lament on the Hearth of Rheged* (ibid., p. 18 f.) is a sustained confrontation of present decay with former princely life and portrays one source of the *outcast* theme, the fall of a royal house. Here some time has elapsed since the fall of Urien, Owein and Elphin and the poet speaks from a middle distance, as it were; whereas in the English poems *Ruin, Seafarer,* and *Wanderer* the former inhabitants are unknown and the setting promotes a more stylized *ubi sunt* treatment. For Old Irish parallels cf. Appendix III.

The antithesis between the happy and the hapless one is developed organically in *Seafarer, Wanderer* and the *Riming Poem*; it is incorporated into *Deor* (35 ff.) and apparently too in the *Penitent's Prayer* (114 ff.). The *Wife's Lament* and *Wulf and Eadwacer* embody the themes of loneliness and separation, and the *Husband's Message,* different in tone from these, shares the situation of exile.

The relation of Old English *penitential* to *exile* poetry referred to above is mirrored in OE Law: *peregrinatio* is a sub-type of exile there and shares with it the designation *wræcsið* (F. Liebermann, Gesetze Der Angelsachsen, Scientia Aalen, 1960, II 617, 706), and the term *wræcnian* 'to be in exile or on pilgrimage'; cf. also *forwrecen* 'peregrinus' Luke 24: 18. Besides, the outlaw (*friðleas, wrecca, utlah, fliema*) is often automatically excommunicated, to become *Godes fliema (utlaga), utlah wið God* (ibid. II, *sub friedlos* 2, 14).

The technical connotation of words occurring in the poems may offer vital clues to the interpretation of these: *freondleas* (*Wanderer* 28) has the legal meanings 'kinless' and 'outcast' (: *friðleas* 'expulsus'); synonyms are *wineleas* and *wrecca* (*Wife's Lament* 10, *Wanderer* 45, *Seafarer* 15 . . .). Here also belongs the term *wulf* 'outlaw': cf. Exeter Gnomes 147 *wineleas wonsælig mon genimeð him wulfas to geferan* . . . 'the friendless unfortunate one makes companions of wolves (very treacherous beasts; very often that companion rends him)'. In OE law the stranger (*ælþeodig, cuma*), wandering unannounced off the highway, is liable to death or capture on suspicion of theft (i.e. as *wealdgenga*); the outlaw is described as (*ge)fah wið þone cyng and ealle his frind, utlah wið eall folc, utlah wið God and men* (ibid. sub *friedlos* 1n, o). This meaning suits admirably the context of *Wulf and Eadwacer* where *wulf* occurs as proper name in 4, 9, 13², 17 (cf. *bireð Wulf to wuda*).

In the *Wife's Lament* the technical aspect is of particular importance. For *fah* cf. 46. The technical meanings of *fæhðu* and *folgað* have been noted by R. F. Leslie, Three Old English Elegies, Manchester 1961, pp. 7, 53, 55. The poem makes it clear that the husband (technically *hlaford*, earlier *ealdor*) strives to safeguard the wife from legal involvement as accomplice in his deed. He is now an absconded *fliema* whose property is automatically forfeit and whose marriage is dissolved unless (as in our poems) it is cemented by love; he may not yet be a *proclamatus exul* (In Cn III 47). Her main dilemma is that the separation may become a permanent one (52–53). If she can prove her innocence in the test by ordeal she is entitled to maintenance in the form of *feoh* and *weotuma*. Although revenge in the blood-feud was directed principally against the blood-relations of the culprit, it seems clear that in the eighth century the culprit's wife and retainers might be the victims of reprisal (Liebermann II, *sub* Blutrache 5 ff.). Hence *Wife's Lament* 25–26 (*fæhðu dreogan*) may include dire as well as merely unpleasant consequences. She is placed under the care of her husband's kin, not only for protection, but because they have certain legal responsibilities towards her: they may be liable for any fine she may incur, and in certain circumstances for administering her estate, as a widow. It is not certain that *folgað secan* in 9 implies seeking her husband rather than another protector, nor, in view of 8, does it seem very likely, though the context in 12–14 may seem to support it. She is estranged from her husband's kin, who wish to establish a permanent separation between the two of them. There can be a clash of interests about the husband's property, which in normal circumstances she would inherit provided they had family, otherwise half of it; she does not inherit, however, if she remarries. (So Wif 4; otherwise in other Laws.) By seeking another protector to represent her interests she widens the breach.

Opposed to the situation of exile is *eðel*, technically, 'home and civil status of landowner '(Liebermann II, s.v.); with this *eard* can be practically identical (*eðles* II Cn 41 = *eardes* VIII Atr 26). In connection with the crux MS. *heard*, Wife's Lament 15, note that in II Cn 1 the late MS. A reads *heard* for *eard* of the other MSS.

The double application of *dryhten* ('earthly lord; God') in *Seafarer* 41, 43 is also found in the Laws.

The importance of the exilic theme outside as well as inside the Old English lyric has been illustrated by way of studies in the formulaic and conventional character of O E poetic diction.[1] The complete apparatus of such studies, a concordance of verbal and thematic formulae in O E poetry, ought to provide a useful basis for its deeper appreciation and clearer assessment. We are inclined to think that a further development of these studies will inevitably lead outwards towards the comparative aspect. For example F. P. Magoun terminates his article on *oral-formulaic character*[2] as follows: 'That tenth–eleventh century scribes at times separate verses (not our typographical lines) by dots may merely reflect a feeling for the basic rhythm, the onset of a down-beat, comparable to a musically unschooled person's tapping time with foot or finger though knowing nothing of the writing of music or of musical composition.' In view of the provenance of O E script and the occurrence of this as well as the feature he previously mentions (i.e. poetry written as prose) in Welsh and Irish manuscripts, it is obvious that the scope of such 'possible problems of the future' transcends the bounds of English philology in the narrower sense.

For the investigation of the Celtic background and the vital elucidation of O E poetry which this can now be expected to provide, Welsh sources alone though important are insufficient. To take a simple illustration: since Sieper's identification of the sad-voiced cuckoo this has been a staple of all treatments of Welsh 'influence' on the O E lyric. In fact however an Old Irish lyric fragment on the district of Femen (in South Tipperary?)—apparently a resort of hermits—is constructed round the association of saintly nostalgia (*ēolchaire nōeb*) with melodious cuckoo song (*cēolchaire chūach*):

Femen indiu is ferr a chách	mēt a thened is a thūath,
ēolchaire na nōeb cen dīth	crīch dian cōem cēolchaire chūach.

'Femen is better than ever today with the number of its hearths and

[1] S. B. Greenfield, 'The Formulaic Expression of the Theme of "Exile" in Anglo-Saxon Poetry', Speculum 30, p. 200 ff. (1955).

[2] 'Oral-Formulaic Character of Anglo-Saxon Narrative Poetry', Speculum 28, p. 446 ff. (1953).

INTRODUCTION

communities; yearning of imperishable saints, land of cuckoo-song so dear.'[1] Cf. the Welsh poem *Kintevin*, p. 67, and *Seafarer*, 53 ff.

The Irish tale of *Suibhne Geilt*[2] demonstrates *par excellence* the nexus between the outcast theme and the penitential motif. Its importance as a source appears from our contention (*infra* p. 198 ff.) that the English term *guilt*, O E *gelt, gylt* derives from Irish *gelt* in this meaning. This is supported by the fact that three British analogues of the *Suibhne* tale are on record: that of the Welsh Myrddin, the Merlin of the *Vita Merlini*, and Lailoken of the *Vita Kentegerni*. These legends belong to South-West Scotland where in the Suibhne tale (§§ 46–50) a fourth figure called Fer Caille 'Man of the Wood' (alias Ealadhan, Alladhan) is encountered by Suibhne. The composite figure which these variants comprise is the prototype of the Wild Man of the Wood, and the tale basic to the several legends is, in the words of K. Jackson[3], briefly this: A man goes mad in a battle (Magh Rath A D 637, Suibhne; Arfderydd in Cumberland A D 574, Myrddin-Lailoken-Merlin) because of the curse of a saint (Suibhne) or a horrible vision in the sky (Lailoken; traces of it in Suibhne) or fear of the battle (traces in Suibhne) and grief for the slain (Merlin). He takes to a life in the woods (all), where he lives on berries, roots or apples, etc. (all). Being mad, he is a prophet, and has dealings with various visitors (all) to whom he prophesies (Myrddin, Lailoken, Merlin). Finally, he makes friends with a saint (Suibhne with Moling; Lailoken with Kentigern) and dies.

What this summary does not bring out is that the guilt-laden prince who is shocked out of his wits and out of normal social intercourse (*shunning mankind, keeping company with wolves*, line 1817) becomes by way of privation and penitence himself a saint before the tale is ended. From the beginning of his life of wandering outcast Suibhne recognizes that he is being justly punished by God for his crimes (§§ 14, 19, 27; lines 1144 ff., 1406 ff.); like a hermit he admonishes others (§ 23) and cries: O Christ, without sin, hear me, love me, sever me not from thy sweetness (ibid.). Indeed his first utterance at the beginning of his frenzied life (§ 14) fits into the hermit pattern: 'God has vouchsafed me here/life very bare, very narrow,/without music and without restful sleep,/without womenfolk, without a woman-

---

[1] K. Meyer. *Bruchstücke der älteren Lyrik Irlands*, Berlin 1919, p. 62.

[2] *Buile Shuibhne*, ed. J. G. O'Keeffe, I T S 12, London 1913; Mediaeval and Modern Irish Series, Dublin 1931 (quoted by line). The tale is a 12th century compilation from earlier originals, one of a cycle centring round the battle of Magh Rath, A D 637.

[3] 'The Motive of the Threefold Death in the Story of Suibhne Geilt', in *Féil-Sgríbhinn Eóin Mhic Néill*, Dublin 1940, p. 546.

tryst. . . . God has severed me from my form/know me no more, O warriors.' His life as an outcast is sinless (line 708), without reproach (2236), or harm to anyone (2242 ff.), and at the end he is the 'king, saint and saintly crazed one' (2186). So too from an early stage he frequents churches and their vicinity (§§ 20, 22, 24). For further detail cf. p. 198 ff.

A reference in the ninth or tenth century *Book of Acaill* to 'all the stories and all the poems which he left after him' suggests that much Suibhne literature must have been lost. But a considerable amount remains. In one of the earliest extant poems (*c.* 800, cf. EIL, p. 112) Suibhne is already established as a hermit with his oratory (*airiuclán*), thatched by 'his darling, God of Heaven', in an ivied tree-top. Poems testifying to Suibhne's association with S. Moling probably from the twelfth century tend to support this: cf. EIL, p. 114, st. 5, where longing (*ēolchaire*) seizes the poet to hear the birds' music (*cēolchaire*) as they chant the canonical hours. Cf. the comparable instance above, p. 24. In st. 8 the poet speaks of the chanting of psalms and in 6 and 11 of Mass and canonical hours in conjunction with sounds of nature. Another poem in praise of the site of Moling's monastery (Anecd. II, p. 22) has been ascribed to the saint himself; it is entirely in the hermit tradition. Its subject is the dear hallowed glen of Suibhne's resurrection which the saint foretold he was to visit. In Suibhne's eulogy local features are suffused with a spiritual glow. In st. 13 he looks backwards: I travelled with hosts; red was my spearpoint;/To the great Lord I return thanks for directing me to this glen.

Suibhne Geilt, the king-saint, prophet[1]-poet and outcast-penitent forms a link between antiquity and medieval thought throughout North-Western Europe from Ireland to Scandinavia. His feather dress is reminiscent of the *tuigen* of the *fili* (likewise prophet and poet originally) and also of the Norse *fjaðrhamr* and of the shaman's costume. But such a (natural) covering is also the authentic dress of the Early Irish hermit (cf. p. 200): a poem on Oengus the Culdee (LB 106 b 25) represents him thus with a growth of young corn through his hair: while in Lism. L. pp. 260, 354 a holy man has a natural dress of bright bird-feathers only. On the scope and importance of bird-symbolization in a pagan as well as a Christian context we treat in some detail below. It has not been sufficiently appreciated that in the story of Suibhne the bird analogy (cf. §§ 11, 12) is developed to

---

[1] The gift of prophecy was a sign of increasing spiritual power, cf. the *Lives* of Antony, Benedict, Cuthbert, Columba . . .

the utmost (which explains for instance his meal and birdlike caution in § 77—points obscure to the editor, p. 172). We have referred above to the concept of the free-ranging soul (p. 20; p. 137 below). From *Guthlac*[1] 557 ff., 729 ff. it would appear that in OE circles the whole body was believed capable of such flight and if so Suibhne's powers of levitation—an original feature not found in his Welsh counterpart Myrddin—have to be taken into account. Connected with this is his role of *wanderer* (lines 91, 389, 416, 589, 1398; §§ 12, 17, 26 . . .) *deformed* (lines 583, 716 ff., 756), expiating his guilt and crimes. His deformation has a clear spiritual aspect and we may think here in terms of the bird-soul in travail. It is also in agreement with the medieval cult of the leper which we discuss below in connection with *Claf Abercuawc*, p. 74.

The Suibhne cycle provides a setting for the comparison of present privation with past splendour, happiness and comfort much exploited in Early Celtic and English poetry. Its whole framework reminds of the Welsh Ysgolan's crimes and penance (BBC p. 81; cf. p. 88 below). It also yields motifs which recur in the related literatures. Cf. the *gjalti* of *Hávamál*; the thickets overgrown with briars of *Wife's Lament*, 31: *Buile Shuibhne* 408 ff., 453 ff., 992 ff. The situation and treatment of the Suibhne/Eorann episode is very similar to that of this OE poem in which the rôles are however rather obscure:/*Buile Shuibhne* § 32, st. 2: Once thou didst utter, O great Eorann, a saying pleasing and light, that thou wouldst not survive parted one day from Suibhne:/*Wife's Lament* 21 ff.: We two had very often vowed that nothing else should part us but death alone . . . ; *Buile Shuibhne* § 32, 3c, d: Suibhne: warm for thee on the down of a pleasant bed, cold for me abroad till morn: *Wife's Lament*, 32 ff.: Very often did the absence of my lord afflict me here grievously. On the earth there are lovers who live dear to each other, sharing one bed, while I at dawn walk alone under the oak-tree through these caves of the earth. There must I sit during the long summer day, there can I weep my miseries, my many hardships. For I can never find rest from my anxiety of mind or from all the longing that has afflicted me in this life: Suibhne (st. 8): No path for a beloved lady is that of Suibhne here on the track of care;[2] cold are my beds at Ard Abhla . . . Eorann (previously): Though the king's son were to lead me/to blithe banqueting halls,/I had

---

[1] Cf. also the vision of Tortgith, Bede's H. E. iv. 9.
[2] MS *sliocht imnidh*; cf. OE *wræc-sìþ*, *wræc-lást*, keywords of the poems.

liefer sleep in a tree's narrow hollow/beside thee, my husband, could I do so. . . .

In both poems tone, basic situation (separation and misery of one partner), and scenery are closely similar. Both are largely built of the same elements: misery, sadness, anxiety, wandering; hostile briars and thorns; comparison with happier circumstances. . . . The *longing* and sleeplessness of the Wife are staple elements in Suibhne poetry (cf. *Buile Shuibhne* lines 968, 562–4, § 43) and the only perceptible difference is that one is in monologue the other in dialogue form. The conclusion is obvious, whatever its more immediate explanation may be.

Plan: The focus of the present work is Section 2, Chapters 6–11 with its study of *Seafarer*, *Wanderer*, and *Penitent's Prayer*; the penitential motif; and OE religious terminology. What precedes is intended— by and large—as a prelude or introduction; what follows as a further contribution to the theme of Hiberno–English cultural and literary connections.

The two opening chapters explore the background of *peregrinatio* (*ailithre*) in Ireland and Britain, the third its treatment as a theme in Irish literature. As the Early Celtic and English lyrics with which we are concerned are characterized in part by the incorporation of gnomic elements, this phase is entered upon in Chapter 4, which treats penitential and sententious poetry on analytic and comparative lines. This is followed in Chapter 5 by a summary account of the gnomic manner and matter of the contiguous literatures English, Irish, Icelandic and Welsh.

The central section (Chapters 6–11) is followed by a short study of *Cædmon's Hymn* as the earliest English poem and of *Finnsburg* as deriving in substance from the early Germanic tradition.

It will be apparent that our study of background and environment historical and literary in Chapters I–V arises out of the critical study of the poems attempted in Chapters VI–IX and is designed to prepare the reader for it. More specifically, it is the elucidation of the *personae* of the OE poems with their problems and circumstances which has called for background study. In a more summary treatment than is here attempted we should have first presented the study of the poems; as it is, we have allowed pedagogical considerations to dictate the order of treatment. Similarly, the interpretation of text in Ch. VI is accorded its logical priority as key to the total interpretation.

CHAPTER I

THE CHRISTIAN EXILE-SEAFARER

a. *Irish*

The *Anglo-Saxon Chronicle* reports in its annal for the year 891: . . . . And three Irishmen came to king Alfred in a boat without any oars, from Ireland, whence they had stolen away because they wished for the love of God to be on pilgrimage, they cared not where (*forþon þe hi woldon for Godes lufan on elþiodignesse beon, hi ne rohton hwær*). The boat in which they set out was made of two and a half hides, and they had taken with them provisions for a week and after a week they came to land in Cornwall, and soon went to king Alfred. Thus were they named: Dubhslaine and Macbeathadh and Maelinmhain . . .[1]

This account[2] admirably illustrates an Irish eremitical tradition which alone and in combination with coenobitical monasticism played a vital role in the history of the Early Irish Church.

The Old Irish term for pilgrim-exile is *ailithre,* that for life-long exile *ailithre cen tintúd,* lit. other-landness without returning. *Ailithre,* one of the three boons begged by Columba (*c.* 521–597), is fully described and motivated in his Life, in the Book of Lismore (Stokes, Lism. L., 20 ff., 168 ff.): this begins with the passage from Gen. 12. 1:

655. *Exi de terra tua et de domo patris tua, et uade in terram quam tibi monstrauero . . .*

658. The Lord Himself gave this friendly counsel unto the head of the perfect faith and of the complete belief, even unto Abraham son of

[1] Here follows the instructive remark: *⁊ Swifneh se betsta lareow þe on Scottum wæs gefor* 'and Suibhne, the best teacher among the Irish, died'.

[2] Cp. the commemoration of Egbert in *Félire Oengusso* (*c.* AD 800) on December 8th:

Buaid nIchtbrichtáin umail	The triumph of humble Egbert,
darrala tar romuir.	who came over the great sea:
do Chríst cachain figil	unto Christ he sang a prayer
hi curchán cen choduil.	in a hideless coracle.

This was probably the famous Ecgberht of H.E. III. 4; V 9, 22.

Terah, that he should leave his own country, to wit, the country of Chaldea, and that he should go for his pilgrimage into the land which God would show him, to wit, the Land of Promise . . .

667.   This is the tale that is made famous: the Lord himself enjoining Abraham to leave the country of Chaldea which was his own fatherland, and to go on a pilgrimage into the Land of Promise, because of the good which was to accrue therefrom to himself and his children, and to their offspring after them.

670. Now the man to whom God gave this counsel, even Abraham, it is he that is accounted in the Scripture as father to all the faithful: as the apostle certifies when he says, 'Verily', saith the apostle, 'the sons of Abraham are all who resemble him in perfect faith' (cf. Gal. iii. 7).

674. Now the good counsel which God enjoined here on the father of the faithful, to wit, on Abraham, it is incumbent on his sons after him, namely on all the faithful, to fulfil it, that is, to leave their country and their land, their wealth, and their worldly delight, for the sake of the Lord of the Elements, and to go into perfect pilgrimage in imitation of him.

679. Now, in three ways are men summoned to the knowledge of the Lord and to the membership of His family.

680. This is the first way: the urging and kindling of men by the divine grace to serve the Lord after the manner of Paul, and of Anthony, the monk, and of the other faithful monks who used to serve God there in Egypt.

683. Men are summoned in the second way (by a human being), to wit, by holy preachers who preach the divine Scripture to men after the example of Paul the Apostle, who preached to the Gentiles until he brought them by the net of the Gospel to the harbour of Life.

686. Men are summoned in the third way by necessity, that is, when they are constrained to serve God by tribulations and by the dangers of the world, or by separation from the temporal goods wherein they sojourn: after that example of the people of Israel, who turned to the Lord from the worship of idols and images when constrained by the tribulations which each of them found in foreign nations, as is related in the Scripture. Wherefore to declare that saith the prophet David: 'Whenever the people of Israel shall undergo tribulations and great

hardships, let them beseech and pray unto the Lord, that the Lord may thereafter free them from those hardships.'

694. Abraham therefore, the head of the perfect faith and of the complete belief, when he was urged by the divine grace, fulfilled the command which had been enjoined upon him by the Lord, that is, he went into the country of Chaldea till he reached the place where his father died; and he came thence into the Land of Promise.

698. Now, three ways there are in which one leaves his fatherland when he goes into pilgrimage; and there is one of these for which no reward is gotten from God, and two for which it is gotten. For when one leaves his fatherland in body only, and his mind does not sever from sins and vices, and yearneth not to practise virtues or good deeds, of the pilgrimage, then, that is made in that wise, there groweth neither fruit nor profit to the soul, but labour and motion of the body idly. For it little profiteth anyone to leave his fatherland unless he do good away from it. For even unto Abraham himself on leaving his own country, and after separating from it in the body, the Lord gave this counsel, and said: *Exi de terra tua,* 'take thy mind henceforward from thy country and thy land, and let not thy thoughts be turning to it again'. As if what God would clearly say to Abraham were: 'Shun both in body and in soul henceforward in thy pilgrimage the sins and vices of the country wherein thou hast hitherto dwelt in the body; for it is the same to anyone, as if he were still dwelling in his fatherland, should he copy in his pilgrimage the custom of his fatherland. For it is not by path (of feet) nor by motion of body that one draws nigh to God: but it is by practising virtues and good deeds.'

713. Now, at another time, one leaveth his fatherland in desire of heart and in mind, though he leaveth not in body; as happens to the ordained, who spend their lives in their own countries until death, for laymen and clerics detain them in the lands wherein they dwell, because of their great profitableness to them. Since it is not for the sake of the body that they continue in their fatherland, their good will avails them with the Lord as a pilgrimage.

720. At another time one leaves his fatherland completely in body and in soul even as the twelve apostles left, and those of the perfect pilgrimage, for whom the Lord foretold great good when he said in the Gospel: 'Take heed of this, for from a few to a multitude ye have forsaken for

my sake your country, and your carnal kindred, your wealth and your
worldly happiness that ye may receive a hundredfold of good from
Me here in the world and life everlasting yonder after the sentence of
Doom' (cf. Matt. xix. 29).

726. These, in sooth, are they of the perfect pilgrimage, in whose
person the prophet speaks: 'I give thee thanks for it, O God: I have
pilgrimage and exile in the world even as the elders who went before'
(cf. Ps. 38. 13).

730. Now, a multitude of the faithful servants of the Lord, both in the
Old Law and the New Testament, fulfilled perfectly this benevolent
counsel, and left their country and their land, and their native place
and their kindred in the flesh, for the sake of the Lord of the Elements,
and went in pilgrimage into far off foreign countries. Even as he
fulfilled it, and left the land of his birth for the love and fear of the
Lord, he the high saint and the high sage, and the son chosen of God,
for whom there is a festival and commemoration on the occurrence of
this season and time, even the archpresbyter of the island of the
Gael, the brand of battle set forth with the divers talents and gifts of
the Holy Ghost, to wit, the holy Colum Cille.[1]

Columba's biographer Adamnan (d. 704) speaks of him as *pro
Christo peregrinari volens,* and a quatrain in the language of the
eleventh century attributed to him when about to leave Ireland,
AD 563, runs:

> Fil súil nglais fégbas Érinn dar a hais;
> noco n-aceba íarmo-thá fíru Érenn nách a mná

'There is a blue eye which will look back at Ireland; never more shall
it see the men of Ireland nor her women' (Murphy, *Early Irish
Lyrics,* p. 64). In another anonymous poem of c. AD 1000 (ibid.,
p. 66) he is made to say: 'Away from Ireland sorrow filled me when I
was powerful, making me tearful and sad in the strange land to which
I came (lit. was put)':

> Rom-lín múich i n-ingnais Éirenn díamsa coimsech,
> 'san tír ainéoil conam-tharla taideóir toirsech.

[1] The perfect pilgrimage is also called *bánmartre* 'white matryrdom', *martre* retaining
the original connotation of 'testimony' in Gk. *martýrion,* and signifying 'the endurance
of tribulation for God's sake'. Cf. the Cambray Homily, Thes. II 246 f. and N. K.
Chadwick, *The Age of The Saints In The Early Celtic Church,* London 1963, pp. 93 ff.
The triad is completed by *dercmartre* 'red martyrdom' = martyrdom in the modern
sense, and *glasmartre* 'green martyrdom', i.e. separation from one's desires by means of
fasting and labour, or suffering toil in penance and repentance.

In fact, Columba did visit Ireland on more than one occasion, and his *peregrinatio* may have been a penance, imposed perhaps by his confessor (cf. J. T. Fowler, ed. *Adamnani Vita S. Columbae* Introd. lxiii, lxxi f. (Oxford 1894); W. Reeves, *Life of Saint Columba* (by Adamnan), p. 9 (Dublin 1857).

Columba's prophecies concerning the abortive voyages of the saintly Cormac Ua Liathain and Baitan in quest of a desert island in the sea are recorded by Adamnan in Books I, 6, II, 42; I, 20. Book I, 6 (A. O. and M. O. Anderson, *Adomnan's Life of Columba*, 222 ff., London, 1961) runs: Also at another time, Saint Columba prophesied and spoke thus concerning Cormac, Léthan's grandson, a holy man who sought with great labour not less than three times a desert in the ocean, and yet found none:

'Today again Cormac, desiring to find a desert, begins his voyage from the district that is called Eirros-domno, lying beyond the river Mód (Moy). But this time also he will not find what he seeks; and for no other fault on his part than that he has improperly taken with him as a companion of his voyage a man who, being the monk of a religious abbot, has departed without the abbot's consent.'

In Book II 42 Columba foresees that Cormac will land in the Orcades from a further voyage and commends him in advance to the king's protection. Cormac's peril on the high seas in a subsequent voyage is divined by the saint, who intercedes successfully for him. Of Baitan, who sought his blessing when about to embark, Columba prophesies (Book I 20): 'This man, who goes to seek a desert in the ocean, will not lie buried in a desert place . . .',—and the prophecy was fulfilled.

We may round off this account of early *ailithre* with the story— parallel to the Saxon Chronicle report—of the three young clerics who were successful in their quest (Book of Leinster, p. 283, Book of Lismore, fo. 84, c. 10 = Stokes, Lism. L., viii): 'Three young clerics of the men of Ireland went on their pilgrimage. It was fervently and heartily they went. There was no provision taken to sea save three cakes. "I will bring the little cat," says one of them. Now when they reached the shoulders of the main, "In Christ's name," say they, "let us cast away our oars into the sea, and throw ourselves on the mercy of our Lord." This was done. Not long afterwards they came with Christ's help to a beautiful island. Plenty of firewood was therein, plenty of water. "Let us build a church in the midst of our island." This they do. The little cat goes from them. It draws to them a veritable salmon, up to three salmons for every (canonical) hour. "O God," say they, "our pilgrimage is no pilgrimage now! We have brought provision with us, our cat to feed us. It is sad now to eat his catching. We will not partake of the cat's produce." Thereafter they abode for six watches without food, until a message came from Christ that (some) was on the altar, to wit, half a cake of wheat for each man, and a piece of fish. "Well, then, let each of us make known his work for Him who feeds us." "I will sing, first," says one of them, "the three fifty (psalms) every day, with celebrating my hours and with mass." "I will sing, then," says another, "the thrice fifty prayers, with celebrating my hours and with mass every day." "I will sing," says the third man, "a hundred and fifty *Hymnum dicats* every day, with celebrating my hours and with mass." ' When the first cleric dies, his religious duties are divided between his fellows, and when the second dies the third assumes the whole burden, which he soon finds intolerable. Whereupon he fasts against God, who seemed to him to love his companions more than him. An angel comes to chide him and to explain that his is the better part. Then he thanks God and is content,—'so he dwelt in his island till he was aged and withered, and till Brendan came from the sea: and Brendan blessed him and gave him communion and sacrifice, so he went to heaven: and a watch of angels is always over them in their island'.

This spirit of *ailithre* chiefly motivates the missionary labours of S. Columban. When he had spent many years in Bangor with S. Comgall 'he began to desire pilgrimage, mindful of that command of God to Abraham, "Get thee out of thy country and from thy kindred and from thy father's house, unto a land that I will show thee" '. (Jonas, *Vita Columbani* I § 4, p. 159 (B. Krusch, Hannover 1905)). Like Columba, he left Ireland without any definite goal, his one idea being to go far from his native soil, spreading the Gospel among foreign peoples on his way (L. Gougaud, *Christianity in Celtic Lands,* London 1932, p. 140). O. D. Watkins (*A History of Penance*, II, 612 f., London 1920) points out that the motive of Columban's departure from Ireland was mortification rather than missionary zeal:

'It will be noted in this narrative (of Columban's life, based on Jonas) that the missionary motive hardly appears. In fact the conversion of the heathen seems hardly to have entered the purview of the Irish monks who at this period began to overrun the Christian communities of continental Europe. When as in the case of S. Gall it came to them it came as the result of circumstances. They were monks, and the going forth into an unknown land seemed to them desirable in the first instance as being a further grade of mortification. It was indeed so regarded generally. Exile characterized the penances assigned in the penitential of S. Columbanus to the two heinous sins of murder and perjury. Absence from the home of his birth had been the saint's early remedy against temptation (i.e. against the entanglements of sex). It was now his louder call to leave his kindred and his father's house to go into a land which *God* would show him.'

Substantially the same conclusion is reached by J. L. G. Meissner (Report of the Church of Ireland Conference, Dublin, 1932, p. 79): 'The chief motive behind all this wandering of the early Celtic Saints was the salvation of their own souls, but it led as a matter of course to the preaching of the Gospel of Christ to the heathen, and produced the most wonderful missionary activity the world has ever witnessed.' The urge to evangelize, which seems to have been a product of the early expansion, became a motive of the later. Cf. J. F. Kenney, *The Sources for the Early History of Ireland* I, 488 (N.Y., 1929).

b. *Hiberno-English*

The concept of pilgrimage which we have discussed and illustrated in the foregoing pages was familiar to and practised by the English before the time of Bede. Irish missionary activity in Britain and the contact it generated are one obvious reason for this,—but Welsh example (*pace* Bede!) must also have counted—as it so generally did in the early Irish Church.

Accordingly, Prof. D. Whitelock applies as a matter of course and without comment to England and the English the definition of *peregrinus* which Kenney (Sources I, 488) specifies for the word 'as used in Ireland', when she says (Interpretation of *The Seafarer*, 268):

'*Peregrinus* had a wider meaning than our "pilgrim", often referring, to quote J. F. Kenney, to 'the man who, for his soul's good, departed from his homeland to dwell for a space of years, or for the rest of his life, in strange countries" .' She continues 'Bede speaks in similar terms of Willibrord, Wihtberht and the two Hewalds, all Englishmen living in Ireland. The presence of two Anglian runic inscriptions on the Isle of Man suggests that English *peregrini* went there also. The Old English version normally renders Bede's various phrases "on elþeodignesse lifian". The Irishman Fursey came to England because "he wolde for Godes lufon on elþiodignesse lifian". Many sought the Continent: Hild wished to lead the life of a pilgrim in the monastery of Chelles, "quo facilius perpetuam in caelis patriam posset mereri"; but Rome was naturally the chief resort . . .'

Here Prof. Whitelock adds examples and details,—as also of pilgrimages in the modern sense across the sea (pp. 268–69). Resuming on p. 270:

'From their correspondence and the statements of their biographers, it is abundantly clear that the Anglo-Saxon missionaries to the Continent regarded their mission as a pilgrimage and trusted to win a heavenly home by relinquishing their native land. Boniface calls himself "exulem Germanicum" and gives "timor Christi et amor peregrinationis" as the cause of his separation from his friends, and Archbishop Cuthbert uses the phrase 'in tam periculosa ac ferocitate plena peregrinatione pro amore aeternae patriae" with reference to his mission. The biographers refer frequently to the disregard for worldly goods and the contempt for transitory pleasures of this world, often quoting the promise of Matthew xix. 29. A few quotations will suffice . . .'

These follow for Wynnebald, Willibrord and Leoba. Then 'Instances could easily be multiplied, but enough have been given to show the prevalence of the desire for pilgrimage and exile as a means of obtaining eternal life.

The "peregrinatio pro amore Dei" or "propter nomen Domini" or "ob amorem Christi" plays, as is well known, a very important part in the Irish Church, and it occurs also in the lives of Welsh saints. In one of these Tatheus journeys from Ireland to Wales with eight companions in a ship, "sine instrumentis naualibus", which at once reminds us of the three Irishmen who . . . came to King Alfred in a boat without any steering gear, "because they wished for the love of God to be on pilgrimage, they cared not where". The wording "hi woldon for Godes lufan on elþiodignesse beon" is almost identical with phrases in the Old English translation of Bede. I submit that the poet of *The Seafarer* meant the same thing by "elþeodigra eard gesecan" and that he has given poetic expression to the impulse that sent numbers of his countrymen to the schools of Ireland, to the mission fields of Germany, and to the shrines of distant saints.'

It is apparent from Bede, H. E. III, 27, that for seventh century England Ireland was the land of instruction and spiritual guidance. The two nations formed a kind of religious and cultural commonwealth, and so Bede often extends his account of happenings in England to Ireland as a matter of course. It is natural for him to proceed from the ravages of a plague in England (AD 664) to the Irish scene (H. E. III, 27): 'This pestilence did no less harm in the island of Ireland. Many of the nobility, and of the lower ranks of the English nation, were there at that time, who, in the days of the Bishops Finan and Colman, forsaking their native island, retired thither, either for the sake of Divine studies, or of a more continent life; and some of them presently devoted themselves to a monastical life, others chose rather to apply themselves to study, going about from one master's cell to another. The Scots willingly received them all, and took care to supply them with food, as also to furnish them with books to read, and their teaching, gratis.'[1]

Then Bede tells a story of Ethelhun and Egbert, two very promising young Englishmen of noble blood, when they were in the Irish monastery of Rathmelsigi. Ethelhun was a brother of Ethelwin 'qui et ipse aeuo sequente Hiberniam gratia legendi adiit, et bene instructus patriam rediit, atque episcopus in prouincia Lindissi factus, multo ecclesiam tempore nobilissime rexit'. The story illustrates the theme of effective repentance before death, which recurs very often in H. E. and which therefore reinforces the traditional view that Bede himself composed the *Death-Song* associated with his name. It shows a certain kinship with the tale of the three clerical students (cited above, p. 33), and with that of the two clerical students who agreed that whichever of them dies first should come to the other with tidings of the other world (Lism. L., x-xii, LL 278a, Rawl. B. 512, fo. 140b, 2). The section most relevant for our purposes may be given in the OE version.[2] *Swelce he eac gehat geheht, þæt he á wolde for Gode his liif in elþeodignesse lifigan ⁊ næfre to Breotone ealonde hweorfan, þær he acenned wæs; ⁊ þæt he buton sealmsonge regollicra tída, gif him lichoman untrymnis ne wiðstóde, þæt æghwelce dæge alne saltere in gemynd þære godcundan herenesse ásunge; ⁊ þæt ælcere wucan dæg mid neahte ætgædre*

---

[1] J. Stevens and L. C. Jane, Transl. Everyman's Library 479, p. 154.
[2] T. Miller, *The Old English Version of Bede's Ecclesiastical History of The English People*, Part I, p. 242 (EETS 95, London 1890).

37

*áfæste. Mid þy he ða his gehat 7 bene 7 his tearas geendade, þa eode he
eft to his huse* . . . 'And he also made a vow, that he would for God's
sake live all his life in a foreign land, and never return to the island of
Britain, where he was born; and that besides psalm-singing at the
regular hours, if not prevented by bodily infirmity, he would every
day sing through the whole psalter in memory of the divine praise;
and that every week he would fast a night and a day continuously.
And when he had ended his vows, prayers, and tears, he returned
home . . .' The theme of pilgrim-exile is also found in combination
with details of religious observance in the Irish *Immrama* and Hermit
Poetry (cf. pp. 46 ff., 50 ff.).

It is clear too from Aldhelm's letter to his friend Eahfrid[1], who had
spent six years there 'uber sophiae sugens', that students flocked to
Ireland in swarms. Aldhelm mentions the subjects taught and is piqued
that the England of Theodore and Hadrian should need to have re-
course to the other island. He himself had benefited from both streams:
he had assumed the monastic habit in Maildub's monastery of Malmesbury while the Irish exile-hermit still lived, and had studied under
Maildub and Hadrian, succeeding the former as abbot.

Other notable instances of English pilgrims in Ireland are: H. E.
IV, 3 (Stevens-Jane, Transl. pp. 169, 245): 'Egbert . . . who long led
a monastic life with the same Ceadda, when both were youths, in
Ireland, praying, observing continency and meditating on the Holy
Scriptures. But when he afterwards returned into his own country,
the other continued in a strange country for our Lord's sake till the
end of his life. A long time after, Hygbald, a most holy and continent
man, who was an abbat in the province of Lindsey, came out of
Britain to visit him . . .'; H. E. V, 12: In the neighbourhood of his
(Drythelm's) cell lived one Haemgils, a monk, eminent in the priest-
hood, which he honoured by his good works: he is still living and
leading a solitary life in Ireland, supporting his declining age with
coarse bread and cold water . . .'; Cynefrid, abbot of Gilling, retires to
Ireland, where he dies of the plague, *c*. 661.

The key to the Hiberno-English religious and cultural nexus was of
course the mission initiated by Aidan in 635, and its symbol the
succession of Scottic Bishops Aidan, Finan, Colman, and Tuda down
to 664. Oswald, Oswy, and Aldfrid, kings of Northumbria from
634–71 and 685–705 were all instructed by the Scots and had an
excellent knowledge of the Irish language. Aldfrid's mother, according

[1] Cf. J. A. Giles, Sancti Aldhelmi Opera, pp. 91 ff. (Oxford, 1845).

to the Irish authorities, was an Irishwoman, Fína, and he was known as Fland Fína and was credited with the authorship of Irish poems still extant. In H. E. III, 25 we are told that Cedd, brother of the Ceadda mentioned above, acted as interpreter at the synod of Whitby, but it is not known whether he learnt his Irish in Ireland, or, for instance, from the Irish monks at Lindisfarne. With the Scot Diuma he was sent by Finan to the Middle Angles, and Diuma was succeeded there by another Scot, bishop Cellach. Irish connections with the more southerly Glastonbury and Bosham are well known.

Eata, 'one of Aidan's twelve boys of the English nation', was made abbot of Lindisfarne on Colman's departure and later became bishop. Cellach's successor in Mercia was also an Englishman, but was educated and ordained by the Scots. The gradated secession of the Scots served to perpetuate their influence on the religious and cultural traditions of the English nation, which monks did so much to shape and interpret.

Hiberno-English relations, established firmly in the seventh century, received a further impetus from the Irish anchorite movement of the eighth, which left its mark too on the neighbouring island.

CHAPTER II

THE ANCHORITE MOVEMENT
IN IRELAND AND BRITAIN

A derivative Irish document with a bias composed probably in the
ninth or tenth century, the famous Catalogus Sanctorum Hiberniae[1]
divides the saints of the Irish Church into three successive Orders of
decreasing sanctity from the time of Patrick to A D 664–65. These
Orders correspond to phases of Church organization which we may
conveniently describe as secular, monastic and eremitical. The
classification sacrifices historical truth to a symmetrical arrangement; it
is summarized by J. F. Kenney (*Sources* I 478) as follows:

(I)   *Ordo sanctissimus* A D 432–544 (or 549). 350 holy bishops,
Franks, Romans, Britons, and Irish, founders of churches, all
under the leadership of Patrick, using the same tonsure, the
same liturgy of the mass, keeping the same Easter, and receiving
women as 'consortes'.

(II) *Ordo sanctior* 544–598 (or 601). 300 saints—a few of them
bishops but many priests—using different liturgies (one was
received from the British saints David, Gildas and Docco) and
different rules of life, but one tonsure and one date for Easter,
and refusing the ministrations of women.

(III) *Ordo sanctus* 598–665 (or 664). 100 saints—a few bishops, but
many priests—who lived as hermits, using different liturgies,
different tonsures, and different dates for Easter. The names
are given of several saints of the second and third orders.

The chronology is based on the older recension in the MSS. A U,
and on MS. S (cf. Grosjean, op. cit., 198–212); together with the lists
of saints of the second and third orders in the same MSS. it may be
due to later interpolation (op. cit., p. 212).

A similar division of the Irish Church is implied in the heading of a
list of twelve saints of the 'Unity of Maelruain', L L 370 γ 38:

[1] Cf. P. Grosjean, Édition et Commentaire du Catalogus Sanctorum Hiberniae,
Analecta Bollandiana 73 (1955), 197 ff., 289 ff.

Lucht oentad Maelruain inso·i· Maelruain Tamlachta ·i· iar Pátraic 7 iarsna da apstal déc insi fail 'The folk of the unity of Tallaght herewith, i.e. after Patrick and after the twelve apostles of Ireland'.

J. F. Kenney (*Sources* I 468) considers it probable 'that the great monastic movement of the sixth and seventh centuries, and the eremitical of the seventh and eighth, were in part at least an attack on what was considered the degeneracy of the older religious establishments'. In evidence of such reaction he adduces: (1) the development of the *disert*, attached or in close proximity to the monastic church, where the more devout monks, and the 'pilgrims' from other establishments, might lead the life of recluses and at the same time share in the religious work of the church; . . . (4) the rise of the *Céli Dé*.

The earlier meaning of the term *céle Dé* appears from Ml.30 c 3 (and its context): *is bǽs linni epert intí charas nech 7 fortét forcertar side iarum hiselbad indfirsin foridtet amal asmberar is cele dǽ infer hisin* 'it is customary with us to say that he whom anyone loves and helps is thrown afterwards into the possession of that man who helps him, as it is said, that man is a servant of God'. This use of *céle* is reminiscent of the legal use of the term ('client') and of the transition from *free* to *base clientship* (cf. D. A. Binchy, *Críth Gablach*, p. 80, Dublin, 1941). *Céle Dé* in this meaning is equivalent to L. *servus (famulus) Dei*; the term *famulorum* (to which gl.25 *inna mogae* properly applies) is used in the L. text. In Wb. 30b26 *servum Domini* is rendered by '. . . mug dæ' and this is also the meaning of *Dé mog*, Fél., p. 4, line 16. *Meudwy*, the Welsh equivalent of *mug Dé* shares with it and with *céle Dé* the later specialized meaning of 'hermit'. In Trip. I 198 *céle Dé* is used of a Briton and in FM 806(811), 919(921) it is recorded that foreign culdees came to Ireland from south and east respectively to preach and to reform monastic regulations.[1]

'Who the *Céli Dé* were' writes Kenney, Sources I 470, 'is not very clear. But it seems certain that they owed their origin as a distinct institution to the reform movement of the eighth century. The term "*céle* of God" had, no doubt, a general sense of perhaps long standing,

---

[1] In O E, *þēow* 'servant' is commonly used beside the heroic terms *cempa*, *oretta* 'champion': e.g. of Guthlac: *se hālga þēow* (157, 896, 922), *dryhtnes þēow* (314, 386, 579); also *godes yrming* 'God's pauper' (272); *Crīstes cempa*(153), *Dryhtnes cempa* (727, 901), *wuldres cempa* (558, 688), *godes cempa* (889), *godes oretta* (569). Guthlac, dwelling in his mountain retreat, is represented as saying of himself (383–89): This mountain dwelling is neither lowlier nor more exalted than befits a man who daily endures his Sovereign's will in suffering; nor must the servant of the Lord (*dryhtnes þēow*) love in his soul more of earth's possessions than a sufficiency for himself alone, that he may have his body's sustenance. Cf. also: Mantat ancer, *Godes wrǽcca*, Cod. Dip. Kmbl. vi. 192, 3.

but its technical application to a special spiritual association dates, on our evidence, from the first half of the ninth century. In the "Notes on the customs of Tallaght" it seems to designate all who were leading a strict monastic life under spiritual direction and in accordance with the ideals of Máel-Rúain, Elair, Máel-Dithruib, etc.; but the Rule of Fothad *na canóine* has distinct sections for *Céli Dé* and for monks. The most satisfying hypothesis seems to be that the *Céli Dé* were the communities of religious who gathered around the reform leaders as the monks of an earlier age had gathered around the primitive church-founders; that their aim was to revive the ancient zeal and discipline of the monastic churches; and that the method followed was to combine the austere life of the recluses or anchorites, already an element in the majority of the larger churches, with a community organization and the close and strict supervision of a spiritual superior. It is probable that in some churches, as Tallaght, they formed the whole monastic body; in others, as at Ros-cré, a distinct community set up in the neighborhood of the old church; and in others, as at Armagh, a group residing within the monastic bounds, perhaps performing most of the sacerdotal and eleemosynary duties, and constituting a community of "stricter observance" in the midst of the older, larger, and laxer organization.'

In *The Age of the Saints in the Early Celtic Church,* Oxford 1963, p. 73, Mrs N. K. Chadwick on the basis of Grosjean's study writes: 'If we can disabuse our minds of the spurious authority of the *Catalogus* and look to the records of the early Irish Church, I think it becomes clear that the so-called Third Order has always been an integral part of the monastic Church; that there is little ground for regarding the religious of this Order as constituting a "Reform"; and that the literary movement with which they are associated is not the expression of a new development, but the formulation in writing of their early traditional beliefs and discipline.' Cf. also ibid., pp. 78, 117.

The anchorite movement, though not peculiar to the Irish Church, was the culmination of tendencies present for centuries which ultimately link it to Egyptian monasticism of the third and fourth centuries. Accordingly, the movement incorporated the traditions of the third order of Irish saints, who are described in the Catalogus as 'dwelling in desert places, living upon herbs and water and alms and possessing nothing of their own'. R. Flower, in his article[1] on our

---

[1] 'The Two Eyes of Ireland'; Religion and Literature in Ireland in the eighth and ninth centuries (Report of the Church of Ireland Conference, Dublin 1932, pp. 66–75).

subject, says (p. 71) 'The movement which Maelruain of Tallaght and Duiblitir of Finglas represented clearly aimed at enforcing an anchoritish severity of conduct in monastic life and in the direction of the lay conscience. For the anchorite was not necessarily a solitary. The rule for anchorites which goes under the name of St. Columcille, a composition of this period, begins with an instruction to the anchorite to "be alone in a place apart in the neighbourhood of a chief monastery, if thou distrustest in thy conscience to be in the communion of many". On the religious side the movement is marked by an anxious scrutiny of conscience and the formulation, after eager debate among the leaders, some records of which have come down to us, of ascetic directions for the guidance of the spiritual life. On the literary side the most intimate documents which we can associate with this period all have this same note of discipline—the tract on the monastery of Tallaght, the Irish Penitential and the curious collection of ethical and religious memoranda entitled the Alphabet of Devotion. And the so-called Rules, really collections of ascetic precepts placed under the name of a popular saint, which begin to multiply at this date, clearly originate in the same school. The Triads of Ireland, a text which we have seen, mentions Tallaght and Finglas with special honour, may well have been compiled under this influence. A marked interest in liturgiology is observable in the tract on Tallaght, and there is good reason to believe that the Stowe Missal, with the explanation of the significance of the Mass which accompanies it, was written in that house. But, above all, these ascetics were interested in the records of the saints. Works like the Félire of Oengus and the Martyrology of Tallaght could not have come into existence without unremitting research into the traditions of the Irish Church, and the hagiological memoranda in the notes to the Félire and the collections of this nature in the Book of Leinster are the obvious continuations of all this activity. It is probable that the marked stress on asceticism which we find in the Lives of the Irish saints reflects the tendencies of this period, and some of them may have been composed at this time and in this environment."

It is now also recognized that Irish *hermit* or *nature* poetry of the ninth and tenth centuries, expressing the anchorite ideal or way of life, is largely the outcome of this movement. For examples and discussion cf. pp. 50 ff. This poetry is obviously the work of monks and hermits and is mostly anonymous, though in some cases attributed to authors of an earlier age. It is the product of a mood in which a personal zest for the simple solitary way of life close to nature and to

God finds its outlet. The tenser mood in keeping with the religious purpose, discipline, anxiety, and typical literary output of Flower's account (*supra*) is reflected in *penitential poetry* such as *Uga Corbmaic Meic Cuilendāin* (cf. pp. 54 ff.) which shows a more direct and necessary affiliation with the movement than the other. Indeed a direct relation between Cormac, bishop-king of Cashel, Tipperary, and the movement can be established. For to him is attributed a versification of the names of its saints, five of whom belong to Tipperary houses. Moreover, Maelruain himself probably came from Lothra, North Tipperary, and seems to have been trained in Munster.

W. Reeves, *The Culdees of the British Islands* (Dublin 1864) has assembled evidence of the incidence of our movement on England north and south, on Scotland, and on Wales. On p. 59 he writes 'When King Athelstan was on his march against the Scotch, in 936, he halted at York, and there besought of the ministers of St. Peter's church, who were then called *Colidei* (i.e. *Céli Dé*), to offer up their prayers on behalf of himself and his expedition, promising them that, if he returned victorious, he would confer suitable honour on the church and its ministers. Accordingly, after a successful campaign, he revisited this church, and publicly returned thanks for the favour which heaven had vouchsafed to him. And observing in the same church men of holy life and honest conversation, then styled *Colidei*, who maintained a number of poor people, and withal had but little whereon to live, he granted to them, and their successors for ever, for the better enabling them to support the poor who resorted thither, to exercise hospitality, and perform other works of piety, a thrave of corn from every plough-land in the diocese of York,—a donation which continued to be enjoyed until a late period, under the name of Petercorn. The record goes on to state that these Colidei continued to receive fresh accessions to their endowments . . .

It would appear that these Colidei were the officiating clergy of the cathedral church of St. Peter's at York in 936, and that they discharged the double function of divine service and eleemosynary entertainment; thus combining the two leading characteristics of the old conventual system, which was common to the Irish and Benedictine rules. But when things assumed a new complexion, and a Norman archbishop was appointed, and the foundation of a new cathedral laid, and a more magnificent scale established for the celebration of divine worship in this metropolitan church, the Colidei, or old order of officiating clergy, were superseded; and while they were excluded from their cathedral employment, they received an extension of their eleemosynary resources, and, in order to mark their severalty, they were removed to another quarter of the city, whither they took their endowments with them, and thus continued through several centuries, under an altered economy and title, till all memory of their origin had perished, save what was recorded in the preamble of their charter book.' In MS. Cotton Claudius A 3 (cf. D. Wilkins, Concilia Magnae Britanniae et Hiberniae I, London 1737, pp. 282–84) may be found a privilege in OE and Latin of King Athelred to the Church of Canterbury. Athelred declares the clerics (on p. 284a of the L. version called *cultores clerici*) to be corrupt, and he wishes to replace them by monks.

On this use of *cultores* J. Lingard (History and Antiquities of the Anglo-Saxon Church, London 1845, vol. II, p. 294) remarks: 'In the charter, the prebendaries are termed *cultores* clerici, a singular expression, which seems to intimate that the collegiate clergy were even then styled *Culdees*—cultores Dei —in the South as well as the North of England.' Cf. Also Reeves, op. cit., 60–61.

Bardsey island, Caernarvon, the famous medieval place of pilgrimage, is the only Welsh Culdee foundation on record. Giraldus Cambrensis refers to the religious there as 'monachi religiosissimi, quos Cælibes vel Colideos vocant', terms which he also uses of the monks of Monahincha Island, al. Inis na mBeo, near Roscrea in Tipperary (Reeves, op. cit., pp. 21, 61).

From a Cotton MS. in the British Museum Reeves lists eight Scottish religious houses associated in the record with the term *Kel(e)dei* (p. 32), and from charter sources a further five (p. 33). This is a conservative estimate, but it greatly outnumbers the recorded Culdee foundations of Ireland. The term *kel(e)dei* did not denote a specific monastic order or rule: in this connection its early connotation was chiefly that of 'asceticism' which later deteriorated to 'irregularity'.

Viking depredations were a serious set-back to the Culdee movement. In Ireland, however, two of the nine centres survived till the Reformation, seventeenth century references to them retaining a version of the ancient designation, *céle Dé*. In Scotland they proved less enduring, their name (*Calledei, Keledei*) and office disappearing by 1332 (Reeves, p. 63); while in York, as we have seen, Norman policy removed them from their ancient church and from the cathedral which rose on its ruins.

CHAPTER III

THE MOTIF OF *AILITHRE* IN EARLY IRISH LITERATURE

a. *The* Immrama (*Voyages*)

In List A of early Irish classified tales (L L Facs. 189 c) *Immrama* appear with the nearly synonymous *Longesa* as a special *genre* distinct from the *Echtrai* (Adventures). Cf. p. 186 *infra*. Of the seven tales (in verse and/or prose) mentioned there two have come down to us: *Immram Maíle Dúin* 'the Voyage of Mael Dúin' and *Immram Ua Corra* 'the Voyage of the Uí Chorra'. A third not mentioned in the list, *Immram Snédgusa 7 Maic Riagla* is also extant. In § 30 of *Imr. MD* it is told that the wanderers reach an island on which they find an old monk who declares himself to be the sole survivor of the fifteen disciples of S. Brendan of Birr who had set out on *ailithre* and landed there. Zimmer (Z f D A 33 (1889), 129–220, 257–338) has shown that this episode gave rise to the later attribution of a marvellous voyage to S. Brendan of Clonfert, and he considered *Imr. MD*[1] the second oldest and also the model and quarry of the other Immrama and of the famous *Navigatio Brendani*. Cf. also M. Dillon, *Early Irish Literature*, Chicago 1948, Chapters V, VI. For the text of the *Immrama* cf. A. G. Van Hamel, *Immrama*, Dublin, 1941.

Immram Brain al. *Echtra Brain Maic Febail* is an early transitional type of heterogeneous content going back to the seventh or eighth century. Cf. K. Meyer, A. Nutt, The Voyage of Bran I, II, London 1895–97. Its main episode is the hero's visit to the Happy Otherworld in the western sea, and its chief subsidiary motif the rebirth of Manannán in the shape of an Irish chieftain. In *Im. Brain* the voyage is an incidental, whereas it is the main theme in the *immrama* proper. *Im. Brain* also shows an incongruous leavening of Christian elements, while the two later *Immrama* (*Im. Snédg.*,[2] and *Im. Ua C.*[3]) are

---

[1] In its extant form the prose version, (earlier than the metrical), is tenth century.

[2] The (earlier) metrical version may be tenth century.

[3] Originally eleventh century? Zimmer supposes an O.Ir. original earlier than *Imr. MD*.

completely Christian in tendency, with *ailithre* as their common theme. *Imr. MD* shows the germ of this development, for on three of the thirty-one islands visited Irish hermits are encountered. In the three *Immrama,* as commonly in the *Lives* of seafaring Irish saints and hermits, the motif of the rudderless boat left to God's guidance is found. The general description of the otherworld in *Im. Brain* and certain details of it are re-echoed in other *Echtrai* and in the *Immrama.* These latter also follow *Im. Brain* in concluding with a specific reference to the recounting or recording of the adventures.

The following short summaries of the *Immrama,* beginning with *Bran,* may serve to illustrate their content as well as something of their manner.

In a poem of twenty-eight stanzas Bran is summoned by a woman to the Isle of Women in the Happy Otherworld. This is conceived as a group of one hundred and fifty islands in the western sea, access to which is guarded by the sea-god, Manannán. In the course of her address on the delights of the distant isle, three stanzas occur in which the woman foretells the birth of Christ. Bran sets sail. On the way Manannán comes riding in a chariot to him and in a second set of twenty-eight stanzas he describes his realm and foretells the birth of Christ and of Mongán. Then he urges Bran on to the Isle of Women. Thereafter Bran comes to the Isle of Merriment and an incident follows which recurs in the Voyages of Mael Dúin and of the Sons of Ó Corra: one of his men is put ashore to reconnoitre but ranges himself with the laughing, gaping islanders and has to be left behind. Then Bran proceeds to the Isle of Women and is drawn ashore by a ball of thread thrown by the leader of the women which cleaves to his palm (a motif also found in *Imr. MD*). They remain with the women for a period of many years—though to them it seems but one. Finally home-sickness (*éolchaire*) seizes Nechtan Mac Collbrain, and Bran yields to the importunities of his men and leaves for Ireland. But there Bran and his voyage have already passed into legend. Nechtan leaps from the coracle, but no sooner has he touched Irish soil than he becomes a heap of ashes. Whereupon Bran sings

> For Collbran's son great was the folly
> To lift his hand against age,
> Without anyone casting a wave of pure (i.e. holy) water
> Over Nechtan, Collbran's son.

When the story has been told to the Irish people gathered there and written in Ogham by Bran, he sails away, no one knows where.

The Voyage of Mael Dúin properly begins when he and his foster-brothers reach two little islands where they hear the murderer of Mael Dúin's father boast of his deed and of his immunity from its consequences. No sooner had the foster-brothers suggested vengeance than a storm arose and carried them away over the high seas. Then Mael Dúin said 'leave the boat to itself and stop rowing, and wherever God wills he will bear it'.

On three of the islands visited by them they find hermits from Ireland clothed in their hair. One of these is the sole survivor of the fifteen disciples of Brendan of Birr (†c. 572) who had put to sea to seek a hermitage. Another had cast his oars and rudder overboard and was carried in his curragh on to the rock where he lived. The wonderful voyage ends where it began, when the foster-brothers encounter the murderer of Mael Dúin's father and are reconciled to him.

The metrical version of the *Immram Snédgusa 7 Maic Riagla* is the original one. This tale opens with the murder of their tyrannous king Fiachu by the men of Ross. When Fiachu's brother, Dondchad, was about to have them burnt to death, it occurred to him to consult his confessor, Colum Cille. Columba sent his two monks Snédgus and Mac Riagla with the advice to have sixty couples of them put to sea for God to judge. On their way back to Iona the two monks decide to do voluntarily what the sixty couples had to do perforce. So they ship their oars and put themselves in God's hands. Eight islands in all are subsequently visited by them, and two of these visits call for special comment.

On one of them the 'exultant birds of Heaven's Plain' sing from a tree-top, and one bird preaches to the others on the Creation, the Nativity, Passion and Resurrection of Christ, and on Doomsday; whereupon the audience beat their wings against their sides until the blood flows (cf. the metrical version on p. 143). On another island—distinct from the Christian heaven, which they visit later—they find the sixty couples who had been cast adrift now living near Elijah and Enoch, 'for good they are, without sin, without wickedness, or crime'.

The whole theme of the sermon and the birds' reaction, as well as the connection with Elijah and Enoch, can be traced back to the text *Dá Brón Flatha Nime* 'The Two Sorrows of the Kingdom of Heaven', which may derive from a Greek apocryphon. Here Elijah, in the company of Enoch, preaches to the souls of the righteous in the form of white birds: 'This is the story that Elijah tells to the souls of the righteous under the Tree of Life in Paradise. When Elijah opens the book to instruct the souls, the souls of the righteous in the form of white birds come to him from every quarter. He tells them, first, the rewards of the righteous, the joy and the delights of the kingdom of heaven, and they are exceedingly glad the while. Then he tells them the pains and torments of hell and the decrees of Doomsday. And a look of sorrow is manifest upon him and upon Enoch, so that those are the two sorrows of the kingdom of heaven. Then Elijah closes the book, and the birds utter a mournful cry and strike their wings against their bodies for fear of the pains of hell and the day of Judgment, so that streams of blood flow from them'.[1]

The symbolism of the earlier text has been split in order to form the two main episodes of our *Immram*. Elijah and Enoch have been attracted away from the birds, to lend colour to the virtue of the Irish folk, who now become attached to the vestiges of the original bird-soul symbolism.

An important feature of this *Immram* is the distinction made between the Paradise of Elijah and Enoch, and the Christian heaven which the monks are made to visit immediately afterwards in the final episode of the poem. It seems to show that Christian Ireland's concept of the other world was eked out by pagan Ireland's Elysium in the new role of provisional heaven.[2] That the description of the happy otherworld in such early *Echtrai* as those of Bran and Condla includes the absence of sin, is added evidence of the fusion of Christian and pagan concepts in this domain. The interplay of pagan and Christian concept is seen too in the ecclesiastical term *tír tairngiri*, a translation of *terra repromissionis*, which was applied both to the promised land of Canaan and to the heavenly kingdom. The composite term *tír tairngiri innambéo* the land of promise of the living ones 'Heaven', Wb. 11 a 19, has a purely spiritual context, though it harks back to the expression . . . *tírib beó* 'Land of the Everliving', to which the woman finally enticed Condla in *Echtra Condla*. The Wb. gloss runs: '(Christ) is the mystical rock out of which

---

[1] Cf. M. Dillon, op. cit. pp. 138–39, rendering a par. from end of FA (cf. LU 2272–2283); cf. also RC 21, 352.

[2] To this a corresponding provisional hell was imagined, which with the conventional Christian heaven and hell made up a fourfold afterworld for the four divisions of the human race. Cf. Zimmer, op. cit. 286 ff; Meyer-Nutt, *Voyage of Bran* I 224 ff. This fourfold division is found in OE in the Visions of Drihtelm (*c.* 696) and the Monk of Wenlock (*c.* 717) and in Aelfric, Hom. I, p. 397; cf. ZCP 14, 196 ff., and p. 205 below.

has broken the mighty stream of spiritual doctrine, which has quenched the thirst of spiritual Israel of the saints in the desert of Life, journeying to the Land of Promise of the Living.'

These facts bring us closer to the concept of heaven which inspired the early Irish *peregrinus* and which is likely to have been transmitted by the Irish to peoples of other lands.

The Voyage of the Uí Chorra is a later composition. Its theme is: 'The three sons of Conall Derg ua Corra, i.e. the robbers and marauders going on their *ailithre* and seeking the Lord on the high seas' (lines 177–180). Among their company of nine were a bishop, a priest, and a deacon. They wondered where they should head for, but the bishop said 'wherever the wind carries us'. So they shipped their oars and offered themselves to God. On one of the islands visited they find a disciple of Andreas who was sent on *ailithre* in the ocean because he forgot to perform his nocturns[1] one night (cf. p. 170). Elsewhere they saw people in torment for their sins, or for neglecting their penance. On three occasions they are told to travel on, as their resurrection is elsewhere.[2] On one island they find the disciples of the (? fifth century) S. Ailbe Imlecha who were permitted by God to live there till Doom singing requiems for the souls of those lost at sea. On two other islands—the one inhabited by a young cleric, and the other by a disciple of Jesus who had stolen away from Him on *ailithre*—they receive their food from Heaven, a common motif in this literature of pilgrimage.

For the instances in this tale of souls in the form of birds cf. p. 142.

b. *Lyric Poetry*

We have already seen that two sub-varieties of Irish anchorite poetry can be distinguished: the hermit-nature, and the penitential (p. 44). The distinction is of course not absolute: it is basically one of *mood*, which in turn depends on the aspect of the total religious experience dominating and inspiring the poet at the time of composition. In general, the hermit-nature sub-variety stems from the real or imagined possession and enjoyment of a predictable set of material and spiritual circumstances. So, for instance, the little secluded hut in wood or on island, trees, wild fruit, animals and birds, fish in the stream, the sounds of nature; on the spiritual side prayer, psalms, contrition, reading, meditation, labour. The attitude is one of appreciation and optimism.

---

[1] *Iarméirge* may perhaps refer to 'matins' here.
[2] I.e. the place where they will die and eventually arise.

The penitential poem is more austere, introspective, generally psychological and tense. Accordingly it neglects the natural environment—by comparison—and tends to treat it as a mere incidental quite subordinate to spiritual need. Pleasure is here rather replaced by pain or discovered in austerity and meagreness.

In practice penitential poems are either characterized by *ailithre*, or not. The latter are then prayers of repentance, or prayers for forgiveness (like Murphy's No. 16 by Óengus Céile Dé II, *c.* AD 987), while the former are either full-blooded poems of *ailithre* oversea or of *ailethrán* 'little pilgrimage' at home (Cf. No. 9, st. 1c). This last type has not hitherto been distinguished from the ordinary hermit-nature poem. The difference in mood and attitude is considerable, however, as may be seen from a comparison of Murphy's *King and Hermit* (No. 8) with his *Hermit Song* (No. 9).[1] The former is briefly considered on p. 158 f.—In answer to the king's leading question why he does not sleep upon a bed (first stanza) Marbán enlarges upon the *pleasant features* of his hermit life in twenty-five stanzas, whereupon the king is prepared to yield up his kingdom in order to live with him (final stanza). The *Hermit Song*, on the other hand, perfectly exemplifies the (penitential) *ailethrán* type:

1. All alone in my little cell,
    Without a soul in my company:
    It were a dear little pilgrimage,
    Before going to meet death.

2. A secluded secret little hut
    For the forgiveness of all evil,
    A conscience straight and clear
    Directed to holy heaven.

3. Sanctifying the body with good habits,
    Trampling manfully upon it,
    With eyes feeble and tearful
    For the forgiveness of my passions.

4. Passions weak and withered;
    Renouncing this wretched world;
    Pure eager thoughts;—
    So to appease God.

He refers both to the ninth century, No. 9 alternatively to the eighth.

5. Heartfelt cries
    to cloudy Heaven,
    Confessions sincere and most pure,
    Copious showers of tears.

6. A chill fearsome bed,
    Rest like rest of the doomed,
    Sleep uneasy and short,
    Early and frequent prayer.

7. My food and possessions
    Were a well-loved hardship;
    Indeed, my diet
    Would not lead me to sin.

8. A ration of dry bread—
    Let us meetly cast our faces down—
    Water from a bright pleasant hillside,
    Let that be the draught you drink.

9. A diet unpalatable and meagre,
    Diligent attention to reading,
    Renouncing strife and visiting,
    A conscience calm and easy.

10. How delightful an image
    A pure holy blemish would be,
    Cheeks withered and thin,
    Skin leathery and taut,

11. Christ Son of God visiting me,
    My Creator and King,
    My mind bent on visiting him
    In His own Kingdom.

12. Let the folly[1] which protects me
    Amid monastic enclosures
    Be a beautiful hallowed little spot
    And I there on my own.

[1] Cf. G. Murphy, Éigse 8, 271 'A hermit's plot ... understood as living in a hermit's plot rather than in a rich mansion, would seem to have been regarded by the poet as a safeguarding folly, just as he regarded asceticism as a lovely hardship (stanza 7) and emaciated cheeks (stanza 10) as delightful.'

The environment and outer circumstance common to these two poems (Nos. 8 and 9) and/or the types they represent is reflected in such significant terms as *díthrub* 'wilderness, retreat' (Murphy, No. 12.1c), *díthrubach* 'hermit, recluse' (No. 8. 1a), *aireclán* 'little cell' (line 1 above, No. 43. 1a), *ailethrán* 'little pilgrimage' (line 3 above), *dísiurtán* 'little hermitage' (No. 11. 1b, 4c); *both* 'hut', (8. 8a, 10a) and diminutives *bothán* (12. 1c), *bothnat* (9.2a, above). Cf. *mennután* 'little abode' (8. 12a) characterized as *diamair, desruid* 'hidden and lowly', more often *deirrit diamair* 'secluded, secret' (9. 2a, above). Cf. SR 6340'*nar ndíthruib,*'*nar nderriteib* '. . . secret places', and *Immram Ua Corra*, l. 478 (*recles diamuir derrit* 'a secluded, secret hut').

Profuse tears seem an almost necessary concomitant of repentance[1] in early Ir. literature, and often seem to symbolize it. So in the eleventh century monastic poem No. 26 which lists the spiritual desires of the would-be hermit, St. 7 desiderates 'vehement waves of tears' (*tonna díana dér*), while immediately afterwards in St. 8 the wish to forsake the world is expressed. The twelfth century *Prayer for Tears* (No. 27) has the same desideratum (*tonna díana dér*) in its first stanza, while its fifth seeks the intercession of 'every venerable elder who has abandoned his inheritance' for the grace of tears.

The other ingredient of the *ailithre* poem may be clearly observed in No. 25 by Máel Ísu Ua Brolchán (d. 1086). Here the accent is on purification by ordeal:

1. Beloved Lord, King of kings, dear Father, pity me.
2. Lest we bring any sin with us to the world beyond, lest we find torment awaiting us there,
3. *Give us tribulation which cleanses us,* Son of the living God, King of mysteries.
4. *Rugged tribulation is a good gift: arrange it for us, beloved Lord.*
5. May the wretched dark demon not prevail over us! Within, without, take us into thy care.

Rugged tribulation which cleanses us (*treblait chorrach norglana*) may be found in leaving our possessions and country and venturing in a

---

[1] This was a general feature of the early Church. The first or lowest class of penitents were the συγκλαίοντες 'weepers' who were stationed outside the door of the church. There they were exposed to the weather as they implored the prayers of the faithful. Hence the name χειμαζόμενοι or *hiemantes*. Cf. RC 40, 63–64. The gift of tears was possessed notably by St. Dunstan, cf. B. Colgrave, *Two Lives of St. Cuthbert*, Cambridge 1940, p. 348.

frail craft on the high sea. The pretence that we can or need govern our own course (destiny) is then cast with the oars overboard. *Cormac's Choice* (*Uga Corbmaic meic Cuilendáin*), unhurried yet tense, represents the bishop-king of Cashel who was killed in battle AD 908, as contemplating this step.—To the same Cormac is attributed a versification of the 'folk of the unity of Tallaght', in LL 370 ε 53 adjoining the prose list of twelve saints headed by Máelrúain who were the propagandists of the anchorite movement! (Cf. R. Flower, *The Two Eyes of Ireland*, p. 70.)

The unique copy of the whole poem is contained in the sixteenth century R.I.A. MS. 23 N 10, pp. 17–18, where it is ascribed to our Cormac. Stanzas 8–9 are well known from their occurrence in the tract on poetry in LL 37c where a Cormac is mentioned as their author. St. 10 also occurs there. Stanzas 9–10 occur too in the Book of Ballymote ff. 323, 328 and in YBL 232. Stanzas 15 and 29 are found in the Glossary in H 3 18 (T.C.D.) and the first line of 29 in Cormac's Glossary § 369 in the 'Additional Articles'. The poem was edited without translation by K. Meyer in ZCP 10, 45 ff. In his *Selections From Ancient Irish Poetry*, London 1911, p. 44 he rendered stanzas 1–2 and 8–9.

The theme of the poem—a projected voyage of lifelong pilgrimage —is outlined and developed in the first eleven stanzas. Deprived of power and its trappings, but in the circumstances of poverty which befit the saintly life, the subject contemplates the preliminaries of his pilgrimage:—confession, tears and penitence, and the visitation of crosses. It is clear from stanza 10 that the pilgrim does not propose to chart a course himself.

Stanzas 12 to 26 relate how a variety of Biblical figures[1] were pardoned by God and taken to everlasting bliss. The ones mentioned by name are Jacob (12), the meek publican (13), Matthew (14), the penitent thief (15, 24–25), Mary Magdalen (16, 17), and Peter (22–23). The last three stanzas are a prayer for help against sin and for eternal salvation.

The poem is called a *trírech* in LL 37c. It is composed in a variety of *rannaigecht mór*, with 7 syllables to the line, which ends in a stressed monosyllable; b and d rime and (the finals of) a, c (should) consonate with them. The final word of a, c often rimes with a word in the

---

[1] Exx. of the *help of God* occur in *Fél.* and in the Ordinary of the Mass of the Stowe Missal. They are a commonplace on Irish High Crosses and form a link with Early Christianity (cf. F. Henry, Irish High Crosses, Dublin 1964, pp. 35 ff.).

interior of the following line, as in st. 1. This ornament is known as
aicill and the metrical type as *duan chenelach* (cf. I T iii 144). Alliteration
should normally occur in each line, but it is occasionally lacking as in
1d, 6c, 7a, d . . . Successive stanzas are often linked by alliteration also.

In spite of the numerous later or M. Ir. forms, many of them no
doubt scribal, the language of the poem (for which see Appendix 1),
seems reasonably consistent with the attribution to Cormac.

The well-known MS., 23 N 10, which supplies a complete text, is relatively
early (sixteenth century), good, and apparently an exact replica of an older
vellum (cf. Cat. of MSS., R.I.A., fasc. 22, p. 2772). Considerable corruption
is not to be expected. But the poem has certain difficulties, and a recent
edition[1] of the first nine stanzas tends to solve them in a manner different
from ours. (Our tendency and practice is to accept MS. readings if at all
possible and to turn from them only as a last resort, i.e. where meaning or
form, including metrical form, demands it.) A comparison of the two
editions sets these cruces in relief and places the reader in a position to
appreciate the processes and the solutions involved. The first four stanzas
according to the O'Connor-Greene ed. (with which cp. ours, p. 58) run:

1

In reg-sa, a Rí inna rún,
  Íar comse clúm ocus ceól,
Mo brogad for mara múr
Mo chúl do thochar frim éol?

Shall I go, O King of the mysteries,
after my fill of cushions and music
to dirty myself on the shore
and turn my back upon my native
land?

2

In mbée i mbochta insin chath
Tre rath in Ríg, rí cen meth,
Cen míad mór, cen carpat cloth,
Cen ór, cen argat, cen ech?

Shall I be in poverty in the battle
  through the grace of the King, a
  king without decline;
without great honour or a famous
  chariot, without gold, without
  silver and without steed?

3

Cen ól medrach mesctha druing,
Cen túaith truim, cen teglach torm,
Cen brasscíath, cen aile n-arm,
Cen cúach, cen cuirm is cen corn?

Without heady drink that intoxicates
the group, without a stout tribe,
without a dwelling over me, without a swift shield or any weapon,
without vessel, ale or drinking
horn?

[1] A Golden Treasury of Irish Poetry: Series 2, No. 9: The Pilgrim (by F. O'Connor
and D. Greene, Sunday Independent, January 10, 1965, p. 19). This series is obviously
intended for a wide public; it omits the critical apparatus.

4

Cen éitiud mín mass ar súil,	Without expectation of fine soft clothes,
Cen clúim nád cara cech naeib,	without cushions that the saints despise
Acht barrán beithe fo búaid	except for beech-twigs of virtue
Fo chuilche crúaid frim dá thaeib?	under a hard quilt that covers my two sides?

Comment: 1a: The MS. has *roghso,* which can only be pres. subj. sg. 1 of *rogaid* 'chooses' + augens *-so;* cf. 2a *In mbeo (sic* MS.), pres. subj. sg. 1. of *biid.* A difficulty arises: the subj. is not normal in direct interrogation; in 5a-8a below the fut. is used. But Strachan (On the Use of the Subjunctive Mood in Irish, Trans. Phil. Society 1897, p. 32) expresses himself circumspectly: 'Of the subjunctive in an independent interrogative sentence I have so far no example.' Presumably he would have accepted these had he observed them. In Old Ir., dependent and independent clauses are not rigidly separated, and M. Ir. shows transitions between subj. and fut. The meaning suggested by the context is 'am I to (choose)?' which belongs to the sphere of the subj. The meaning 'choose' fits in with the title in the MS.: *Uga (<uccu)* 'Choice' and with the syntax and seeming intent of the stanza. St. 8c, d with the fut. *in rag . . . 'shall I go . . .'* seems to resume more directly the content of st. 1; but it is not evidence for *In reg-* in 1a. With this, st. 1 is neither syntactically viable nor meaningful, for **In reg-sa . . . mo brogad* 'shall I go to dirty myself' would need to read **In reg-sa . . . do mo brogad* or the like; the verb *brogaid* 'dirties' is quite rare, while *brogaid* (O. Ir. *mrogaid*) 'presses forward' is common. Cf. Ériu 4, 136 *brogsat* (v. l. *lodsat) for sáile.* It is construed with reflexive pron. in *nosbrogat do . . . i nUachtar Fine,* LL 117 a 12 (= R C VIII 60. 21). Cf. also *mrogaid* Contribb. M, p. 177, intrans. and trans. Hence there is no difficulty here about taking the plausible and obvious meaning 'goes forth'; the proposition of the pilgrim dirtying himself on the sea-wall hardly bears inspection.

The emendation *inna* in 1a is unnecessary; besides, it supplies an extrametrical syllable which has to be elided.

1b MS. *comso* is clearly intended to rhyme with *roghso* of 1a (cf. the later specific rules for internal rhyme in the *rannaigechta);* but the augens in *roghso* is late for *-sa* (cf. Thurn. Gr. p. 252). *Comso* is not a gen. of *commus* in pre-position in view of the form of *clúm* (: *rún* 1a), and of the rest of line 1b. The meaning 'sufficiency' and the form *comsa* (dat. of *comse)* fit in well; one problem remains: is *ceol* governed by *comse,* —or by *iar?* If by *comse* then we might expect a gen. sg. *ceoil* (unless a pl.[1] be construed, as commonly in Mod. Ulster Ir.); if by *iar,* then we should expect a repetition

---

[1] Cf. *Hail Brigit,* LL 49 b 38: a ceóil binni.

of this word. It could be argued that *clum ocus ceol* is a collocation and that a governing *iar* is not repeated before *ceol*: cf. L U 9631, 9635: *do náemaib 7 ecailsib 7 bochtaib . . . do sáeth 7 galur 7 cech aingcis . . .* The same anecdote in BLism. 86 c 32 reads *allan do or 7 argat* where LU 9630 has *a llan di or 7 d'argut.* We prefer the other alternative: *ceol* gen. pl., gov. by *comse.*

The final of 2c reads cl~ in the MS. The expansion to *cloth* satisfies the requirement of consonance between the final of c and the rhyme b/d; but the collocation *carpat cloth* seems to us dubious, cf. Meyer, Contribb. sub *cloth*; whereas the association in *carpat cleth* is known and accepted.

The emendation *mesctha* (MS. *mescthar*) is very neat; but is it necessary? We think it is not, construing 'without heady drink (merry mead) by which the group is intoxicated'; here the indirect relation is expressed without prepositional complex as in early rhetorical prose marked by parallelism such as Tecosca Moraind A 26 (Z C P XI 83): *Blaī Tige móir Midchūardda medrait soír 7 doír, medrait baíth 7 gaíth, medrait gnáith 7 ingnaith* 'The freedom of the great Tech Midchuarda, (where) foolish and wise, acquaintances and strangers make merry'. Cp. B 28 (p. 93, ibid.) with *medharthar* (MS. *n*). (Further: *tongu do día tongas mo thúath* 'I swear by the God by whom my people swears' (Strachan-Bergin, Stories from the Táin, Dublin 1944, p. 104); and *is hed dáthar dom* 'that is why people are vexed with me' Wb. 21 c 9.)

The emendation *torm*, 3b, for MS. *trom* supplies a more obvious rhyme with *corn* (3d) than does the MS. form (by metathesis). But the translation offered is impossible, as *teglach* means 'household'. The MS. reading can be retained. MS. *brosciath* (3c) 'pronged shield' or 'shield like a quern-stone' offers a sufficiently plausible basis without emendation. *Cen aile n-arm* has to be construed with *aile* 'fence' on account of the position of this word vis-à-vis *arm* (the adj. *aile* follows its noun: cp. Wb. 22 d 14 *nábat nacha arm aili* 'let it not be any other arms').

In 4a the concrete meaning 'before the eye, visible' seems more appropriate for *ar súil*, cf. Wb. 27 c 9. The finals of 4b/d (MS. *naomh: taob*) represent in late orthography an old rhyme (i.e. *toíb: noíb*) with broad final consonance, and the proposed palatalization is unnecessary.

Stt. 7 and 17 are the only ones not bound to the preceding st. by linking alliteration (*conachlann,* or *fidrad freccomail*; Welsh *cyrchgymeriad,* cf. Z C P 29, 91–99; Ériu 17, 36–37; G. Murphy, Early Ir. Metrics, 38–39, J. Morris-Jones, Cerdd Dafod, 293). But st. 17 is bound by sense and construction, which leaves 7 a unique exception (exceptional too inside the sequence 5–9 where the absence of *f. freccomail* might perhaps be justified on similar grounds as in Fél. Ep. 193–205). There may then be some corruption in 7a, though the self-inflicted wounds mentioned there are in keeping with what we know of austerities practised by the Irish saints (cf. Lism. L. cviii; V.SS. Hib. cxvi f.). *Tiur(r)* is fut. 1 sg. of *do·fúairc* (**to-org-*) 'crushes'.

MS. *toirbe*(7b) I take to represent O. Ir. *torbai*, gen of *torbae* 'injury', itself an old v.n. (formed like *fubae, tóbae*) from**to-ro-ben-*, beside *derbaid* (**di-ro-ben-*) and *turbaid*. Cf. Contribb. sub 2 *do·rorban* 'hinders', and reff. there. Cf. *torba* 'injury' Ériu IX 32, where instances are cited from the Laws. In Laws III 168 18–19 it occurs beside *torba* 'profit' which seems excluded in our context (cf. stt. 8–9). Note that *bárc* (f.) precludes a finite verbal form governing it.

The solutions proposed for other problems (which we cannot discuss further here) will appear from translation, footnotes, and other notes (Appendix 1).

We do not normalize the text of the sixteenth century scribe; the lenition mark (*h*) is supplied with expansions and in some other cases (21b, 23d, 28b, c), but not generally; length marks are not supplied in the basic text, where they are rare. Our English version does not aim at reproducing Irish syntax (cf. 3a, 11b . . .).

Uga Corbmaic meic Cuilendain

(From 23 N 10, with readings from LL, BB, YBL, H 3 18)

1

In roghsa[1], a Ri[2] na run,
iar comsa[3] clum *ocus* ceol
mo brogad for mara mur,
mu cul do tochar frim eol?

Shall I choose, O King of the mysteries,
after a sufficiency of down and music
to fare forth over the sea's wall
and turn my back on a familiar road?

2

In mbeo i mbochta isin cath
tre rath in rig[4], ri cin meth,
cin miad mor, cin carp*a*t cl*eth*,
cin ór, cin arg*a*t, cin ech?

Shall I be in poverty in the battle
through the grace of the imperishable King,
without much honour or a wattled chariot,
without gold or silver or steed?

3

Cin ol medrach mescthar druing,
cin tua[i]th truim, cin teglach t*r*om[5],
cin b*r*o-sciath[6], cin aile n-arm,
cin cuach, cin cuirm is cin cor*n*d?

Without merry mead which intoxicates men,
without great territory or retinue,
without pronged shield or fence of weapons,
without cup or ale or drinking horn?

MSS Readings: [1] roghso. [2] rig. [3] comso. [4] ri. [5] *read* torm [6] brosc nia *vel* brosciath.

4

Cin etiud min mas ar suil,
cin cluim nat caro ce*ch* naomh,
acht barran beithe fo buaidh[7]
fo cuilche cruaidh *f*rim da taob?

Without fine soft clothes before my
   eye,
without down which no saint loves,
but birch twigs in virtue
under a hard sheet against my sides?

5

In tim*ger* celebra*d* coir
d'in*n*si moir m*a*c Mil*ed* muaidh?
inna*m*tairber fo Christ cuing
ria te*cht* tar tui*n*d maro ruaidh?

Shall I say a fitting farewell
to the great isle of Ireland?
Shall I subject myself to Christ's yoke,
before going over the wave of the
   mighty sea?

6

In radiubhsa rad ndiuit[8] ndian
mo coibsen cia*n*, co*m*al cruaid?[9]
in *f*erfat, a Ri[10] na nell,
*f*rasa mo der dar mo gruaidh?

Shall I make a candid, eager,
and full confession, a hard covenant?
Shall I shed tears copiously
down my cheek, O King of the
   clouds?

7

In tiur[11] mo laim do cach cre*cht*
*f*or bru tuinde toirbe barc?
in fuiceb oc maro mur
sli*cht* mo da glun isin tra*cht*?

Shall I smite my hand with all
   wounds
on the edge of the barque-destroying
   sea?
Shall I leave at the sea-shore
the track of my knees in the strand?

8

An toigeb[12] mo curchan ciar
os oigen u*cht*letan an?[13]
in rag, a Ri[10] richid réil,[14]
as mo toil fein *f*oran[15] sal?

Shall I launch my dusky little coracle
upon the great broad-breasted ocean?
Shall I go, O King of bright Heaven,
by my own will upon the brine?

9

Im ba sessoch, im ba seng,
im ba *t*ressach folingg tond[16],
a *Christ*, an cuingena lium[17]
o thi co[18] techt tar[19] lind lond?[20]

Whether the sea be steady and
   smooth
or whether it spring fiercely,
O Christ will you help me
when the time comes to go over the
   wild wave?

MSS: [7] boaidh. [8] ndiut. [9] *vel* nuag (i.e. n-uag). [10] rig. [11] *read* tiurr. [12] in tóceb L. [13] aigen N, forin n-ocian n-uchtlethan n-án L. [14] *sic* L, in rigthigh rel N. [15] arin L. [16] torgib droṅg L, turme glonn B, turme nglounn Y. [17] in cuṅgene frimm L, in congebha linn B, in congena friom Y. [18] oc L. [19] for L, ar B, tar for Y. [20] long B, lounn Y.

10

Ced[21] leth co bráth[22] iar coaird[23] cros
coslafe[24] mo coblach[25] cres?
in[26] ba soir no[27] siar, ni suaill,
in[26] ba fothúaid[28] no fodess?[29]

Whither till doom after the visitation
of crosses will my narrow boat go?
East or west?—no trifling matter—
to the north or to the south?

11

Fa mba[30] tre fochaid congrain
romficfa andail bratho buain?
fa mba[30] las mbess det oc toir
dilgud mor ar monar suaill?[31]

Or shall it be through hateful tribulation
that I shall come to eternal judgement?
Or will He be disposed to help?
a great forgiveness for trifling toil?

12

Saorsa Iacop na cet cloth,
ba moch robo rigmac raith,
trocaire indhlighthech an breth,
resiu dogne[th] ni do maith.

You freed the illustrious Jacob,
who soon became a prosperous
prince;—
the judgement was mercy not due
in law,
before he had performed something
of merit.

13

Maith slecht in puiplecain blaith
fo cetaip crecht, comal cruaid,
do Él[32] tempuil nirbo tlaith,
ar beluip caich dobert buaidh.

Good was the prostration of the meek
publican
under many wounds—a harsh covenant;
to God in the temple he was not
feeble;
he was victorious before everyone.

14

Bui Matha mor, monar ndur,
fo mur annaigh oirgce sluaig;
luid lat, leigis leabaid lain,
mainc[h]ine rig Roman ruaid.

The great Matthew—difficult strait—
was in the evil dwelling where many
were slaughtered;
he went with You, left a comfortable
berth,
the service of the strong king of the
Romans.

MSS: [21] *sic* L, cia N, B, Y. [22] cobra N, gubrat B. [23] cuaird L, cuairt B. [24] cos
lafe L, cossalua N, cosluidfea B, cusalua Y. *If the clause is relative, prototonic* coslafe *can
stand in place of deuterotonic* con·slafe; *cf.* T B C *1791* Cia ragas . . . (Otherwise Ped. II
622). [25] coblach N, B, chouplauch Y, bachlach L. [26] im L, Y. [27] imba L, ba B.
[28] *sic* L, uthuaidh N, tuaid B, buthuaidh Y. [29] imba fodess L, *no* budes N, *vel in* bodes
B. [30] *sic* MS (in place of len.). [31] soaill N. [32] MS Ɫ; *Meyer reads* no.

15

Ni rocéss an laoch do*n* leirg
i tigh pin*n*e, bes iar faidg,
ar do saordeis a baois buirb
adaig daoib im aonmeis aird.

The hero from the slope did not suffer
in a penitentiary after compline.—
At night ye are at the same high table among your noble band, away from rude folly.

16

A mboi in ballglandu, ba cain,
Moire Magdallda, miond oir,
aonta demna, dreman cleir
foi for g*r*ein i*n* crotha coir.

When the pure-limbed gentle Mary Magdalen—the golden diadem—was alive,
A company of demons—hardy band—
laid siege to her, the radiant one of fair form.

17

Dob*ir*t di la dilgud pian
beith ar do dreich, dilgud mar;
meruidh a coissce*l*u[33] cian
cen mer*us* soisce*l*a slan.

With a remission of punishment You granted her
to be in Your presence—a great dispensation.
The remote tale of her will endure as long as the Gospel remains intact.

18

Saithemail b*reth* romb*ir*t tall
ar ban*n*scail n-an*n* o roell,
o tarmairt an*n* aibel drong
cloch gach oīnfhir[34] ina cean*n*.

Shrewd was Your judgement of yore on a woman when she went astray,
when each of the hasty throng
was about to cast a stone at her.

19

Coi*certuis* in dine ndian,
a ri side, sorcha dal,
arạ-nda-clochad[35] ria gach cuain
do cuail pecuid fer ba slan.

You rebuked the violent crowd
O King of Peace,—happy event!:—
that one who was free from the burden of sin
should stone her before the rest of the mob.

20

Saor docuaid it*er* da re*ch*t,
ni fuair let le*ch*t ar a lo*ch*t,
in adoltroch rodom*er*t,
in malort*ach* im a corp.

She went free between two laws,
she got not death from You for her sin,
the adulteress who beguiled them,
the one who bartered her body.

MSS: [33] *Read* coiscēla. [34] MS aon*f*hir. [35] MS ar na clochad.

21

Caín dorolgis do cach naill,
do gach pect[h]ach, brat[h] cech cind,
nirb ard n-aithisech a greim,
inge nad n-aithersed inn.

Gently You have forgiven every
other,
every sinner his every crime,
the punishment was not great or
loathsome,
but that he should not relapse into it.

22

An fer maith is moam rotcar,
petar aupstal, aurtaig tor,
nachatfedir, a De bi,
atcuitig fa tri, ba col.

The noble one who loved You most,
the Apostle Peter, trustworthy hero,
thrice swore he knew You not,
O living God, how wrong!

23

Cia rotsenustar ar tlas
do muinterus, mo gach druis,
dorolgis dó, demin scel,
iar sceit[h] a der tar a gnuis.

Though through weakness he denied
Thee,
that he was of Your band—worse
than lust!
You forgave him, indeed,
when he had shed tears down his
cheeks.

24

Gabuis diabul cacht cin clith
for laoch roalt frie cech toich,
o tarcuib for doma[i]n dreich,
for leith co farguib a croich.

The devil took in open bondage
the hero who had been brought up
to thieve;
since before the world he had
sinned,
he left his cross on one side.

25

O creidis inniut a recc
medon laithi, nirbo lag,
hi parthus iar n-oidche uair
is e gilla do cuaid lat.

Since he believed in You forthwith
at noon he was not weak;
he was the one that went with You
to Paradise after the cold night.

26

In lin roleicis fot barr[36]
it lir gainim maro min,
in[37] lin ronescmart[38] as cach n-ing
at lir na rind fil a nimh.

The number You have allowed under
Your roof are as numerous as the
fine sands of the sea,
The number You have delivered
from difficulties are as numerous
as the stars in heaven.

MSS: [36] or bair. [37] elide. [38] Read donescmairt (?).

27

A nasadh na n-aingel n-an
don riched ran rechta reil
do*m*ficib-sa[39] cobuir coir,
fo bithin is toir a n-eimh.

From the assembly of the radiant
  angels
of the splendid kingdom of clear
  rule
let due aid come to me,
since it were now timely.

28

Ar do cesad, ar do croich,
o cotris do muin*tir* mait[h],
nimfargbadh-sa amuic[h] dodt eis
a n-in*b*a*id* noteis it fla*ith*.

Since by Your passion and cross
I may reach Your good people,
May I not be left behind You,
when You enter upon Your kingdom.

29

Pecud buanoll brath gach mbi,
nir*b*o fla*ith* i*m* cri co*m* cro,
am[40] dao*n*nacht a m*ei*c De bi,
cid tu ba[41] ri ni *b*o ro.

May ever-powerful sin which betrays
  everyone
not reign in my body till death;
O Son of the living God, it were
  not too much
wert Thou King over my nature.

To Cormac, Columba and—plausibly—to abbot Celedabhaill of
Bangor (d. 927) is attributed another poem of *ailithre* expressing the
urgency of a penitential journey and habitus for its fifty-eight-year-old
subject. This second poem on the twin themes of pilgrimage and
penitence is one of self-admonition to the courses which ensure salvation. The urgency here, expressed by the constantly-resumed theme-
word *mithigh* is one of redeeming the time. In *Cormac's Choice* it was
embodied in the subject's presentiments and in his vehement prayer.

The references to stability in stt. 4, 8 c, d may reflect the decline
of the earlier concept of pilgrim wandering legislated against in the
Benedictine Rule on the Continent, in favour of later types: pilgrimage
abroad at a fixed residence, or to a shrine. Irish monastic reformers of
the eighth and ninth centuries were more sceptical of pilgrimage over-
seas. Cf. K. Hughes, The Changing Theory and Practice of Irish
Pilgrimage, Journal of Ecclesiastical History 11 (1960), 143 ff.[1]

MSS: [39] *Read* domiced-sa. [40] im H. [41] bu H².

---

[1] Miss Hughes cites from BNnÉ i 310–11 the anecdote of Mochuda's desire for pilgrim
wandering, which is dissipated when S. Comgall exorcises from his shoe the 'mocking
devil' who 'puts the spirit of restlessness into everyone'! Cf. Rawl. B 512 fo. 142 b 2,
BLism. 86 d 38. A similar moral is found in Plummer VSH ii 260 (cf. R. Flower, *The
Irish Tradition*, p. 58) and in Thes. II 296.

II. Colum Cille (Cormac mac Cuillionáin) cecinit. Ed. K. Meyer, Arch. III, 311 from the fifteenth century MS. Laud 615, p. 108 and 23 N 3, p. 175. Cp. also Lism. 95 d 16 (23 H 6), FM II 618, F VI 1 and 23 H 24. Our text is based on L(aud) with readings from the other MSS., for which cf. Notes, App. I. Of the older MSS. L alone is liberal with the length mark, cf. *dúalach* 2a, but *sualach* 2c; in 4c, L, N, F, H read *fós* for *fos(s)* of the other MSS. I have not considered it necessary to supply the mark of length in all cases.

1

Mithidh[1] damhsa tairired[2]
do thríall o thoraibh teghl*aig*h,
asccnamh am*ail* ailit*her*[3]
tar tuin*n* múaidh mara
  medhr*aig*h.[4]

Time for me to proceed on a journey
from the domestic throng;
to advance as a pilgrim
over the great wave of the joyous sea.

2

Mith*idh* fretech dúalach
ocus derna f*r*i deamhan,
mithidh ascnamh sual*ach*,[5]
saltra*d*h *for* toil co dreamhan.

Time to renounce vice
and to reject the devil;
time to seek virtue
and to trample vigorously on the will.

3

Mith*idh* anadh dh'in*n*laghadh[6]
colla co lí*n* a caire,[7]
mith*idh* íar*um* imradhadh
cora f*r*i[8] m*a*c mór Maire.

Time to cease pampering
the body with its many faults;
time then to contemplate
peace with the great Son of Mary.

4

Mith*idh* corp do cairiug*u*dh[9]
dáigh isí i*n* crí notbrena,[10]
mith*idh* fos íar taiririudh,[11]
tír a[12] teilcmís ar ndéra.

Time to rebuke the body,
for it is the body that corrupts;
time to stay after journeying
in a country where we might shed our
  tears.

---

[1] *Read* -gh (FM). [2] taireradh L, toirired Lism., tairir FM. [3] oilither Lism., do asccnamh imm ailither FM. [4] tar tuinn mara muaidh menmnaigh FM. St. 3 follows, then 2 with inverted order of couplets in Lism., FM,N,F,H. [5] sualcha Lism., N. [6] dinntladhadh FM, dinnbhaghadh N,F,H: cf. *Ériu* 19, 119. [7] coire (:Muire) L., caire (:Maire) Lism., N. [8] co ro frith FM. [9] chairiucchadh FM, cairiugh- L, coiriged Lism. [10] fódbrena L, is aigi notbrena Lism., (notbreána N), isa cion ron brena FM. [11] sic FM (tt-), taireradh L, toirired Lism. [12] airm i FM.

5

Mith*idh* fr*im*[13] corp credhbaidhe[14]
costadh im chrabhadh ngl*i*ndi,
mith*idh* reic[15] na hercraidhe[16]
ar th*í*r na flatha f*i*ndi.

Time for my wasted body
to get used to constant devotion;
time to sell that which is transient
for the land of the fair King(dom).

6

Mith*idh* lámh fri tarbhata[17]
domhain cé cétaigh chaingnigh,[18]
mith*idh* grés fri hernaighthi
ag adhr*adh* airdr*i*gh a*i*ngl*i*gh.[19]

Time to turn from the tribulations
of this engrossing and troublesome
    world;
time for continual prayer
adoring the High-King of angels.

7

Mith*idh* faichill tiughlaithi,[20]
treasa luai*n* laithi brátha,
mithidh iar*um* idhnaidhi,[21]
terbódh fri gn*úi*se gnátha.

Time to watch out for the last day of
    life,
the Day of tumult and of Judgement;
time thereafter to wait,
to part from familiar faces.

8

Inge *acht* d*í* aonbl*iadhain*
n*í* theasta dom tr*í* fichtibh,
toirisiu*m* fó áonriaghail
*i*n nach maighi*n* budh mith*idh*.[22]M.

Only two years
are lacking of my three score;—
it were time
to remain in some place under one
    rule.

9

N*í* mharat[23] mo co*m*a*í*si
b*í*d*í*s im crab*udh* cr*i*thir[24],
anadh do*m* rith robha*í*si,
a Dé mhóir, do b*udh* mith*idh*[25]. M.

My contemporaries are no more,
who were given to trembling devo-
    tion;—
it were time, O Great God, for me
to desist from my career of folly.

10

N*í* mhar[26] Corm*a*c Cuireadhach,
rogaet[27] co sleghaibh sithibh,
I*n*drech*t*ach muadh Muiredhach,
Máo*n*ach máol molbh*thach*
    mith*idh*. M.

Cormac of the hosts lives no more—
he was killed with long spears—
nor the great Indrechtach, Muiredach,
Maenach, nor the famed Maelmith-
    idh.

[13] *sic* L, lámh FM, fam N,F,H. [14] cr*a*ibhdhighi Lism., cr*a*ibhthighi N, F,H.
[15] rem N. [16] nearchraidhe FM. [17] turbhaidhe FM, t*er*bodadh Lism. [18] domhnain
cé cétaibh caingen FM, do̅m truagh ot chaingnig N. [19] airdrigh aingeal FM, Isu
ainglidh N. [20] focuil tighláithi FM, faichibh tiughlaithi N,F,H. [21] omhan indnaidhe
FM. [22] airisemh fo naomh riaghail in nách maighin ba mithigh FM, gach L., tairniu*m*
fo ei*n*riag*ail* . . . Lism.; . . . dam do badh mo i*n*a mithid Lism., N. [23] *sic* FM, marat
Lism. mharait L. [24] bhitt*í*s fri crábhaidh crichidh FM (crithid Lism.). [25] ba (mithigh
FM), Lism. [26] ba liach FM, Lism. [27] *sic* Lism., roghaot L.gaeta FM.

The penitential theme is similarly treated in a Mid. Ir. poem published by Meyer in A C L III, p. 321. Its first stanza runs:

Alithre idan inmain,
trāethad cinadh, corp genmnaid,
betha bocht dereōil derrit
ticc co menicc fo menmain.

A dear pure pilgrimage,
subduing faults, a body chaste,
a life of poverty lowly and secluded
occur often to my mind.

In a short poem of four stanzas the above-mentioned Máel Ísu (cf. p. 53) asks four gifts of God, the first being that of pilgrimage (A C L III, p. 230):

Būaidh crāb*uidh*, būaidh n-ailithre,
būaidh n-aithricche dom anmain,
a Chrīst gan cuid cairighthe
érni damh huile amhlaidh!

The gift of piety, the gift of pilgrimage,
the gift of repentance for my soul,
O Christ without reproach,
grant them all to me.

Būaidh treabhlaite tocc*aidh*e
damh fri deiredh mo shaoghail,
gurbham fīrēn fonaide
iar mbruindiudh duit ce*ch* bæghail.

The gift of chosen tribulation
for the end of my life,
that I may be perfected in goodness,
when you have smelted all flaws.

In the first of three stanzas on the way of salvation and of the Culdee associated with Adamnan (though it contains Mid. Ir. forms) pilgrimage is mentioned as one of the three best possible steps (A C L III, p. 215):

Trí cémenn cindti do chách
is ferr cingfes nech co bráth:
céim torroma lobair lis,
céim d'ailithri, céim d'eclais.

Three steps designed for all,
the best that any will ever take,
a step to visit the sick,
a pilgrim step, a step to church.

CHAPTER IV

THE WELSH BACKGROUND:
PENITENTIAL AND SENTENTIOUS POETRY

Our first Welsh poem[1] is found in the late twelfth century Black Book of Carmarthen, pp. 33–34:

Kintevin keinhaw amsser.	Maytime, fairest season,
Dyar adar glas callet.	Loud the birds, trees are green,
Ereidir in rich. ich iguet.	Ploughs in the furrow, the ox in the
4 Guirt mor brithottor tiret.	yoke,
	Green is the sea, dappled the fields.
Ban ganhont cogev ar blaen guit guiw	When cuckoos sing on the top of fine trees
Handid muy. vy llauuridet	My sadness grows;[2]
Tost muc amluc anhunet.	Smoke stings, (my) grief is revealed,
8 kan ethint uy kereint in attwet.	For my kinsmen have passed away.
Ym brin in tyno. in inysset mor	In hill, in dale, in islands of the sea,
Impop fort itelher.	Wherever one may go,
11 Rac Crist guin nid oes inialet.	There is no refuge from the White Christ.
Oet in chuant in car in trosset	It was our desire, our friend, our merit
Treitau ty tir dy alltudet.	
Seith seint a seithugeint a seithcant[3]	To cross over to the land of Thine exile.

---

[1] *Kintevin* belongs to the Old Welsh period (800–1100). Criteria of age are: the type of *englyn* employed: in the second st. an early crude form of *englyn unodl*, in the third *englyn penfyr*. Secondly the Irish rime -*er*: -*edd* in stt. 1,3,5. Thirdly, the form of the preposition *ddi* (Mod. W. *i*) in line 13.

[2] 'From its song emanates ("handid") "my murder" ' (!) (ZCP 29, 217 (1964)).

[3] Note the identical collocation in the Ir. anecdote of Mochuda's projected pilgrimage (p. 63, f.n. 1 *supra*): in his community were *morseiser ⁊ secht fichet ⁊ secht cēt* 'seven and seven score and seven hundred', every third one of whom had converse with angels (ZCP III 32).

A want in un orsset.
16 Y gid a Crist guin ny forthint-ve
   vygilet.

Seven saints and seven score and
   seven hundred
Went to one Throne,
With the White Christ they were
   unafraid.

Rec a archaw-e nim naccer.
Y rof a duv. dagnouet.
Ambo forth.y porth riet.
20 Crist ny buv-e trist y'th orsset.

A gift I ask; let me not be refused:
Peace between me and God.
May there be for me a way to the
   noble gate!
Christ, may I not be sad before Thy
   Throne!

The poem is based on the twin themes *leaving this world* and *Peace with God*. H. Lewis (*Hen Gerddi Crefyddol*, Caerdydd, 1931, p. 5) aptly entitles it *Tristwch ym Mai* (Sadness in May), thus defining its mood. Its opening combines universal gnome with particular descriptive statement and conjures up a picture of brightness and activity in Spring beside the sea. But the most characteristic sound of this splendid season is the one to which the subject's soul responds most sadly; the call of the cuckoo brings a sharp stab of pain: the memory of departed kinsmen suffuses the entire poem. From the first mention of the cuckoo (lines 5, 6) the poem reflects a grey shade of anxiety back on the opening stanza and draws it into harmony with st. 3, which, also discursive, is dominated by the silver of *Crist guin*.

The *tone* of this poem—a vital consideration—is as near to being identical with that of *Seafarer* 48–66a as seems possible—and this is set in l. 47 *ac a hafað longunge se þe on lagu fundað* 'but he who is eager to go to sea always feels a (spiritual) yearning'; in both passages the cuckoo is a harbinger of sorrow; in both the nature description gives way at the mention of the cuckoo to serious issues of life, death, and the hereafter:

    The woods blossom forth, the cities become fair,
    The fields begin to look bright, mankind begins to stir itself;
50   All these things urge to fare forth
    The heart of the eager one who thinks
      To depart far on the paths of the sea.
    Then too the cuckoo urges him with its sad voice,
    The herald of summer sings, forebodes bitter
55   Sorrow to his heart. He does not know,
    The man happy and prosperous, what some of those endure
    Who print their tracks of exile furthest.

The English passage has not only the same selection of detail, practically, as the Welsh, but it has it in a closely similar (though not identical) sequence (*Kintevin* 1–4: *Seafarer* 48–49; *K.* 5–8: *S.* 53–55a; *K.* 9–10: *S.* 50–52; *K.* 12–16 echo the central themes of pilgrimage and holy death dealt with in another way in *S.* 58–64a, while the prayer for peace with God and happiness in heaven in *K.* 16–20 finds an echo in *S.* 64b–66a). The treatment of detail in the two passages is, naturally, not always quite the same, but though divergent in the narrow view, it will be found to harmonize in the broad. For the two poems (as well as the *Wanderer*) are dominated by the White Christ who found our Welsh poet's kinsmen on hill and dale and in islands of the sea. As C. O'Rahilly puts it: 'It was to men such as these, men of piety and learning, who "sought Christ in the wilderness" (*Christum in eremum quaerere*), that it was given to know and love nature in all her moods' (*Ireland and Wales,* p. 126). So that the Welsh background—like the Irish—reveals the motif of *ailithre* and suggests the coincidence of poet and hermit.

The opening stanza of *Kintevin* might lead us to expect a seasonal poem, but the linking of seasonal manifestation or sententious remarks on natural phenomena to a human mood or situation is part and parcel of Welsh artistry and it is found in the individual *englyn* as in the individual poem. It is the human situation that counts. This subtle mixing of the sententious with the personal or emotional is also a feature of the OE *Seafarer, Wanderer* and *Wife's Lament.* It is characteristically Welsh and it becomes Cymro-English. It may at times be almost impossible to unravel the thread of the human situation from its gnomic setting; hence the modern impression of almost deliberate obscuration in Early Welsh and OE poetry. We shall now proceed to illustrate these points.

Welsh *Kintevin* corresponds in etymology and meaning to Ir. *cétemain* 'May', and an Old Ir. poet too has rendered the season in 14 stanzas, of which the first two are (EIL, p. 156; cp. K. Meyer, *Four Songs,* p. 8, and ECNP, p. 23; ninth century):

Cétemain, cain cucht,	May-day, fair showing,
rée rosáir rann;	splendid season;
canait luin laíd láin	blackbirds sing a full lay
día laí grían gaí ngann.	when the sun casts a slender beam.

Gairid cuí chrúaid den;   The hardy vigorous cuckoo calls,
is fo-chen sam saír;   welcome to splendid summer;
suidid síne serb   it settles the harsh weather
i mbi cerb caill chraíb.   in which the wood of boughs is
    torn.

The resemblance in the opening of the Welsh and the Irish poem is offset by the following characteristic differences: the manifestations of the season are not linked (or applied) in these Irish verses to a human mood or situation[1] as they are in the Welsh, where the associations awakened by the cuckoo's call cause the season of actual experience to recede into the middle distance as the last link in a perennial chain. And so phenomena subtly change into universals and description into gnome, and a poem becomes a subtle mixture of the personal (emotional, lyrical) and the sententious. In neither literature has the combination been generally understood, for the surgery formerly practised on the English poems was also fashionable in Welsh. To a certain extent the urge to see *pure* (unmixed) exponents of some notional genre such as *nature poem, gnome, description,* was responsible for the fashion of excision. The assumption that complexity is a late, and single-minded simplicity an early condition is also involved here and in the historical treatment of the 'elegy', since Sieper (wrongly) sought the origin of the OE genre in the Germanic *lament for the dead,* explaining its complexity as the later attraction of other features to this nucleus (p. 13 ff.).

Characteristic, then, of Welsh—and a puzzle in OE—lyric poetry is the highly functional use of the gnome and the occurrence of sententious passages in a context of deep or poignant feeling. The germ of the nature-man synthesis is found in some early Ir. lyrics; but these are commonly more explicit and descriptive where the Welsh are highly-fused and cryptic. We have referred above to st. 14 of *Cétemain;* another notable example is the *Old Woman of Beare* (E I L p. 74 ff., stt. 15, 22, 34: *c.* AD 800):

Is labar tonn mora máir;   The wave of the great sea is noisy;
ros-gab in gaim cumgabáil: winter has begun to raise it:
fer maith, mac moga, in-díu   neither nobleman nor slave's son
ní freiscim do chéilidiu.   do I expect on a visit today.

---

[1] But the final stanza (14) does link the two in a gnomic manner reminiscent of Welsh.

A-minecán! mórúar dam;
cechn[d]ercain[1] is erchraide.
Íar feis fri caindlib sorchuib
bith indorchuib derthaige!

Truly, (or often enough), I am very
  cold;
Every acorn is transitory.
After feasting by bright candles,
  to be in the darkness of an oratory!

Céin mair ailēn[2] mora máir:
dosn-ic tuile farna tráig;
os mé, ní frescu dom-í
tuile tar éisi n-aithbi.

It is well for an island of the great sea:
flood comes to it after its ebb;
as for me, I expect no flood
after ebb to come to me.

The *Old Woman's Lament* is essentially a *reflective* lyric, leisurely
rather than intense. It depends greatly on contrast and paradox, and
its dominant figure is the movement—particularly the ebb and flow—
of the sea, which is made to carry the brunt of the theme (: *on growing
old*). The above stanzas do remind one of the Welsh manner; but the
differences, too, are clear: the natural phenomena cited here stand in a
clear and immediate relation to the underlying human situation, whereas in much Welsh poetry the two merge into a problematical gnomic
unit, requiring thought and even ingenuity to unravel. In other words
the Welsh poets, like the English, give the uninitiated modern reader
the impression of deliberately obscuring their theme. And now let
us observe a Welsh scholar at work on one such poem untangling the
thread of the human situation from its gnomic setting. The poem in
question is from the *Black Book*, p. 89 ff. It begins (quoting I.
Williams, LEWP, p. 14 ff.):

'Llym awel; llum brin; anhawt caffael clid.
Llicrid rid; reuhid llin. Ryseiw gur ar vn conin.

"Keen is the wind, bare the hill. Hard it is to find shelter. The ford
gets worse. Lake freezes. A man can stand on a single stalk." And so
on. Withered are the reeds. Snow falls. White is the fringe of the
mountain. Bare are the trees. Weak the songs of birds. White cloaked
is the ridge. Long is the night. Bare the headland, gray the slope.
Rivers in flood. Meagre is the stag, etc. But there is something else
here—like a mountain brook making its way through and under
reeds and heather, now in full view, then disappearing for a while,

---

[1] Cf. cechnercain H 3 18, and cach dér choin, gach dercaoin of the 'Y' group of MSS.
(EIL, pp. 78–79, PRIA 55 C 4, p. 100); Murphy reads *dercu*.
[2] *sic* MSS. Murphy emends to *insi* to accommodate *dosn-ic* of the next line.

but sure to emerge further on, so there runs a trickle of dialogue right through the 38 stanzas. The theme is cowardice. Omitting all the nature poetry, I shall give you only the relevant lines. One voice dwells on the severity of the weather: "Warriors will not go to war (st. 5, the first intimation of battle is embedded in a sequence of nature poetry). Idle is the shield on the old man's shoulder." The other voice counters with "Fine is the shield on the shoulder of the brave", and so on alternatively, though sometimes several lines of padding separate their remarks. . . ." '

This theme is worked out over the first 23 (25) stanzas; the next 7 contain a dialogue between men on a raid, and then we have a final retrospective 6 on the raid itself. I. W. continues '. . . though there is a heavy overlay of nature poetry in the first half, almost burying the dialogue, at last the drama, as it were, breaks loose. Yet every scrap of description is relevant to Act I, Scene 1, portraying the unwilling warrior, wounded and dispirited by a presentiment of death, goaded on by his counsellor. Once he is convinced of his duty the weather does not count any more, and we have pure dramatic dialogue to the end (of Act 1, Scene 2).'

Two Irish poems from the Finn-cycle which have been compared to this Welsh one are printed and translated by Meyer, *Four Songs* pp. 14 ff., 18 ff. Cf. also his *Selections From Ancient Irish Poetry*, London 1959, p. 56 ff., and ECNP, p. 26. The first is short (EIL, p. 160: ninth or tenth century):

Scél lem dúib: dordaid dam,	My tidings for you:—the stag bells,
snigid gaim, rofáith sam.	Winter snows, summer has gone.
Gáeth ard úar, ísel grían,	Wind high and cold, low the sun,
gair a rrith, ruirthech rían.	Short his course, sea running high.
Rorúad rath, ro cleth cruth,	Deep-red the bracken, its shape is gone,
ro gab gnáth giugrann guth.	The wild-goose has raised his wonted cry.
Ro gab úacht etti én;	Cold has seized the wings of birds;
aigre ré; é mo scél.	Season of ice: these are my tidings.

The *Song of Winter*[1] (*Four Songs*, p. 18) does offer evidence of a conflict embedded in nature poetry in the manner of the Welsh poem:

[1] Tenth century.

72

1. Fuitt co brāth!
   Is mō in donenn ar cāch,
   is ob cach etrice ān,
   [ocus] is loch lān cach āth.

   Cold till doom!
   The storm is greater than ever;
   Each shining furrow is a river,
   And a full lake each ford.

2. [Is] mēit muir mōr cech loch lonn,
   is droṅg cech cuiri gūr gann,
   mēt taul scēith banna dond linn,

   Big as a great sea is each angry lake,
   Each keen thin company a host;
   Big as the boss of a shield each drop of rain,

   mēt moltchrocann find cech slamm.

   Big as a white wether's skin each flake.

4. Ro-fad rēod rōta gribb
   īar nglēo glicc im Choirthi Cuilt,

   Quick frost has bound the roads
   After a sharp struggle round Colt's standing- stone;

   congab donenn dar cach leth,
   co nā abair nech acht fuit!

   The storm has spread on all sides,
   So that none say aught but 'Cold!'.

This poem occurs in two different settings and it may belong to a story now lost (cf. ibid., pp. 16–17, LEWP p. 17). In one of its settings it has a companion piece on Summer which closely resembles *Cétemain*. The last stanza of this poem[1] illustrates how the poet's mood reflects his environment (*Four Songs*, 23):

Tibid grīan dar cach tīr,
dedlaid lim fri sīl snon,
garit coin, dāilit daim,
forbrit brain, tānic sam.

The sun smiles over every land,—
A parting for me from the brood of cares(?),
Hounds bark, stags tryst,
Ravens flourish, summer has come!

We now turn to an Ir. elegy in which nature mourns the beloved dead as it did Baldur and 'the restless wild creatures die of grief for him'; where accordingly the Welsh fused manner might be expected. The first stanza of *Créide's Lament for Cáel* runs (EIL, 148 ff.: *c.* AD 1175):

Géisid cúan
ós buinne rúad Rinn Dá Bhárc;
bádud laích Locha Dá Chonn
is ed chaínes tonn re trácht.

The haven cries out
over the fierce stream of Reenverc;
The drowning of the warrior from L.D.Ch.
is what the wave against the shore laments.

In the sequel animals too are made to mourn a similar bereavement, but the inferences are always clear and the element of obscurity or mystery

---

[1] Tenth century.

is lacking. The same applies to the famous hermit poem in which the sea is much more than a mere setting (cf. p. 159 *infra*).

A second feature of the Welsh poem *Kintevin* is the sad-voiced cuckoo which recurs in *Seafarer* 53 and *Husband's Message* 23. We have referred above (pp. 24, 26) to an Old Ir. instance and to one in a Suibhne Geilt poem which combines longing with liturgical bird-song (EIL, p. 114, st. 5). A less specific association of Spring with death or pain is found in Latin poetry, cf. *The Return of Spring* by Horace, Penguin Book of Latin Verse 1962, pp. 29–31, and a poem with the same title by Pentadius, ibid., 69; S. Augustine's poem in Penguin Med. Latin Lyrics 1962, p. 168; also Alcuin's *Lament For the Cuckoo* ibid., 88–90. For the wider incidence of the sad-voiced cuckoo motif cf. E. Sieper, op. cit., pp. 70 ff.

I. Williams suggests (LEWP, 13) that the sound of the cuckoo's cry aroused the association with *cw* 'where?' in Welsh, as with *ku* in Persian. Cf. also J. G. Evans' ed. of BBC. p. 135. One could point to the homophony in Ir. of *coí* 'lamenting' with *coí* 'cuckoo' in nom. and voc., but this may have little significance.

No reason for the sad association is given in the OE instances but it is in *Kintevin* (8) and in *Claf Abercuawc* where the theme of cuckoo song is sustained throughout 8 stanzas (3–10).

In W. B. this poem[1] is entitled *Englynion mab claf* 'stanzas of a leper' and its association with the Llywarch cycle is ultimately due to its position before poems of that cycle in the MS. (cf. CLlH, pp. lvi, 174). An important preliminary question is whether the choice of a *leper* subject has a special significance or not. In a Mid. Ir. anecdote S. Moling Luachra (+ c. 695), numbering himself among the *Culdees*, is made to say: *intan do theiged Crist do acallaim na cele ndé nipo chorcarda na rigda do theiged. acht i rrechtaib na tróg. i. na llobor 7 na clam. no bíd Críst* 'When Christ used to go to converse with the Culdees, not in purple nor regally would he go but in the shapes of the wretched, to wit, of the sick and of the leper was Christ wont to be' (LL 284 b 2–5; cf. Fél. 154 (L.)[2]. Another story of a leper is told in BLism. p. 156,

---

[1] Dated 'tenth or eleventh century?', ECNP, p. 76.

[2] For legends of Patrick's leper, Comlach, cf. Trip. 84, 556; for Lomman, Brigit's leper, BLism. 195; for Ciarán, Senán, and the lepers ibid., p. 218. Fél. commemorates 'lucid Fínán the leper' on March 16th, 'Colmán the zealous leper' on May 21st, and another Colmán on November 14th. In Lism. L., p. 304, we read that Cámmine would like to fill his new church 'with disease and sickness and every ailment that is worst to man',—and so it befell him. Fergal's army doom themselves by outraging a leper-anchorite before the Battle of Allen; the leper (*clam*) curses them and foretells their defeat.

Trip. pp. 447, 449. The devotion bestowed on lepers in the Middle Ages is referred by F. W. Farrar (*The Life of Christ*[17], p. 149, London 1874) to Isaiah's delineation of our Lord as a patient and afflicted sufferer and to David's description of a smitten and wasted outcast (Isa. 52, 14: 53, 4; Ps. 21: 7–8, 15–17). 'The Vulgate rendering of Isa. 53.4 is, "Nos putavimus eum *quasi leprosum,* et percussum a Deo, et humiliatum" and this gave rise to a widespread fancy . . . that He who healed so many leprosies was Himself a leper' (Farrar, ibid. p. 149). Stanzas 31 and 32 *infra* remind one of this connection. For the text of the poem cf. CLlH pp. 23–27; we translate as follows (cf. ECNP pp. 53–56 for K. Jackson's version):

1 It is my mind's desire to sit upon a hill
   and yet it does not rouse me;
   short is my course, deserted my homestead.

2 Keen the breeze; bare the cattle-track[1]
   when the wood puts on the fair hues of summer,
   very ill am I today.

3 I am not active; I do not keep soldiers.
   I cannot move around,
   Let the cuckoo sing as long as it list.

4 The loquacious cuckoo sings with the day
   a loud song in the meadows of Cuawc.
   Better too much than too little.

5 In Abercuawc cuckoos are singing
   on flowering branches.
   Loquacious cuckoo, let him sing on!

6 In Abercuawc the cuckoos are singing
   on flowering branches,
   alas for the leper who hears them constantly.

7 In Abercuawc cuckoos are singing;
   sad is my heart
   that he who has heard them will not hear them more.

8 I have heard a cuckoo on an ivy-tree,
   my shield has sagged,
   the longing for one I loved is the greater.

[1] Reading *beuder biw,* cf. CLlH 161. *Beuder*: Ir. *bóthar,* cf. M. Richards, Lochlann II 130 and T. F. O'Rahilly, Celtica I (1946), 160. In Mod. W. Kerry Irish *bóithrín* means 'cow-track'.

9 In the crest of the moving oak
  I have heard the voice of birds;
  loud cuckoo, everyone remembers what he loves.

10 Singer of perpetual song, nostaligic its cry,
   with the roving course and the flight of a hawk
   loud cuckoo in Abercuawc.

11 Loud the birds, wet the streams,
   the moon shines, cold the midnight hour,
   sad my heart with the affliction of disease.

12 White the hill-top, wet the streams, long the midnight
     hour,
   the accomplished are held in honour,
   I deserve the sleep granted to old age.

13 Loud the birds, wet the shingle,
   the leaves fall, the exile mourns;
   I deny it not, I am ill tonight.

14 Loud the birds, wet the strand,
   bright the sky, broad the wave,
   the heart is withered with longing.

15 Loud the birds, wet the strand,
   bright the wave of wide course,
   (?) my vigour in youth—
   I would I had it again.

16 Loud the birds on Edrywy heights,
   and the cry of the dogs in the waste,
   loud the birds once more.

17 Early summer, all growth is fair,
   while warriors hasten to battle;
   I go not, my wound does not let me.

18 Early summer, pleasant on the bank
   while warriors hasten to the field,
   I go not, my wound prevents me.

19 Grey the hill-top, fragile the ash-tree tips,
   the bright wave flows forth from the river-mouths,
   laughter is far from my heart.

20 Today it is the end of a month
   that I have been in the lodging which he has left;
   sad is my heart, disease has laid hold of me.

76

21 Clear is the eye of him who looks on,
   he who is secure can be magnanimous;
   sad is my heart, disease preys on me.

22 Cattle in the shed, mead in the bowl,
   the fortunate one does not desire discord,
   patience is the fringe of understanding.

23 Cattle in the shed; beer in the bowl,
   slippery the ways, fierce the shower,
   and deep the ford; the mind concocts treachery.

24 The mind concocts an evil deed,
   there will be pain when it is atoned,
   a selling of little for much.

25 (?) Hell is in store for the wicked
   when God judges throughout the long day,
   dark will be falsehood, bright the truth.

26 (?) The chalice is upraised, the assailant in bonds,
   men are merry over mead;
   withered the reed, the cattle in shelter.

27 I have heard the resounding wave
   loud among the shingle and pebbles,
   my heart is heavy with depression tonight.

28 Branching the tip of the oak, bitter the taste of the ash,
   sweet is cow-parsley, laughing the wave;
   the cheek does not hide the affliction of the heart.

29 Frequent the sighing which comes upon me
   after what I've been used to;
   God does not allow good to the wretched.

30 Good is not allowed to the wretched
   but only sorrow and care;
   God does not undo what he has done.

31 The leper was a page; he was a bold warrior
   in the court of a king;
   may God be kind to the outcast.

32 That which is performed in an oratory (viz. penance)
   he is hapless who reads it,
   hateful to man below, hateful to God above.

A feature of the poem is the grouping of stanzas into *gostegion* by two varieties of linking (*cymeriad*): that in the opening lines of stanzas, as in 5–7; and linking by resuming a closure in the beginning of a following stanza as in 23–24, 29–30. By invoking the first variety we may amend the first word of st. 25 to *Creator* which then enters into a K-group with 26 and 27 (*Kreator-Kerygyl-Kigleu* as first words of their respective stanzas), cf. CLIH, 171. By applying the second variety of *cymeriad* to stt. 29–32 we arrive at a different order of these. St. 29 ends and 30 begins with *da y diryeit;* st. 30 ends with *ar a wnel* and 32 begins with *or a wneler* (*yn derwdy* / *Ys tiryeit yr a'e derlly*) . . . which clearly suggests a sequence, especially since the intervening stanza looks like an explanatory addition to the poem proper which would form a natural conclusion for it, and since it is not formally linked with 30. The case-history of the leper emerges clearly from st. 31: he was attached to a royal house first as page (*mackwy*) and later as a soldier of the king's war-band (*teulu*); then he contracted leprosy and became an outcast, one separated by God from worldly kin, according to A.L. x 556. Cp. the term *gwahanglwyf.*

The linking of stanzas by recurring formulae in their opening lines lends to such sequences something of the effect of a litany. It raises the problem of the precise contextual value of the repeated elements in relation to the individual stanza. This problem is more acute still where the main theme in the third line of an englyn is preceded by lines containing apparently irrelevant matter in the form of nature or human references, the so-called *llinellau llanw* (cf. CLIH xliii), which sometimes coincide with the *cymeriad*. Examples of such formulae are: 2a *Llem awel; llwm beuder byw* which uniquely realizes a structural mould found elsewhere; 11a *gwlyb neint* 'wet the streams' is reproduced or varied in 12a, 13a, 14a, 15a according to requirements of *cymeriad,* structure and rhyme. In stt. 11, 12 it appears beside formulae with *deweint* 'midnight': *cold* (*long*) *the midnight hour,* where the temporal reference is at variance with that of 4a; and beside 13b *the leaves fall,* which conflicts with the seasonal data in stt. 2, 17, 18. These inconsistencies suggest that the formulae in question are irrelevant from the point of view of the poem as a whole, and that sequences tend to be episodic and autonomous: the second section (11–16) retains the night reference in 13c, and while a temporal progress might be argued for the first 10 stanzas, the seasonal disparity is against it. Temporal references in this poem are, however, mainly conventional (cf. p. 82 below); moreover, we have to take into account the fact that sequences tend to be somewhat episodic and autonomous. The episodic and repetitive structure of the poem has to be seen in relation to its *mood,* and a logically consistent development is not to be expected. The fact that the choice of nature formulae seems often to be determined by formal requirements does not entitle us to dismiss them *en masse* as 'irrelevant'; for the importance of nature as a structural element in Celtic poetry is too pervasive to be lightly dismissed in an early lyric such as this (cf. ECNP, pp. 110 ff., 187 ff., and p. 81, f.n.1, *infra*). In the following analysis we try to determine what if any significance for the poem as a whole can be attached to formulae of the kind in their context.

In the opening section, stt. 1–10, the cuckoo theme is clearly an important vehicle of the poem's intent and so the references to cuckoos and birds in this section are relevant. The introspective character of the poem and its concentration on *mood* is set in relief by st. 31 with its welcome biographical gloss on the persona of the leper. In a poem of this class motifs from the natural environment are used to orchestrate the thoughts and feelings which form its main preoccupation. Let us consider this in more detail:

Line 1a strikes a familiar note: it is a common opening in early Ir. poetry. Cf. ECNP No. XXI *Benn Boilbin that is sad today . . . it was lovely to be upon its crest*; in No. XLI Deirdre is made to say: *Glen of fruits and fish and lakes,*/*peaked hill of lovely wheat,*/*it is distressful for me to think on it . . .*; No. VI *Delightful I think it to be in the bosom of an isle*/*on the crest of a rock . . .*; No. XVII *High and delightful hill*/ *to which the fair Fiana used to come . . .*

The leper is out of harmony with the joys of his environment (1b, 2c) and he greets the singing cuckoo somewhat querulously (3c), *let it sing on!* And throughout the following seven stanzas it does sing on with others in a splendid early summer setting while the leper's sad thoughts range from his own plight to his dear departed and back again. Cf. *Kintevin* supra, p. 67. The references to nature in stt. 3–10 are organic and necessary. Stanzas 11–16 form a group[1] linked in their first lines by *gordyar adar* (No. 12 alone showing a different, lighter link in the *g* of *Gwynn*). Is this merely a mechanical device, or does it not also sustain the contrast in the previous section? At all events stt. 17–18 which follow do resume the antithesis between, or dissonance of, subject to environment. Cf. 17a/c, 18a/c. He is preoccupied with his own plight and the natural phenomena observed from his hill-top seat are woven into and around this basic strand and serve to carry it. This we expect from st. 1, where the leper's great love of nature is made to blend with his still greater despondency.

---

[1] Note the firm delimitation of this group by the repetition in 16c.

Line 4c *Gwell corrawc no chebyd* is rendered closely by K. Jackson: better is the spendthrift than the miser. This gnomic observation we interpret as a grudging acceptance of the loquacious cuckoo and render accordingly. St. 10 offers a poetically relevant picture of the singing, roving cuckoo. St. 11 adds to the bird reference descriptive comments on the outer environment in the shape of englyn-building formulae, which are taken up and varied in stt. 12–19 and 27–28. These comments are linked by a casual and loose association of ideas with the leper's frame of mind. This is demonstrated by the transition in st. 13b, c: *the leaves fall, the exile mourns, I am ill tonight.* Such an association may be implicit in other cases whether the phenomena mentioned are in consonance with the leper's feelings (11b cold the midnight hour), clearly dissonant (17a (18a) 'Early summer, all growth is fair') or apparently neutral (12a–15a wet the stream, shingle, strand). The latter have the gnomic property of specifying states native, natural, or normal to phenomena, statal observations parallel to and linked locally with the instrospections of the leper about himself. He has a double focus and sees all nature about its own business while he broods on his. He loves nature even when he chides it and he 'composes' as a child of it. So he may even forget to brood, as in st. 16.

St. 20 on the other hand omits the nature references altogether, offering instead a rather cryptic biographical datum. Prior to this there are rather few proverbial references to man: st. 12 shows a transition from the properties of natural phenomena to what is proper to man: as the accomplished merit honour so old age too has at least the modest right to sleep and to the suspension of pain claimed by the leper for himself. St. 21 juxtaposes the attitudes of the disinterested and the uninvolved to that of the leper.

A very significant contrast is offered in stt. 22/23: the former represents the case of the *detwyd* or fortunate man content with his lot, peace-loving and wise because patient. St. 23 deftly depicts the destiny of the *dirieit* or unfortunate one who chooses the wrong path. In consequence he must atone in great travail (st. 24) before facing the day of Judgment (25). Note the adroit use of *cymeriad* in 22a, 23a to etch the antithesis. (Alternatively these stanzas are packed with empty and irrelevant formulae which render their cohesion questionable and their overall intent doubtful.)

The final echo-phrase in 26c (*cattle in shelter*) probably marks the conclusion of a thematic sequence, as 16c more obviously does. Stt. 27–28 return to the theme of depression in conjunction with nature references. In 27a these are expressed in the personal manner of 8a, 9b (*I have heard . . .*) and in organic connection with the leper's mood. St. 28 is the last of its kind and its nature references are of the neutral, sympathetic and antipathetic varieties mentioned above: the face reveals the inner mood (28c) as the wave smiles in the sunshine, as cow-parsley and ash reveal their specific taste and the tip of the oak-tree its shape.

In retrospect we notice that the thematic treatment in the poem is repetitive and would seem by external standards to lack a logical development. But this is in keeping with the nature of poetry whose primary function is to delineate a mood—or an attitude, as in prayer. The *Penitent's Prayer*, for instance, combines these related facets and its repetitive structure has to be assessed accordingly. Cf. Ch. ix.

It has been pointed out above that the organic connection of man with nature[1] characteristic of Welsh poems such as this is paralleled in Early Ir. poems like the *Old Woman of Beare* where the fusion of the two aspects is less complete and the result less cryptic. It may be illustrated too from a seventeenth century poem on Cathal Óg O Connor, RIA MS. C IV I. In three opening stanzas his character and life are silently treated in terms of bees expelled from the hive, a

---

[1] Cf. J. M. Synge, The Aran Islands (Dublin, 1912), p. 51: 'In Inishmaan one is forced to believe in a sympathy between man and nature, and at this moment, when the thunder sounded a death-peal of extraordinary grandeur above the voices of the women, I could see the faces near me stiff and drawn with emotion.' P. 121: 'At one moment she is a simple peasant, at another she seems to be looking out at the world with a sense of pre-historic disillusion and to sum up in the expression of her grey-blue eyes the whole external despondency of the clouds and sea.' P. 153: 'The sense of solitude was immense. I could not see or realise my own body, and I seemed to exist merely in my perception of the waves and of the crying birds, and of the smell of seaweed.' A. E. Housman finds in nature a responsiveness lacking in his fellowmen: Shropshire Lad XLI: In my own shire, if I was sad,/Homely comforters I had:/The earth, because my heart was sore,/Sorrowed for the son she bore;/And standing hills, long to remain,/Shared their short-lived comrade's pain./And bound for the same bourn as I,/On every road I wandered by,/Trod beside me, close and dear,/The beautiful and death-struck year:/Whether in the wood-land brown/I heard the beechnut rustle down,/And saw the purple crocus pale/Flower about the autumn dale;/Or littering far the fields of May/Lady-smocks a-bleaching lay,/And like a skylit water stood/The bluebells in the azured wood.

The bearing of our theme on English poets such as Cowper and Wordsworth appears from W. Leisering's *Das Motiv des Einsiedlers in der englischen Literatur des 18. Jahrhunderts und der Hochromantik* (Diss. Halle/Salle, 1935). For Irish and Welsh poetry cf. further K. Meyer, Selections From Ancient Irish Poetry, p. xii f.; R. Flower, The Irish Tradition, p. 42; H. I. Bell, The Development of Welsh Poetry, Oxford 1936, pp. 6 ff., illustrated also pp. 22, 31 ff. Cf. R. T. Davies, ed. Medieval English Lyrics, London 1963, *passim*, and p. 309: 'In nos. 2, 3 and 4 [thirteenth century] the inner world of the poet's mood is expressed in relation to the outer world of nature which is presented in concrete detail.'

healing herb and a drink of nectar. In st. 6 his mother is referred to as the fallow-land in which he was tempered; in st. 8 his strength 'is like the coming in of the tide, or the keen speed of rowing'. Cf. st. 15b, c, d of our Welsh poem above. In St. 17 he is endowed with traditional attributes of the true prince: He made every forest fully fruitful, and bitter weather serene; he soothed the roaring of the breakers . . . In st. 18 he is said to have set on fire the fury of winter (*Budh adhnadh goile Geimhridh*).

The essential loneliness of the speaking subject in surroundings of hill, sea, trees and the sounds of nature relates this poem to a wide complex of outcast poetry and lyrical lament dealing with a reversal of fortune in Welsh, Irish and OE. A comparison suggests a derivative application of Celtic means in the OE fragments.

Take the conventional use of temporal forms, for instance. Common to Ir. and W. is the use of *anocht/heno* 'tonight' and of *indiu/hediw* 'today'. Cf. ECNP 119 ff., and EIL 154, stt. 1, 3–6. Stt. 1 and 6 of this poem have the topical reference *innocht* 'tonight'; stt. 3–4 adopt *deired aidche* . . . at the end of a night' and st. 5 *i matain* . . . 'on a morning ...' In the *Buile S.* poem, § 45, beginning *Duairc an bhetha-sa* 'Gloomy this life', st. 3d specifies as temporal point *madain ghlaisreódha* '(faring through greensward)/on a morning of grey frost'; st. 7d *madan mhuicheirghe* '(mind on early departure),/morn of early rising'. In W. and OE this point of time is very prominent. For W. cf. *Claf A.* 4a above (*gan dyd*); and CLlH XI stt. 59c, 60c *Duhunaf wylaf uore* (*bylgeint*) 'I awake and cry at morn (dawn)' in a sequence with *heno* as the stock reference. For W. *deweint* and OE *uhte* 'dawn' cf. p. 170.

To this complex belongs also the W. use of *gwedy* 'after', as in CLlH XI 72a, XII 1a, 2a, 7a, 8a. Ex. *Gwydi gurum a choch a chein* (BBC 64) 'after purple and red and fine (clothes)' which has immediate parallels in a comparable context with the Ir. use of *iar, d'éis*: cf. *Cormac's Choice* 1b *iar comso clum ocus ceol* 'after a sufficiency of down and music' (p. 58); *Ind ráith d'éis cach ríg ar úair* 'the fort (remains) after each in his turn' (EIL xvi). T. H. Parry-Williams also cites the W. use of *kynn bu* 'before' (Procc. Br. Acad. 32, p. 274 (1946)).

The same is true of the seasonal involvement in *Husband's Message* 22 ff. and *Seafarer* 48 ff. which may be taken with *Menologium* in a wider context of seasonal poetry (cf. ECNP, Ch. IV). The closest analogy is with *Claf A. and Kintevin* which also have the cuckoo reference. Stt. 6–8 of *Cân Yr Henwr* (CLlH, p. 8 ff.) too have the

context of cuckoos, lovelessness and longing. Cf. the Ir. counterpart of this poem, *The Old Woman of Beare,* st. 19, where however the birds are lacking. In passing we may note the analogy between st. 22 of this poem and the closing stanzas of *Claf A.*:
'Truly, (*or* often enough), I am very cold;/Every acorn is transitory./ After feasting by bright candles/to be in the darkness of an oratory!' The Suibhne poem mentioned above, *Gloomy this life,* also includes a schedule of seasonal visiting towards its close, and the Suibhne stanza cited on p. 26 has the association of bird song and longing in a winter setting.

We refer above, p. 80, to the antithesis between the fortunate and the hapless man[1] and on p. 22 to O E instances. To the hapless one (*dirieit*)[1] belongs a characteristic semantic field comparable to E. D. Grubl's inventory of forms connected with *sorg* and *cearu* (*Studien zu den angels. Elegien,* p. 180). The following reff. are to page and stanza of CLlH: he is *direit,* 26.30a and passim, *edein* 'outcast' 27.31c, *divro* 'exile' 24.13b. He is oppressed by *etlit* 'sorrow' 24.8c and passim, *hiraeth* 'longing' 24.14c, *hoet* id. 10.16c, *tristit a phryder* 'sorrow and anxiety' 26.30b, *lletvryt* 'depression' 26.27c. He is *divryt* 'depressed' 24.13b, *truan* 'wretched' 9.3c, *trwm* 'dejected' ibid., *unic* 'lonely' 10.17a, *crei, oergrei* 'sad' 25.20c, *digarat* 'loveless' 9.6c, *cas* 'hateful' 27.32c. With these are often combined terms expressive of age and sickness.

Closely connected with the concept of the *dirieit* in CLlH is the attribution by Llywarch and Heledd of their manifold misfortunes to the operation of a malevolent personal destiny (*tynged*). Cf. CLlH lxvi ff. This is paralleled by the attitude to *wyrd* in *Wanderer* (5, 15–16, 100) and to its operation in the *Riming Poem,* where riches, pride and treachery are the forerunners of disaster; pride as in the case of Llywarch and Heledd (CLlH lxvi ff.), treachery as in *Claf A.* stt. 23–25. The analogy between the W. *dirieit,* the Ir. *tróg,* and the Icel. *feigr* 'doomed one' is obvious though not complete, and the O E operation of *wyrd* generally fits into this wider frame. The *anhoga* of the *Penitent's Prayer* with whom the Lord is angry (77 ff., 91) stands in relation rather

---

[1] In the gnomic poem *Bidiau* II, stt. 2, 10, *diriaid* and *dedwydd* are contrasted: st. 2b, c: *dirieid bid ymgeingar,/dedwydd yr a' i gwyl a' i car* 'the misfortunate one is quarrelsome; happy he on whom looks the one who loves him'; st. 10b, c: *bid dedwydd ar ei naid,/gnawd aflwydd ar ddiriaid* 'the fortunate one can depend on his destiny; usual is disaster for the misfortunate'. For *dedwydd/diriaid* cf. CLlH lxvii, 173, 175, and EWGP 53–54. Exx. in EWGP are *diriaid*: II 2c, III 3c, 22c, 31c, V 4b, VII 2c, 10c, 11c, VIII 8a. *dedwydd*: II 3c, III 29b, IV 11c, VIII 9c.

to the anguished David of Ps. 37 who prays for mercy in his affliction. A comparison with this psalm rids the OE poem of many obscurities. Cf. p. 180.

Kintevin is preceded in BBC (29–33) by another religious poem to which it is closely related. The theme of this one is *Ren new a'n roto ran trugaret* (12) 'May the Lord of Heaven grant us a portion of mercy', and this mercy is echoed at the opening and the close of the poem as it is in the *Wanderer;* cf. 1–3:

Moli Duu in nechrev a diuet.
Ae kyniw ny welli ny omet.
Vn mab Meir modridaw teernet.

The praise of God at the beginning and in the end,
He does not reject, He does not refuse him who attempts it,
The one Son of Mary, the Lord of lords.

The last two lines are:

An eirolve ne Mihagel.
ar ren new ran trugaret.

May Michael intercede for us with the Lord of Heaven for a portion of mercy.

Lines 10–17 are similar in theme and treatment to *Cormac's Choice* (pp. 58 ff. *supra*). Cf. H. Lewis, op. cit., pp. 3, 112 ff., and K. Jackson, A Celtic Miscellany, London 1951, p. 328:

10 Teyrnuron, tanc yrom-ne heb imomet,
   Diwyccom-ne a digonhom o gamuet.
   Kin myned im guerit, im iruet,
   In tywill heb canvill im gorsset,
   Ym gueinvod, im gorod, im gorwet.
15 Guydi meirch ac imtuin glassuet,
   A chyuet, a chid im a graget,
   Ny chisgaw, gobuyllaw om diwet.

10 'O Lordly Heart, may there be peace between us;—refuse me not!
   May we make amends for the wrong we have done.
   Before going to my tomb, to my green grave,
   In darkness without candle to my grave -mound,
   To my burial, my retreat, my repose,
15 After steeds and indulgence in pale mead,
   and feasting and consort with women;
   I will not sleep, I will meditate on my end.'

Lines 18–35 closely resemble *Seafarer* 80b–102:

> Gulad it im-ne, ys agro y massvet,
> Mal deil o vlaen guit daduet.
> 20 Guae agaur agraun maur uerthet,
> Ac onys guataul y riet;
> Kyn gatter ew in ryred pressen
> perygil uit in y divet
> Ny vir drud nid yscrid in y timhyr,
> 25 Ny chiuid uore, ny chiueirch, nid eistet,
> Ny chan wen, nid eirch trugaret;
> Bit chuero y talhaur in y diwet
> Syberuid a maurwrid a maret.
> Meithrin corph y lyffeint a nadret
> 30 A llevuod, ac imtuin enwiret;
> Ac agheu dydau urth gluydet,
> Ew in luth dychinull, dychiuet.
> Dynesa heneint a lled arnad,
> Dy clust, di trem, di teint, neud adwet.
> 35 Dychricha croen di uisset,
> A'th una heneint a lluidet.

'We are in a world of grievous wantonness;
Like leaves from the tree-tops it will pass away;
20 Woe to the miser who hoards great riches,
For unless he devotes it to God
—though he be permitted to run his course in this world—
There will be peril at the end.
The foolish man knows not in his heart to tremble,
25 He will not rise early (for matins), nor beseech (God), nor keep vigil,
He will not chant a prayer nor crave mercy.
Bitter in the end will be the retribution
Of pride and haughtiness and pomp.
He pampers his body for toads and snakes
30 and lions, and practises iniquity.
And death will come to the door
And gather him up and carry him off greedily.
Old age and infirmity of mind will draw nigh;
Thy hearing, thy sight, thy teeth are failing,
35 The skin of thy fingers will wrinkle
And old age will make thee grey.'

The underlying theme here and in *Seafarer* 80b–102 is *this transitory*

world, seen from a religious point of view. The two passages open on
this note. Exponent of the argument in the Welsh passage is the figure
of the *miser* (*agaur* 20) which corresponds to the OE *everyman* (*monna
gehwylc* 90). Indeed, in lines 97–103, the latter is represented as a
miserly sinner (cf. 100, 102) that seeks to do with gold hoarded in his
lifetime what only God's mercy can accomplish—thus reproducing
20–23 of the W. poem. The content of the W. opening (18–19) is
developed in 80b–89 of the OE poem where it passes into the description of *everyman* ageing (89–91) to correspond to 32–35 of the W.
poem. Lines 92–93 of the OE poem refer to the passing of friends,
while in the W. poem (31–32) Death the Reaver is delineated with all
the vividness of the later *morality.* Cp. the striking figure of Death in
Guthlac B, 1139 ff.

From a sequence concerning the things which are best for the soul
in BBC 79.12–85.6 we select for comparison with OE penitential
poetry the following poem of pilgrimage:

1 Kyntaw geir adywedaw.
  y bore ban kyuodaw.
  croes Crist in wissc ymdanaw.

  The first word that I will say
  In the morning when I arise:
  Christ's cross be a vesture round me!

2 Ar helv uy ren yguiscav
  hetiu. un trev a glyuaw.
  nid ew wy duu niscredaw.

  To-day I shall don what is the Lord's;
  One home I shall frequent;
  He is not a God in whom I will not
    believe.

3 Guiscaw ymdanaw inberth.
  ny credaw coel canyd kerth
  y gur am creuys-e am nerth.

  I shall dress myself becomingly,
  Believing no omen, for it is not right;
  The One who made me will strength-
  en me.

4 Y mae vimrid ardebed.
  arowun ar mor wyned.
  etyl butic bitaud ked.

  My mind is (bent) on a journey,[1]
  Intending to go to sea;
  A beneficial design;—it will be a
  boon.

5 Y mae vymrid ar kighor.
  arowun myned. ar mor.
  etyl butic bitaud ior.

  My mind is (set) on a plan.
  Is purposing to go to sea,
  It will be a beneficial design, Lord.

6 Dyrcheuid bran yhasgell.
  arowun myned. impell.
  etyl butic bitaud guell.

  The raven will lift her wing
  intending to travel far;
  A profitable design;—it will be
  better.

---

[1] *Tebed*: Ir. *teiched* 'flight'; but cf. I. Williams, Canu Aneirin, p. 304.

7 Dyrcheuid bran y hadein.
arowun myned ruvein.
etil butic bytaud kein.

The raven will lift her wing,
Intending to travel to Rome;
A profitable design;—it will be splendid.

8 Ystarnde wineu fruin guin.
redech. hiraethauc raun rin.

ren new. oet reid duu genhin.

Saddle the bay with the white bridle;
With the nostalgic gait and the rough hair;—
Lord of Heaven!—Him we would need with us.

9 Ystarnde winev birr y blev.
ruit ygniw rygig. otew.

mynyd vo truin. yd uit trev.

Saddle the bay with the short hair,
With the easy movement and the ambling pace.
Where there is a nose there will be a sneeze.

10 Ystarnde wineu hir y neid.
Ruit ygnyw rygig. woteid.

ny lut ar lev trev direid.

Saddle the bay with the long bound,
With the easy movement and the sprightly (?yearning) pace.
The sneer of the vicious will not check the brave.

11 Trum kyduod daear.tev
deil dris.
chuerv vuelin met melis.

ren new ruita-de vyneges.

Heavy the consistency of earth; thick the leaves of the briar.
Bitter the drinking horn of sweet mead.
Lord of Heaven, facilitate my enterprise.

12 O eissillit guledic. a gueith
wtic.wosprid. a phedir pen pop ieith.
Sanffreid suyna-de inimdeith.

O Royal Offspring, Redeemer victorious
in battle, Peter head of every nation,
St. Bride, bless our journey!

13 Heul eirioled arouned
argluit. crist kely. colowin ked.

Dywyccviff wympechaud am gueithred.

O Sun of intercession, Desire(d One)
of the Lord, Christ of Heaven, Pillar of Bounty,
may I atone for my sin by my deed!

The theme of the poem is a proposed pilgrimage to Rome whereby the pilgrim hopes to expiate the sins of his past life. The first 11 stanzas are in one of the earliest measures, *englyn milwr*, 3 7-syllable lines with one rime. In the first line of stt. 9, 10 *y* is not reckoned, in the 11th *daear* is monosyllabic as sometimes in Old W. and in some modern Southern dialects. This eleventh st. splendidly realizes the psychical texture of abnegation on the one hand and preparation on the other so appropriate to the pilgrim. It forms the transition from the plan visualized so clearly and in such detail in the preceding section, and it leads on to the final prayer. On the whole the poem brings to pulsating life the dry chronicle entries of British pilgrims who undertook the hazardous journey to Rome.

This poem is preceded in BBC by the famous and puzzling *Ysgolan* verses. Ysgolan, like the Irish Suibhne Geilt (cf. pp. 25, 199 ff.) committed several depredations outlined in st. 3 of our poem against the Church. The penance imposed on him was a year's banishment to a precarious existence on the sea at Bangor—which seems quite in accord with early Welsh penitential codes. The word *du* 'black' so heavily concentrated upon in the first stanza symbolizes no doubt the state of Ysgolan's soul until the expiation of his crimes. This view is supported by the whole tenor and progress of the poem which leads us from the sinner's state to his misdeeds and thence to his punishment and repentance:

1 Dv dyuarch du dycapan.
du dy pen du duhunan.
iadu ae ti yscolan.

Black your horse, black your cloak,
Black your head, black yourself,
Black skull, is it you, Ysgolan?

2 Mi iscolan yscolheic
yscawin y puill iscodic.
guae ny baut a gaut guledic.

I am Ysgolan the clerk,
the frenzied one is deficient in judgment,
Woe to him who suppresses not what offends the Lord.

3 O losci ecluis.allat buch iscol.

allyvir rod y voti.
vy penhid.ystrum kynhi.

For burning a church and killing school cattle,
and the drowning of a gift book,
my penance is heavy upon me.

4 Creaudir y creadurev.
porthidev muyhaw.kyrraw de imi vy gev.
ath vradaste am tuyllas ynnev.

Creator of creatures,
Our greatest Help, forgive my wrong;
He that betrayed You deceived me.

5 Bluytin llaun im rydoded.
ym. bangor ar paul cored.
Edrich de poen imy gan mor pryued.

I was given a full year
In Bangor on the stake of a weir;
See the pain I have had from seaworms.

6 Bei yscuypun ar vn.
mor amluc guint. y vlaen bric guit fallum[1].
arav vneuthume bith nys gunaun.

If I had known what now I know
Plain as wind in tree-top twigs,
I would never have done what I did.

[1] *Ffallwm*, an obscure word, perhaps a compound of *llwm*. Cf. Lloyd-Jones, GBGG, s.v.

The reference in 5c to the pain from vermin recalls the austerities of SS. Finnchua and Íte who allowed themselves to be gnawed by chafers or beetles (Lism. L., pp. cviii, 89).

I. Williams (BBCS 6,352) would derive the personal name Ysgolan of our poem from a Welsh *scaul, ysgawl*: Ir. *scál* 'champion, hero' and adduces the Breton forms Scolan, Ker-scoulan from Loth, *Chrest. Br.*, 230. The word *ysgodig* (2b) 'wild' is derived from *ysgawt* 'shade': Ir. *scáth* 'shade; fear; phantom, spectre . . .'. From this Ir. word is derived the name of the amazon *Scáthach*, a daemonic figure from whom Cúchulainn learnt the arts of warfare. Cf. *Scáth*, name of a phantom, Heldensage, 283. The W. cognate of *scáthach* is *ysgodog*, a synonym of *ysgodig*. These affinities support I. Williams' contention (*Canu Aneirin*, 388) that *ysgodig* is synonymous with *gwyllt* 'wild' and strengthen the comparison with the Suibhne Geilt motif referred to above. For a similar use of W. *ellyll* 'phantom' cf. R. Bromwich, *Trioedd Ynys Prydein*, 170: in triads 63, 64 *ellyll* has the force of men who went 'outside' themselves, which reminds us of Cúchulainn's battling metamorphosis and the Norse *berserksgangr* as well as of the *geilt/gwyllt* transformation. A late sixteenth century poem in praise of the Welsh translation of the Bible testifies to the Sgolan tradition. Cf. G. Williams, *An Introduction to Welsh Poetry*, London 1953, p. 41, who cites the lines:

pob kelvyddyd a dysc ffraeth, ddoedd gwir wybodaeth ganto
nes y Scolan gythrel gay ddinistro llyfray'r kymro.

'Every art and fluent learning, all true knowledge he had
till the false devil Scolan destroyed the Welshman's books'.

The *Ysgolan* poem confirms for W. literature what is so thoroughly exemplified in the Ir. *Voyage of Snedgus and McR.* (cf. pp. 48, 143, 187): the line of tradition from pre-Christian times which regards the sea, first, as a place of punishment for crime, and then as a place of atonement for sin.

The life of St. Tysilio perfectly illustrates the ideal of peregrinatio without return (*ailithre cen tintúd*, cf. p. 29): the chieftain's son turns his back on home and prospects and joined a monastery in Eifionydd. Thence he proceeded to Inis Suliau on the Menai where he founded the monastery of Llandysilio. In his ode to the saint, Cynddelw first considers his life (H. Lewis, op. cit., p. 33, lines 20–28):

Gorpu nef yn Eiuyonyd duded.
Mat gyrchawd garchar alltuded,
Kyrch kyflawn kyfle difroed;
Mat gymerth arnaw, praw pruded,
Prif obrwy, obryn trugared; . . .
Mat goreu madeu marthoed,
Ac yr Duw diofryt gwraged.

He conquered Heaven in the land of
  Eifionydd.
Well he sought a prison-exile,
A perfect resort, a place of pilgrim-
  age;
Well he undertook—proof of
  wisdom—
to merit mercy, the chief prize . . .
Well he behaved to renounce
  affliction
And for God to turn from women.

Later Cynddelw refers to a pilgrimage to Meifod and declares (93 ff.)
that the one who goes there cannot lose God; and that those in im-
minent spiritual danger are drawn thither and their deficiencies made
good.

CHAPTER V

THE GNOMIC MANNER AND MATTER OF OLD ENGLISH, IRISH, ICELANDIC AND WELSH

Gnomology may be approached in two ways: by definition of the term *gnome* and subsequent analysis of admitted gnomic material; or by analysis first, followed by identification of the gnomic *ethos* in its varying manifestations in the different literatures. Of the two approaches that by definition is the more clear-cut, particularly where the aim is a comparative study, and it is the one which has found most favour. It has tended however to promote the anatomy of the subject at the expense of the living organism and to deal in norms rather than in facts.

In the Introduction of her *Gnomic Poetry in Anglo-Saxon*, N.Y., 1914, B. C. Williams gives *inter alia* a survey of definitions of the *gnome*, including that of Aristotle (*Rhetoric* II, 21). The distinction between gnomes and proverbs as defined by others she rightly finds to be inapplicable in practice; Old Norse *máls hættir* includes both; the gnome (Denkspruch) can become a proverb (Sprichwort) by dissemination. She adopts gnome in the general meaning of 'sententious', applying it to a generalization of any kind whatever, and in her treatment of the subject she includes sententious sayings in epic and lyric poetry.

The latter are not specifically treated by the Chadwicks in their comparative study of Greek, Norse, Irish and Welsh gnomic poetry (*Growth of Literature*, Cambridge 1932, Ch. 12; cf. p. 399; on 380 brief reference is made to *Wanderer* and *Seafarer*). The Chadwick classification is based on Aristotle's definition of the gnome and it may be summarized as follows: Type I: Gnomes of Action and Conduct coming within Aristotle's definition i.e. statements relating *not to particulars* but to such *universals* as are the objects of action and are to be chosen or avoided in our doings; Type II: Gnomes of Observation, further subdivided into (a) human gnomes in which a course of action is not envisaged; (b) gnomes dealing with destiny and the gods;

(c) gnomes concerned with beings other than human. Aristotle's concentration on Type I agrees with the tendency of Hesiod's *Works and Days* which is concerned with what should be done rather than with observations of fact.

The chief merit of the Chadwick treatment is that its criteria facilitate comparison; its chief demerit that the criteria can be applied without a really close analysis of the material.

In his valuable studies of Celtic Gnomic Poetry (ECNP, Ch. 3; EWGP, p. 1 ff.) K. Jackson also uses a normative approach, without adopting the Chadwick frame. In spite of his efforts (EWGP, 1–2) the distinction between gnome and proverb remains elusive. Professor Jackson also differentiates rigorously between pure gnomic and quasi-gnomic poetry, i.e. poems in which gnomes are combined with descriptive statements about a particular scene (ECNP, p. 127), or with a particular human reference. For the earliest poetry (as apart from problems of the origin and development of 'quasi-gnomic' poetry, Jackson, Ch. 5) it does not seem to us helpful to press the distinction; not only do nature-gnome and description frequently merge, but the actual distinction between the two types may be difficult to establish. The gnomic awareness in the seasonal opening of *Kintevin* (p. 67 *supra*) is developed as description of a particular scene, while the final stanza of Irish *Cétemain* (EIL, p. 158) shows the merging of the two types:

Ecal aird fer fann,	The frail man fears loudness,
fedil fochain ucht;	The constant man sings with a heart;
uisse ima-cain	Rightly does he sing out
'Cétemain, cain cucht!'	'May-day, fair aspect!'

In Ir. gnomic literature we find the same combination: cf. *Bidh Crínna* 126 (Ériu V, p. 140) *Da mola tu duine ara saidhbhris on saogal tic sin* 'if you praise one for his wealth, it is from the world it comes'. In *Tec. Mor.* (pp. 105 ff. below) principles of individual and of general behaviour are brought together; individual precepts are offered in the light of universal experience. On p. 44, B. C. Williams quotes from Lawrence, JEGP IV 477: 'It was characteristic of Anglo-Saxon thought to connect the particular and the general, to make a man's experiences point a moral as well as adorn a tale. The Saxon in misfortune found consolation in philosophy long before King Alfred translated Boethius. Deor's refrain *þæs oferēode, þisses swā mæg!* is of a piece with the Wanderer's conclusions on reviewing the fates of men.

The reflective mood which leads to moralizing is closely akin to the elegiac spirit. . . .' A similar point is made incidentally by Williams (op. cit., 31) in speaking of gnomes in the epic: 'Such a saying is irrelevant in the sense that it is a generalization, which, though possibly called to mind by a particular circumstance or concrete situation, yet stands alone, independent; but it is not irrelevant with respect to the large unity of the early epic, which was ample and inclusive. . . .'

a. *English: The Gnomic Manner*

The chief O E gnomic sources are the collections in the *Ex. Book* (edd. W. S. Mackie (Part II), London 1934, which we use for our treatment below, and Krapp–Dobbie, Columbia 1936, pp. 156–163) and in MS. Cotton Tiberius B i (ed. Dobbie, *The Anglo-Saxon Minor Poems*, London 1942, pp. 55–57); cf. also B. C. Williams, op. cit. pp. 118–29. Subsidiary sources are the homiletic poems *Fates (Fortunes) of Men*, Ex. Book 154–156; the *Gifts (Endowments) of Men*, ibid. 137–40, and *Vainglory (Warning Against Pride)* ibid. 147–49. These are characterized by the occurrence of the distributive *sum* in connection with the homiletic theme of God apportioning different dispositions, gifts, or destinies to different people. Further, *A Father's Instruction (Precepts)*, Ex. Book 140–43, with contents in correspondence with these titles. Then come the occasional gnomes of lyric, epic, heroic and religious poetry. In the Exeter Gnomes, *Vainglory, Father's Instruction*, as in the miscellaneous *Order of the World (Wonders of Creation)*, Ex. Book 163–66, the figure of the communicating sage or wise speaker appears.

The corpus of sententious sayings comprising the Exeter and Cotton gnomes is characterized by the verbal forms *biþ, sceal* and simple present–future forms of other verbs; by the attribution to phenomena of characteristic qualities, activities and states (e.g. Cotton 16–17 *Ellen sceal on eorle, ecg sceal wið hellme/hilde gebidan* 'a man ought to be brave (courage is proper for a man); the sword will do (i.e. properly does) battle against the helmet'); by the inventory of items expressing superlative qualities (e.g. Cotton 5 ff. *wyrd byð swiðost. Winter byð cealdost* . . . 'fate is the strongest; winter the coldest'; cp. *Grímnismál* 44 (G. Neckel, Edda I, Heidelberg 1936, p. 64) and our Ir. gnomic texts for lists of superlatives similar to Cotton 3b–12); by verbal forms implying what is fittest (*geriseð* Ex. 66 and *passim*); and by adverbial and other forms implying frequency, custom (*oft, á* . . .).

The frequent occurrence of *sceal* makes the detailed investigation of its meanings in the gnomes an obvious starting-point of their study, the more so as this question has a direct bearing both on the gnomic spirit and on the principle of organization it mainly employs. The question has been previously treated[1] but without an adequate survey of the material. It has an obvious bearing for instance on the justification for the title *Maxims*, sometimes applied to the Exeter and Cotton gnomes (e.g. in the Krapp–Dobbie editions).

The first instances in the Exeter Gnomes are (4 ff.):

> gleawe men sceolon gieddum wrixlan god sceal mon ærest hergan
> 5 fægre fæder userne forþon þe he us æt frymþe geteode
> lif ond lænne willan he usic wile þara leana gemonian.
> Meotud sceal in wuldre mon sceal on eorþan
> geong ealdian god us ece biþ . . .

To interpret *sceal* (*sceolon*) in these lines, we have to consider the context.—Lines 1–3 invite an interlocutor to an absolutely free, full, and uninhibited exchange of ideas and information;—reservation will be met by reservation (2b–3). All this is generalized and summed up in 4a: *wise men should exchange sayings*. 4b (*first one should fittingly praise God*) is not irrelevant here: to praise God in the beginning (and in the end) is a proper practice frequently invoked and illustrated in the poetry.[2] The reasons for praising God are given in 5b–6. The sequel, to 18a, develops the theme of 4b–6, namely the relations between eternal God the benefactor and transient man who must render an account of His *gifts*. Thorpe (Codex Exon., London 1842) construes 'must' in 4b, though the context suggests propriety rather than compulsion. Mackie and Williams silently use their customary 'shall', which expresses some nuance between obligation and compulsion, and serves rather to obscure our problem. Lines 7–8a are translated

---

[1] In his survey of the semantic field of *skolo* in the Edda, Neckel (op. cit. Vol. II 154) considers the significance of the term as gravitating between the personal will of the subject and an impersonal fate; a third factor is the relation between the subjective will and the individual circumstance. Like *skolo* in Háv. 46.6, O E *sceal* may function without an infinitive, cf. the frequent *Ðys sceal on twelftan dæg* 'this is the proper gospel for the Epiphany' of Matthew 2: 1. For *sceal* cf. also Growth of Lit. 380 ff., Jackson, E W G P 61 f., Sweet, Anglo-Saxon Reader[11], 222, and B.T.

[2] Cf. *Cædmon's Hymn*; and *Black Book of Carmarthen*, p. 29, l. 1 ff. (p. 84 *supra*). Also *Preiddeu Annwn* (cf. J. Rhys, Lectures on the Origin, p. 248: 'The poem opens with the usual tribute to Christianity which not infrequently begins and ends the Welsh poems most replete with heathen lore.'); similarly *Book of Taliesin*, poem xiv; for O E poems cf. further p. 102 *infra*, and for the doxology in Middle English Romances Z C P 29, 1962, p. 95.

by Mackie as follows: 'God shall exist in glory. Man shall live on the earth, and the young man grow old', which leaves the precise force of *sceal* unexplained. Obviously the facts expressed in these lines apply to the present rather than the future, and just as the modern *'ll* form brings out the element of custom, closely allied to and often merging into that of certainty in present time, so *sceal* here expresses the states proper to God and man and the fact of senescence as predictable, certain, because natural and characteristic.

The translation with 'shall' in 7–8 does violence to the whole sequence (1–13) which is pitched in the present tense, the first half only (1–6) containing normal instances of future and past in agreement with this. The same argument from the context applies to the next example in 18b–19:

> þing sceal gehegan
> frod wiþ frodne biþ hyra ferð gelic

in Mackie's translation: 'Sage shall hold a meeting with sage; they are congenial spirits'. Here 19b with *biþ* seems to prove our point: as the minds of wise men are congenial they *should* hold communion together —it is fitting, proper, recommendable, but in no sense compulsory. The next examples occur in 22 ff.:

> Ræd sceal mid snyttro ryht mid wisum
> til sceal mid tilum tu beoð gemæccan
> sceal wif *ond* wer in woruld cennan
> 25 bearn mid gebyrdum beam sceal on eorðan
> leafum liþan leomu gnornian
> fus sceal feran fæge sweltan
> *ond* dogra gehwam ymb gedal sacan
> middangeardes meotud ana wat
> 30 hwær se cwealm cymeþ. þe heonan of cyþþe
> gewiteþ . . .

'Good counsel shall go with wisdom, justice with the wise, a good man with good men. Two are consorts; woman and man shall bring children into the world by means of birth. The tree shall suffer the loss of its leaves upon the earth, and lament its branches. The dying man shall depart, the doomed man die, and every day shall struggle at his parting from the world. (God alone knows where goes the pestilence that departs out of a land;)' (M.)

In 22–23 we have a series of things which go together; in 24–25a the function characteristic of one such pair. In 25b–29a the related phenomena of the tree losing its foliage and man dying are developed,—thus balancing and supplementing the reference to birth in 24–25a. 29b–30 on pestilence naturally follow what precedes on death; they also betray what the writer is up to: here his search for the cognate, the characteristic attribute fails: he is unable to tell us the homing place of pestilence. Cp. the ending of Cotton Gnomes 57b–66 on the theme *Meotod āna wāt* (57b), *drihten āna wāt* (62b), and *Fates of Men* 8b–9. An apt rendering of *sceal* in these lines (as elsehwere) would be: 'Good counsel 'll go with wisdom . . .', *'ll* (for *will*) expressing the inevitable recurrence of the characteristic, the natural, the proper.

In 22 ff. a *sceal* sequence is interrupted by the verb *to be* (23b), which expresses the customary occurrence of mating; procreation is seen, however, as an inevitable outcome—and so with *sceal*. Similarly in 25 ff. *sceal* brings out the *inevitable* and recurrent character of actions (states) which belong to the nature of things.

In lines 29b–50a the poet is interested rather in the interrelation and meaning of things than in their recurrence or inevitableness. *Sceal* is rare (38–39, 45b, 48a, 49a, 50a); other verbs with a fairly clear habitual value are found in 35a, 37a, 41b (*biþ*), and 45a (*behofað* 'requires'). The *sceal* instances are: 37–40

> (eadig bið se þe in his eþle geþihð earm se him his frynd geswicað).
> nefre sceal se him his nest aspringeð nyd[e] sceal þrage gebunden.
> bliþe sceal bealoleas heorte blind sceal his eagna þolian.
> 40 (oftigen biþ him torhtre gesihþe . . .)

Mackie renders: 'Happy is he who prospers in his home, wretched he whom his friends deceive: never shall he be happy whom his store fails, for a time he shall be bound by distress. The innocent heart shall be glad. The blind man shall be without his eyes; he is deprived of clear sight.'

Sceal in 38–39 is flanked by *biþ* (37, 40), and in 40a is actually represented by it, for this clause extends 39b. As 37a with *bið* also corresponds closely in circumstance with 38a which has *sceal*, we can expect but a minimal difference in usage and force between these two verbs. It should be remembered that beside its habitual force, *biþ*, like the present of other verbs, can express the future; so that *biþ* and *sceal* can stand in close relationship and both fit in well in the OE present-future category which is widely represented in 31–50. The force of *sceal* in 45 ff. is indicated by *behofað* of 45a:

45 lef mon læces behofað læran sceal mon geongne monnan
trymman *ond* tyhtan þæt he teala cunne oþþæt hine mon
átemedne hæbbe

'The sick man needs a physician. The young man shall be taught, encouraged and incited to have good knowledge, until he has been civilized . . .' (M.)

One ought to teach, encourage, civilize, feed and clothe the young man (45b–47), *for he needs all this.* One should not rebuke him before showing him (what to do); whereby he will prosper among the people and become resolute (48–49). But one needs to govern a mind of this kind (50a), for the storm which dashes the sea against the cliffs avails only to buffet both (50b–53). The rendering 'must' for *sceal* in 50a (cf. Klaeber, Eng. Stud. 49, 430) can only have hortatory force (i.e. *has to* in the sense of 'should'), for obviously one is free also to behave like the stormy sea;—50a is really a development of what precedes: having developed a strong, resolute mind by right education, one should learn to govern it.

The passage on storm and calm (50b–55) is in the habitual form, as also its application to humankind in 56 ff. In 58b we find *cyning biþ anwealdes georn* 'a king is eager for power' where the absence of an habitual present form in Modern English tends to obscure the meaning. Cp. Cotton Gnomes 1 *Cyning sceal rice healdan* which is best interpreted as 'to rule is the property of a king', 'a king will rule'. Incidentally, the Cotton Gnomes are usually held by editors to be disconnected; it ought to be pointed out, however, that the gnomes in 1–13a relate to things outstanding in degree (3b–13a), or in kind (king 1a, cities 1b).

In Ex. 60–64 we find a coupling of items (60) and an inventory of appropriate states and actions (61–63a) as in 22 ff., where *sceal* is similarly used. In 63b–70 *sceal* alternates with habitual forms (*biþ* 69a; *oft . . . bilihð* 64b, *oft . . . abreoþeð* 65b);—of special significance for the meaning of *sceal* is the verb *geriseð* 'befits', which occurs twice: *fæmne æt hyre bordan geriseð* (63b) 'a woman is in her fitting place at her embroidery' and *sceomiande man sceal in sceade hweorfan scir in leohte geriseð* (66) 'a man who feels shame will walk in the shadow, an upright man has his place in the light'. The correlation is very close here, and *sceal* must be correspondingly close in meaning to *geriseð*. 66b merges naturally into the impressionist picture of the lord distributing treasure to his retainers (67–69): hand will rest upon head, and treasure lie in its place; the throne will be decorated when men divide it; eager is he who receives the gold, of which the man in the high seat has sufficient. Here *sceal* suggests that what is customary and proper is predictable. In 70 (*lean sceal gif we leogan nellað . . .*) it expresses the future.

Exeter B[1] (71–137) opens with the famous seasonal gnomes: *Forst sceal freosan . . .* 'frost will freeze . . .' i.e. now and always, for that is its peculiar property. Lines 74b–75 refer to God unbinding the fetters of frost (*an sceal inbindan/forstes fetre felameahtig god*): here *sceal* has the same force as in 76 (winter will pass) and in 71 ff. The context with *an* (74b) and *felameahtig* (75b) tends to add in 74b–75 the nuance: '(only) God (can and) will unbind . . .' Lines 79–92 have *sceal* in the senses: what is habitual (proper), becoming, certain and predictable (*will*); what is to be recommended (*should*).

In 93–94a *sceal* rather closely approaches the meaning 'must': the ship usually is—and ought to be—nail-studded, the shield clamped together. It seems to me that the Frisian wife passage following arises out of or is connected with 93–94a: the (*Shield*-bearing?) sailor leaves his *ship* and comes home to his welcoming wife. He is the *agen ætgeofa* (97a) 'own proper provider (husband)' to whom is granted all that he requires (97–99). In the light of the accent here on the proper, appropriate (and necessary) I should hesitate to extend the meaning of *sceal* in 93–94a quite as far as the idea of compulsion ('must'). Neither does this idea correspond with the facts of 93a (a ship *did not have to be* nail-studded).

Lines 100–102, 103–106 are in context with what precedes. In 100— as suggested by its sequel—*sceal* means 'ought', also in 103b and 114a (one should nourish strength with food). The passage from 117 (118b) to 131 is interspersed with terms expressing custom (*bið* 118b, 120a, 123) affinity (*lenge* 120b), what is fitting and necessary (*geriseþ* 125, *þearf* 124a); and the attribution of characteristic concomitants, qualities and actions with *sceal* merely adds a nuance of certainty and predictability. Note the force of 132–133a: the *characteristic product* of Woden was idols, that of God glory and broad skies:—Line 131 (a holy man (will have) housel, and heathens sins) partly prepares us for the theme of 132-135 (: the Lord himself), which forms a proper homiletic close. (Woden, like the heathen of 131, serves as contrast). A deeper structural bond with what precedes is formed by the combination of the *customary* and the *characteristic* in 132–133a.

For this section cf. K. Malone, *Medium Aevum* 12 (1943) 65–67, and R. MacG. Dawson, J E G P 61 (1962), 17 ff.

The remaining Exeter (C) and Cotton gnomes (1–66) offer several noteworthy points: a clear example of *sceal* in the sense of 'must' (Ex. 172: *earm biþ se þe sceal ana lifgan* 'wretched is he who must live alone'). This does not apply to 144: for the habitual aspect of what follows (cf. *oft* 145, *ful oft* 147) clearly suggests a meaning 'should' for *sceal*: nor to 152 with its sequel which clearly expresses what is fitting and proper; (nor to any instance in Cotton). The context of 155a suggests that *sceal* there is intended to bring out that gold *is for* giving away.

Sceal of Cotton 1 (*Cyning sceal rice healdan*) has not the prescriptive—compulsory force of *Widsith* 11 ff., for instance. It expresses rather that ruling is the characteristic activity of a king (cf. Ex. 58b, Cotton 28–29), and so fits into the list of attributions with *byð, bēoð* which follows in 1b–13a. From 3b these are an inventory of things with superlative, or pronounced, qualities of the type *Winter byð cealdost* 'Winter is coldest'. The last of these statements is 13a *Wea*[1] *bið wundrum clibbor* 'Grief is exceedingly tenacious' where the transition from the preceding items in the ordinary superlative is marked by *wundrum*. It is followed in 13b by the transitional *wolcnu scriðað* 'clouds glide by' with its change of verb; the two halves of this line may well be antithetical in intent; their juxtaposition reminds of the Welsh manner. The effect of rude rime between the finals of 12, 13, 14 tends like the alliteration inside 13 to bind together elements which may by processes of gnomic association appear in sequence. 13b may be associable with what follows on the grounds that both express action appropriate to their respective subjects. At all events 13b is clearly transitional. It is followed by the maxim: *good comrades ought to encourage a young prince to battle and to liberality* (14–15). This theme is retained in 16–17a (*a man ought to be brave*, or *courage is proper for a man; the sword will do battle against the helmet*). In the succeeding series *sceal* expresses state or action which is characteristic (proper) and so customary and predictable. Cotton 43b ff., which edd. have found puzzling (cf. Dobbie, op. cit. p. 176, Williams, op. cit., p. 150) can be construed as follows: the girl who does not wish to prosper among her people and be sought in marriage frequents her lover secretly. This fits perfectly into the sequence of thief on the move in the darkness (42) and demon dwelling alone in a marsh inland (42b–43a); it may also be related to welling sea and stream and to teeming cattle in 45b–48a. Note how naturally the final section

---

[1] The emendation *weax* (cf. Dobbie, op. cit., 56, 175) seems unnecessary and inappropriate.

(57b–66) on the whereabouts of the soul after death grows from the reference to capital punishment in 55b; and how its formula *Meotod* (*drihten*) *ana wat* (57b, 62b), posing ignorance, systematically complements the *sceal, byð* type (of observation and experience, i.e. knowledge), in the earlier parts of the poem.

The meaning of *a scyle*, Ex. 177, calls for special comment in view of its occurrence in the *Wife's Lament* 42 ff. In 174 ff. it is observed that the lone dweller would be better off if he had a brother,—for preference son of the same father, in view of such perilous situations as a joint attack on boar or bear. Then it goes on: *a scyle þa rincas gerædan lædan/ond him ætsomne swefan.* Here *scyle* is clearly hortatory: 'those warriors should always (Let those warriors always (M.)) bear arms and sleep together'. *Á sceal* occurs twice: in Ex. 103b, where it clearly has the same meaning as *á scyle* (yet one should always expect the dear man . . .). The other instance is one with which editors seem reluctant to come to grips: Cotton 54b f. *Á sceal snotor hycgean/ymb þysse worulde gewinn.* The contention of rival forces in the world has been detailed in the previous lines (50–54a) so that we are clear at least about the meaning of *þysse worulde gewinn.* Fortunately *á sceal* applies from 54b to 57a, and so clues to its precise force may be sought in the content of these other members. Lines 56–57 (. . . fairly pay for his crime(s) against mankind) suggest that the meaning is 'should always'; this seems to be supported by the fact that the criminal did not always hang (cf. 55b *wearh hangian*). Nor can *á sceal* apply in 54b in any other sense than as exhortation (the wise man should always bear the contentions of this world in mind): —to do this is to profit from observation and experience as behoves the wise man. Cf. *Wanderer* 6–7, 64–65a, 88–91, 106, 111 ff.

Hence the meaning of *a sceal* (*scyle*) in these instances is 'should always'. This convergence of *sceal* and *scyle* is to be seen too in *Seafarer* 109, 111–112 (*Stieran mon sceal strongum mode, ond þæt on stapelum healdan* 'one should control a strong mind and keep it within bounds'; *scyle monna gehwylc mid gemete healdan/wiþ leofne ond wið laþne . . . bealo* 'everyone should use moderation in loving friend and hating foe'). Cf. also *Order of the World*, 17 (*forþon scyle ascian . . .* 'wherefore (he) should inquire about' . . .)

The *Wife's Lament* instance of *a scyle* (42) follows the account of her own predicament and heartache (27–41). It precedes and is fitted into a similar, though short, pen-picture of her husband's plight abroad (47b–53). The passage runs:

A scyle geong mon wesan geomormod,
heard heortan geþoht, swylce habban sceal
bliþe gebæro, eac þon breostceare,
45 sinsorgna gedreag, sy æt him sylfum gelong
eal his worulde wyn, sy ful wide fah
feorres folclondes, (þæt min freond siteð
under stanhliþe storme behrimed . . .)

Line 44a resumes 21a (*bliþe gebæro*) and 44–45a the thought of 19–21a,
which relates to the husband. For this and other reasons we do not
doubt that Lawrence (Mod. Phil. V, 389) and Williams (op. cit., 49 ff.)
are right in seeing here a gnomic use of *sculan* and a case of generalization. Williams does not translate, however, and Lawrence alters the
actual meaning to produce a more common gnomic pattern. Before
offering our own rendering two further observations on the text may
be made: *geong mon* (42a) has a force similar to that of *everyman*, so
we may either coin a corresponding form (*young-man*) or render less
archaically 'youthful man', 'every young man'; Kershaw (op. cit.,
p. 175) invokes Sweet, *New E. Gr.*, Oxford 1898, II, p. 13 to the
effect that the *sy . . . sy . . .* of 45–46 expresses an alternative hypothesis
(*whether . . . or . . .*)[1]. Sweet has however nothing to support this view,
and the *sy* of these lines too obviously continues the gnomic prayer
(or spell) begun in 42 (*a scyle*), to be otherwise interpreted. We
translate: May youthful man be ever sad of soul (*or* youthful man
should ever be . . .) and steadfast of mind; likewise, he should have a
blithe demeanour, also grief of heart and a host of constant anxieties.
May all his worldly joy depend on himself (alone); may he be outlawed
far and wide in a distant land, as (since, because) my lover sits under
a rocky hill covered with sleet by the storm . . .

The poet in true gnomic manner generalizes (to perpetuate) the sad
picture conjured out of her own misery and lovelessness: that of a
husband who once hid sorrow with a smile now exiled, outlawed,
friendless, exposed to all weathers, alone with his memories, and, like
herself, sadly awaiting reunion. The vague link-word *þæt* (47b) may
be interpreted with Timmer (English Studies 24, 1942, p. 36) as
'because, since'. But Beowulf 2699a has *þæt* in the meaning 'in so
much as, in that'; which (as Timmer points out) is also found in
Beowulf 88, *Maldon* 221, 251, and *Dream of the Rood* 19. While these

[1] Similarly R. F. Leslie (Three Old English Elegies, Manchester 1961, p. 58). But the
clauses have the same drift and do not really contain alternative hypotheses. Besides, the
rest of the passage suggests an additive gnomic treatment of detail.

two meanings are in any case closely related and either will serve, the second ('in so much as', 'as') seems to offer a somewhat smoother transition from the generalization (gnome) to the particular case which gave rise to it.

The transition from the gnomic corpus proper to the occasional gnome of epic, heroic, lyric and religious poetry is formed by the *sum* sequences of *Gifts of Men* 30–109 (Krapp–Dobbie, *The Exeter Book*, pp. 138–40) and the kindred *Fortunes of Men* 10–92 (ib. pp. 154–56). Both poems have interesting structural features: like the *Wanderer* they re-echo at their close the reference to God in their first lines, the *Gifts of Men* specifically resuming the attribute of divine bounty. Cp. also the close of *Seafarer* and of *Vainglory*. Moreover the opening of the *Fortunes of Men* (1–9) forms a neat prelude to its theme:—it describes how the parents bring on the child to the point at which one wonders what his destiny will be. Only God knows this (8b),—and here the poet smoothly begins to detail the various fortunes of men.

The gnomic catchword in the *Fortunes of Men* is chiefly *sceal*: *biþ* is less frequent, *mæg* and *con* rare. The pattern is (10–20): To one it will happen in youth that his end becomes a woeful tribulation to men; the grey prowler on the moor, the wolf, will eat him, (and) his mother will mourn his death, which is beyond man's control. Famine will waste another; another the storm will carry away, another the spear will kill, another war will destroy. Another will pass through life sightless, will grope with his hands . . . *Gegonged* (10), *weorþed* (12), *bimurned, bið* (14) are present-future forms; in among them we find, in 12b, *sceal (etan)* which we also render with *will*, and which apparently has a similar application. The potential aspective coincidence of the *sceal* form with the simple verb is the chief lesson in gnomic manner which this poem offers.

In the *Gifts of Men* the gnomic symbol is *bið;*—*mæg* and *con* are also found, beside a unique instance of compulsory *sceal* in 71b. In *Christ* 659–685 where the same theme[1] (i.e. God's gifts) is treated, the accent is on the capacity communicated, and *mæg (con)* becomes the symbol. (Cf. *Beowulf* 930b *ā mæg God wyrcan.* . . .) Lines 1348–1356 from the final passage of *Guthlac* contain some typical gnomic catchwords: *Selast* 'best' (1348 a), cp. *selre* 'better', *Beowulf* 1384b (*sēlre bið æghwǣm* 'it is better for each one'), 1839a; *oftost* (1348b, 1355b; cf.

---

[1] Cp. also *Hyndlolióð* 2–3 with its invocation to the 'Father of hosts', Óðinn, in his capacity of gift-giver.

Beowulf 1663b–1664a); compulsory *sceal* in 1351b, 1353b, beside the more gnomic *sceal* of 1348.

Beowulf has relatively few instances of compulsory *sceal* in gnomic passages, as in 455b, 1386a, 1534b and 3077a. Compulsory *swa sceal* (*man don*) of 1534b is hortatory in 20a and 2166b[1]. A different nuance is apparent in 24b–25: *lofdædum sceal/in mægþa gehwære man geþeon* 'by praiseworthy deeds a man is sure to (will certainly) prosper in every people.' Not quite this degree of certainty can be construed from *Wanderer* 73ff.:

> Ongietan sceal gleaw hæle hu gæstlic bið
> þonne eall þisse worulde wela weste stondeð . . .

'A wise man will perceive how unearthly it will be when all the wealth of this world lies waste . . .'. The set of maxims which precede in 65b–72 contain hortatory *sceal*. This occurs too in Seafarer 109a (which re-echoes Exeter Gnomes 50a); while in *Seafarer* 111a we have hortatory, in 74b compulsory *scyle*.

Of particular value as indices of gnomic intent are terms expressing what is *fitting*, *gerisan* (Ex. 66, 125 ff., 165); cf. also *mid gedefum* 188b; what is *customary*: with *oft* (35, 64, 65, 100, 145, 147, 190); with *á* (103b, 177a, 205a and Cotton 54b); with *hwær* (Ex. 192). Cf. also *fela* 14a, 101, *monig*, *monge* 13b, 15a. The function of explanatory accounts (with verbs in the preterite) such as Ex. 193–201 should not be missed. This one, for instance, explores the basis of bickering and warlike readiness outlined in the gnomes which precede and follow it.

It will appear from the foregoing analysis of the Exeter, Cotton, and other gnomic material that gnomic *sceal* typically expresses the notions of customary action or state, inherent quality and characteristic property, passing over on the one hand to ideal or hortatory action, (state), expressing on the other that sense of certainty which current dialectal varieties of the future (with *will*) bring out and which is also a feature of that future in Shakespearian English. Cf. Jespersen, *Mod. E. Gr.* IV, pp. 240, 244, Schmidt, *Shakespeare-Lexicon*, 1902, p. 1372, and the writer's *Anglo-Irish Dialect of North Roscommon*, pp. 165 ff.

---

[1] Cp. *Atlakviða*, 19. 5. On the basis of monitory gnomes and passages like 2166b ff., Brandl, following Earle, writes of *Beowulf*: kein anderes ags. Erzählungswerk, weder ein weltliches noch ein geistliches, kommt einem Fürstenspiegel so nahe (*Gesch. der altengl. Lit.*, in Paul's *Grundriss der germ. Philologie*, Vol. II, 2nd ed. 1908, p. 1001). Cf. *Beowulf* 2144. Fürstenspiegel, mirror for princes, is also the title given by Thurneysen to the earliest Ir. gnomic text, (*Tec. Mor.*, cf. p. 105 below), which typifies the *genre* influence of the Speculum Principis throughout the corpus.

This meaning of *sceal* relates it closely to that of the other gnomic means referred to above, particularly *biþ*. It suggests moreover, a criterion of unity, cohesion and organization hitherto lacking(cf. Dobbie, *The Anglo-Saxon Minor Poems*, p. lxvi f.): Phenomena in series which seem unrelated may, as pointed out above, be of the same order (things outstanding of their kind, Cotton 1–13a); be in series as exemplars of characteristic properties, concomitants or actions (Cotton 16–54a, Ex. 22–29a, 71–74a); be fitting or proper (152–154a, 165–166, 202–205); be customary (as in Ex. 190–192), predictable (67–68), recommendable (45b–49); or inevitable (as in Ex. 25 ff.). The transition from section to section can be quite deft (as in Cotton 13–15).

The thematic development and relation of phenomena to one another in sequence appears to be much closer than has been previously admitted, so that from this point of view also the gnomic corpus deserves more attention than it has hitherto received.[1]

b. *Irish*

A Brief Sketch

The bulk of the early Irish gnomic corpus is made up of Instructions addressed to a prince or prince-elect by father or foster-father. Not to be separated from these are the cognate *Senbriathra Fithail* 'Proverbs of Fithal (Cormac's judge)' addressed to his son, and *Briathra Flainn Fína maic Ossu* 'the Sayings of Flann Fína, son of Oswy', i.e. Aldfrid, King of Northumbria. Besides these there are anonymous and miscellaneous texts with which we do not deal, such as the *Triads of Ireland* (ed. K. Meyer, Todd Lecture Series, Vol. 13, Dublin 1906) and *Bidh Crínna* (ed. C. Marstrander, Ériu 5, 126 ff.).

Of the Instructions, we discuss the following: *Tecosca Morainn*[2] 'the Instructions of Morand'; the inter-related texts *Tecosca Cormaic*[3] 'Instructions of Cormac', *Senbriathra Fithail*[4] and *Briathra Flainn Fína*[5];

---

[1] Cf. now R. MacGregor Dawson, *The Structure of the Old English Gnomic Poems*, JEGP 61 (1962), 14 ff. E. G. Stanley points out that it is in the nature of the *Maxims* to combine things in contrast (Anglia 73, p. 426) and refers to the cohesive function there of balance and parallelism (427).

[2] Also known as *Auraiccept M., Audacht M.* 'Morand's Instruction, Bequest', ed. Thurneysen, ZCP 11, 56–106.

[3] Ed. K. Meyer, Todd Lecture Series 15, Dublin, 1909. Cp. Thurneysen, Zu Ir. Hss. und Litteraturdenkmälern, 3 ff., Berlin 1912.

[4] Edd. Thurneysen, op. cit., 11–22; R. M. Smith, Revue Celtique 45, 1–92 (1928). Cp. also R.C. 46, 268–271.

[5] Ed. Smith, op. cit. 61 ff. Cf. K. Meyer, Anecdota From Ir. MSS. III 10–20 (Dublin 1910). We cite Smith's editions below.

Briatharthecosc Con Culaind[1] 'the Instructions of Cú Chulainn', and the *Advice to a Prince*[2]. We leave aside the brief *Instructions of Conall Cernach*[3] and the partly gnomic *Rights of Every Lawful King*[4]. Our texts save the last-mentioned (*Advice to a Prince*) are in prose.

Of the two recensions of *Tec. Mor.* published by Thurneysen which we consider here, B is the older and the more comprehensive. In § 1 of this we are told that the young king Feradach Find Fechtnach ('the fair and prosperous') was brought in his mother's womb to Scotland after the rising of the Aithechthuatha or subject peoples, to return later to his patrimony in Ireland. The Instructions are addressed to him by the wise Morand through the herald Nere and so are often preceded by *Apair fris . . .* 'tell him . . .'. They are to inculcate *dīrge dligther* (*dlegar*) *cech flatheman* 'the righteousness due from every ruler' and *fīr flathemon* 'the justice of a ruler' (B 2, 12 et seq., A3). On the Act of Truth, the Prince's Truth and the power of Truth cf. M. Dillon, The Archaism of Irish Tradition, pp. 3–7 (Sir John Rhŷs Memorial Lecture, London 1947).[5]

After the introduction in § 1 (B, A) and the exhortation to the herald in §§ 2–5 (A 2–4), parr. 6–11 (B) outline the reciprocal effects of promoting truth, mercy, and the best interests of the people; to these correspond A 5–9 on promoting truth. Then follows in both recensions (B 12–28, A 10a–26) an inventory of blessings and dispensations which stem from a king's righteousness. Up to this point each recension contains items not found in the other. Then follows in A 30–43 a series of precepts and injunctions with *Abbair fris* to which B 29–57 roughly corresponds. But here again each recension has items not found or not as fully developed in the other; of these the chief ones are the *dligid* series in A 34 (not in B); the *ad·mestar* series in B 32 ff. (only one mixed version[6] of A has some of these); the *do·llēce* set in B 54, which has no equivalent in A. The series with *dligid* 'deserves' is a gnomic pendant to the injunction against evil qualities of character which it follows, outlining what each of the unapproved types of person merits. The series with *ad·mestar* 'he should assess' in B follows a

---

[1] In *Seirglige Con Culaind* § 25, ed. M. Dillon, Dublin 1953.
[2] Ed. T. O'Donoghue, Ériu 9, 43–54.
[3] In *Battle of Airtech*, Ch. 3, ed. R. I. Best, Ériu 8, 170 ff.
[4] Ed. O'Donoghue, *Miscellany presented to K. Meyer*, 258 ff.
[5] Cf. Culhwch and Olwen (J. G. Evans, White Book Mab., p. 460): *Gwir dyw im ar hynny. a gvir dy deyrnas.* 'God's truth thereon to me, and the truth of thy kingdom?'; also the 'spell of truth' (*ór fîrinde*) in the bull-feast ritual for determining the succession to the kingship (BDD § 11, SC² § 23).
[6] The ending of A (54–57) follows this version (*I*), which uses B 63.

similar pattern: first it is enjoined on the prince to estimate the things which God has created according to their true value, for otherwise the result will be defective; then individual items are taken and the manner of their assessment illustrated. The gnomic series with *do·llēce* 'yields to' (54) could be interpreted as arising out of the injunction in 53 and leading on to the specific precepts of 55; it has at any rate a general relevance here. It opens with 'darkness yields to light', 54a, and closes with 'falsehood yields to truth', 54n.

The next section is A 44–48 (= B 58–62) where a fourfold classification of princes is given. It is followed in B by the final exhortation to the herald (63) in which the prince Feradach, recipient of the instructions, is generalized to include 'every prince who rules justly' (not so the derivative ending of A (54–57 from MS. *l*), though 55 is general and gnomic. A 49–57 includes precepts, injunctions and gnomes; in 52 a series with verbs in the future (mainly *bid* 'he will be') outline the beneficent effects which Feradach can expect from complying with these counsels. In 53 this particular case is generalized.

The two recensions are marked by the following rhetorical devices:

(1) Copious alliteration, sometimes binding the first word of a phrase with the last word of the preceding one as in the early rhythmical *retoiric*: B3: *Ma thēisi co-rrīgu, reisi co Feradach Finn Fechtnach fóbéo; bid sīrflaithech, suide lānflatha, luifith iltuatha tathat co muir, moaigfid a chomarpa comlān co ngreit* 'If you go to kings, hasten to Feradach F. F. of happy life; long will he reign; (he will possess) the seat of a full ruler; he will press many thieving tribes to the sea; he will magnify his heir with valour'. Exx. of packed alliteration as in A 2, 13, B 14, 16 are frequent.

(2) Parallelism, Repetition and Variation. The passages selected for illustration here are important alike for content as for form and will serve as an introduction to the text.

A simple form of parallelism occurs in A 4 which may be written as follows:

Sluind dó ri cāch bréthir,[1]	Express to him the word before all,
beir dó ri cāch brēthir,	bring him the word before all,
indid dō ri cāch brēthir,	tell him the word before all,
brīg dō ri cāch brēthir.	declare to him the word before all.

Parallelism also appears in A 5–8 (B 6–11):

[1] But cf. B *re cech mbrēithir* (L *ri cach ṁbrethir*).

Mórad fírinni, na·mmórfa.
Nertad fírinni, na·nertfa.

Comad fírinni, cot·n-ōfadar.
Tócbad fírinni, cot·n-uicēba.

Let him exalt justice, it will exalt him.
Let him strengthen justice, it will
strengthen him.
Let him safeguard justice, it will
safeguard him.
Let him elevate justice, it will elevate
him.

In these exx. we observe an interesting *variation* between morphologic
alternants of the same verb, here in Imperative and Future. This is a
widespread feature of both recensions, cf. B 6–11 et passim, and it
suits our overall purposes to illustrate it in some detail. Beside it and
frequently combined with it is the rhetorical mode of actor acted upon
or reciprocal action. We classify according to the tenses employed,
illustrating from A (which often supplies a full context) and pointing to
corresponding sections of B where such occur; note the wider frame
of parallelism in many exx.: The *Pres. Indic.* of verbs occurs; morphologic alternance zero: the emphasis is on reciprocity: A 46–48
(cf. B 62):

(*Cíall·flaith immurgu* . . .) *nī·déni di neoch, nī·dēni nech de* '(the wise
prince . . .) takes from no one, no one takes from him'. Par. 47 re-
produces the content of 5–8 (above) in more truly gnomic form:
*Fírflaith immurgu, immus·mórat immus·nertat immus·bágat immus·
cumtagat 7 fírinne immalle* 'the true (just) prince however and justice
magnify each other, strengthen each other, contend for each other,
build each other up'. The second sentence of 48 (= B 62) runs:
Do·slaid do·sladar, fo·fich fo·fechar, con·clich con·clechar '(The bull
prince, i.e. unjust ruler) strikes, is struck, injures is injured, dashes is
dashed'; the beginning of 38 reads: *Abbair fris, fingal nīs·nderna.
Mairg fors·ndōirter, mairg ō·ndōirter!* . . . 'Tell him he should not slay
a relative. Woe to him on whom it is carried out; woe to him by whom
it is carried out.'
Pret. Perf./Future: Par. 37 (*Abbair fris, nī·lua úarlommann fola for
úarmírenn crōdai, for fēolai fine; ar* (*is* supplied by ed.) *étarbae n-inderb
n-indless etir cach ar ūair, ar cach die in bith sa.*) *Do·bebae do·beba,
do·rerae do·rera cāch boī cāch bias* 'Tell him he should not drink cold
draughts of blood on cold gory mouthfuls, on the flesh of his kinsmen;
for this world is profitless, uncertain, a transient possession of everyone
in turn, every day. Everyone that has been, everyone that will be,
has died, will die, has departed, will depart.'

Pres. Subj./Fut.: Par. 49 (cf. B 57) *Cach flaith nad ·bí co fīrbēssaib fírinne follnathar, do·bá do·beba, do·rá do·rera, con·gaib con·scara* 'Every prince who rules not according to the true usages of justice, should die, will die, should depart, will depart; what he establishes he destroys'. The possibilities of achieving an effect of contrast inherent in our rhetorical modes is illustrated in this final phrase where the semantic relation is held in focus by formal similarity, i.e. by the recurrence of *con·*. In par. 51 an injunction expressed contrastively in a parallel frame is followed by the application in the future: *Abbair fris, ní·n-erbba do sōebfáthib, na·n-erbba do fírinni, bid ferr cot·n-ófathar* 'Tell him he should not trust in (entrust himself to) false prophets, he should trust in truth, it will protect him better'.

Pres. Rel./Fut. Pass.: Par. 40 *Abbair fris, gonas gēntair, marnas mērthir* 'Tell him, whoso slays will be slain, who betrays will be betrayed'.

From the foregoing it will be clear that the gnome occurs either in more or less pure form as in the last instance (40); combined with exhortation as in our opening exx. A 5–8, and in B 6–11, all of which are susceptible of a more universal rendering and interpretation; or with recommendation, as in 50. The gnome is expressed with the future, as in 40, with the present as in 47–48, or without (substantive) verb, cf. some *sententiae* introduced by *Is tre fír flathemon* 'it is through the righteousness of a ruler (that)'[1]. . .: Ex. A 14 *Is tre fír flathemon cach tír toirthech, cach lámnad lánchóir* 'it is through the justice of a ruler (that) all land (is) fruitful (and) every birth completely normal'; similarly A 55 *Búaid cacha flatha a fírinne, fáilte cach maige, mógad cacha tūaithe* 'The excellence of every ruler is his justice, the joy of every field, the advancing of every people'. Cf. also A 45. Exhortation is expressed with the subjunctive, less often with the imperative; between the two forms there may be little to choose, cf. the subj. use of *erbaid* 'entrusts oneself, trusts in' in 50–51 and the imper. use in 56–57, where the injunctions have the same force in closely similar contexts. A feature of the text is the widespread use of the future in sententious statement.

(3) Word-Order: This is rather free; cf. A 23[2] *Is tre fír flathemon aibne*

[1] But B 19 introduces the substantive verb where A 15 omits it: *Is tre fír flaitheman rob·bí cech etha ardūasail imbeth* 'It is through a ruler's justice that there is abundance of all high and lofty corn'.

[2] Cf. also B 33–44 where sometimes the subject, and sometimes the prepositional complex follows the verb *ad·mestar*.

uisci īasc a tonnaib do·snāmaib segar, construed by Thurneysen p. 100, f.n 7: *do·segar íasc a tonnaib uisci aibne snámaib* 'Through the ruler's justice fish is captured by swimming from the waves of the water of rivers'. Here we have quite a series of features which can be instanced elsewhere in the text:

Type a) Cases of nouns in pre-position: the gen. precedes the noun it qualifies: *aibne uisci;* cf. also 15: *cach hetha ardhūasail imbeth* 'abundance of high and lofty corn'; in B 2, 63 (A 54) we have *mo chenēul (chenēol) clith* 'the desuetude of my kindred', which does not show the form of the gen. we might expect due to the preceding *ar*.

In 22 the acc. precedes the subject in a subordinate clause: *Is tre fír flathemon do·cuiredar ildelba muir* . . . 'It is through a ruler's justice that the sea casts up many forms . . .'

Type b) Case-forms without prepositions: *snámaib* 'by swimmings'; B 30 *faebraib* 'with sword-blades', B 50 *dagaicdib* 'by good works'. Further exx. in B 48–49.

c) Post-position of verb: the verb is separated by tmesis from its preposition as in *do·snāmaib segar* above; this is frequent in both recensions: cf. A 3 *Ad·mestar dar midrīana ad·mōrchlotha miditer* 'it should be assessed above streams of mead aimed at great renown'. Cf. also A 10a, 11, 16; B 13 (with perfective *conat·*), 15, 17–18. By a second type of post-position simple or compound verbs may appear in final position; cf. A 10b *Is tre fír flathemon mortlaidi mōra di dóenaib dingbatar* 'It is through a ruler's justice that great plagues are averted from people'. Further exx. in A 13, 17, 20, 22, 25, cf. also B 22–24 *et passim*. Note that the position of the verb in these cases agrees with that of the predicative adjective, as in A 14 *Is tre fír flathemon cach tír toirthech, cach lámnad lánchóir* 'It is through a ruler's justice that every land (is) fruitful, every birth fully proper'.

(4) Absence or suppression of (a) verb, especially the copula *is*; (b) the link-word *ocus, is*; (c) the def. art.

(*a*) Exx. A 12–15, 17–18, B 14. We have just cited A 14, and one other ex. will suffice: B 14 *Is tre fír flaitheman foss síd sāime suba soad sláine sādaile* 'It is through a ruler's justice a state of quiet, peace, tranquillity, happiness, well-being, health, ease'. Here the substantival character of the language is clearly shown.

(*b*) The suppression of the link-word 'and' is a feature which in some linguistic systems goes hand in hand with parallelism.[1] In our text it is properly characteristic of verbal elements and complexes only; we do not consider its suppression between nouns in the ex. just cited (B 14) to be in any way significant, for instance. Indeed it is likely to appear between all save verbal complexes in the forms 7 'et, ocus' and *sceo*; it occurs once in the form *os* (B 22). *Sceo* is rather common in B; cf. 22: *remi·déce īarmo·dēce tairsceo* (MSS. *tairscu, tarsce, tairrsce*; leg. *tair sceo) desiul scēo tuathbi[u]l do·féce* 'he looks before, he looks behind, he looks in front, to right and left'. Note here that the verbal forms are linked by parallelism, the others by *sceo*. This is the common pattern; for the occurrence of '7' between nouns linked in alliterating pairs, cf. B 56. For another ex. of verbal forms without a link-word cf. B 53, 63 *At·ræ tochumlai* 'Arise and go'. As lenition after *to-* is regular here, it seems unnecessary to entertain the possibility that *-ch* 'and' is infixed.

(c) The suppression of the def. art., also characteristic of the text, is in part relieved by the use of *cach* 'every'. For the relation of this gnomic use to ordinary syntactical usage cf. Contribb. I, fasc. 2, sub *in* (B, C) 187, 188.

The gnomic ideal is expressed by a wide selection of approving epithets throughout the text. Cf. the opening exhortation A 2 (B 2); and A 3: *Fō būan bithsuthain sír fír flathemon suithi cluines* 'Good, lasting, perpetual, constant is the justice of the ruler who listens to wisdom'. Cf. also *caín* 'beautiful', *téchtaide* (A 25) *téchta* (26) 'due', *lánchóir* 'fully right' (14) ... In A 13, 52 there are lists of such epithets. Qualities undesirable in a prince also find expression, as in A 34. That which is due, meet, fitting also comes into its own in the *ad·mestar* series in B 32 ff. Cf. B 32: *Apair fris, ad·mestar duile duileman doda· rōsat amal do·rrōsata; nach rēt nad asa maínib míastar, nícope lān-torath do·bēra* 'Tell him, he should estimate the things of the Lord which he has created for him as they have been created; any object which shall not be estimated according to its value will not give a full result'.

Gnomic catchwords in series—a feature of *Tec. Corm.*, of *Senbr. F.* and of *Br. F. F.* are not rare in this work. Apart from the *ad·mestar* series there is the *dligid* series in A as in the other texts mentioned, cf. 34c *dligid cach diumsach tairniud* 'every arrogant one deserves to be

---

[1] Cf. E. Lewy, Zur finnisch-ugrischen Wort- und Satzverbindung, Göttingen 1911, p. 99; Ernst Lewy: Kleine Schriften, Berlin 1961, p. 662 ff.; Der Bau der Europäischen Sprachen, PRIA 48 C 2, Dublin 1942, p. 83; H. Wagner, Das Verbum in den Sprachen der Britischen Inseln, Tübingen 1959, p. 205 ff.

humbled'; cf. *Senbr. F.* § 5 with 27 exx., and *Br. F. F.* § 3 with 38–most of them identical: *Tec. Corm.* § 15.1 (= *Senbr. F.* § 5.1 = *Br. F. F.* § 3.1) is a solitary example: *Dligid ecna airmitin* 'Knowledge deserves to be honoured'. Cp. passive *dlegar* 'is required of, incumbent upon', *Advice* 17: *Cetharda dlegar do flaith* 'there are four things incumbent on a prince'.

Seven of the 8 exx. of *dligid* in *Tec. Mor.* 34 have the very common catchword *cach* 'every' (*cách* 'everyone') found in A 12–15, 17–18, 20, 24–26, 28–29, 35, 37, 39, 42, 48, 52, and also in the nominal sentence in 55. *Cech* (*cách*) is found in *Tec. Corm.* in the nominal phrases of §§ 13, 15, 31, and *passim*; in *Senbr. F.* § 9, 24 exx. occur. Cf. also *Advice* §§ 13, 16, 20–21, 23, 26, 35.

Further, we find forms of the verb 'to be' in series: cf. A 52 *bid* 'he will be' (cop.): *bid sen, bid suthain . . . bid lán do cach maith* 'he will be old, lasting . . . full of all good'; in B 55 a series with *ba* 'he should be' occurs: *Apair fris, ba trōcar, ba fírién . . . ba fírbrethach* 'tell him he should be merciful, righteous, . . . of just judgment'. This feature is common in the later texts.

In *Tec. Mor.* B 54 there is a series with *do·llēce* not found in the later texts, cf. 54a *Do·llēce dorche do sorche* 'Darkness yield to light'.

In *Tec. Mor.* A 42 a category of things which are *better* (*ferr*), *dech* 'best', and which are a feature of the later texts is faintly adumbrated: *Abbair fris, níp sotal soisil sainairlech. Ar it ferr airli oldās airle, it ferr cīalla oldās cíall, it ferr gāesa oldās gāes. Is ed as dech cacha gāese dōenachtae: dílse 7 díute, tuae 7 trebaire; dech áilche ainmne foss fiss feidle age airle* 'Tell him he should not be proud, haughty (and) self-opinionated. For counsels are better than (one) counsel, the intelligence of several is better than the intelligence of one, the wisdom of several is better than the wisdom of one. The best of all human wisdom is: propriety and simplicity, silence and prudence: the best virtues are patience, quiet, knowledge, perseverance, courage, and counsel.' Cf. *Tec. Corm.* §§ 1; 3; 11; 16.106–112; 17.8–9; 36: *Senbr. F.* § 4 (52 exx. with *ferr*), § 11 (*Cid as dech ban?* 'which is the best of women?'); *Br. F. F.* § 6 (90 exx. with *ferr*); *Advice* §§ 4, 6, 8, 18, 26.

Scarcely significant enough to be considered a forerunner of later lists or other mention of things which are 'good' (*maith, fó*) is the instance of *fó* in *Tec. Mor.* A 3. Cf. *Tec. Corm.* §§ 12; 16. 99–100;—also *Br. F. F.* § 7, I, which is followed in 7, II by an illustration of what is 'troublesome, hard, bad' (*doilig*). Much more frequent than these, especially in *Tec. Corm.*, where they are elicited by question, are the things (kinds) which are worst: cf. §§18, 21–28; also *Senbr. F.* §12; *Advice* § 8.

Gnáth 'usual' occurs in A 45, 50. Par. 45 runs: *Flaith congbála co slūagaib dianechtair, gnāth flaith lobur ēlaithech do suidiu* 'the prince who establishes himself with forces from outside has usually a weak, fleeting kingdom'. Cp. also *nūallgnāth* 'accustomed to proclaim', an epithet of the herald Nere (A, B 2). For the later texts, curiously, *gnáth* is unimportant, although the concept behind Tec. Corm § 7–8 *Cia bátar do bésa (gníma) intan ropsa gilla?* 'What were your habits (deeds) when you were a lad?' is closely related to it.

The *Instructions of Cormac* (mac Airt) are in the form of answers by this accomplished king to the questions of his son, Cairbre Lifeachair. A survey of its themes will also serve for its catchwords (the chief of which is *cech* 'every', see above): What is best (*dech*) for king and tribe (1, 3); the true (proper) right (*cóir rechta*) of a king (2); the dues or rights (*ada*) of chief and ale-house (4); the proper qualities of a chief (*téchta flatha*) (6); the sources of chieftaincy (5); the *habits* and *deeds* (*bésa, gníma*) of the young Cormac (7, 8): the sweetest sound he has heard (*bindem*) 10. For sweetest (*milsem*) in other connections cf. 31.24–27; things *good* (*fó*, 12), *best, better* (*dech, ferr* §§ 11; 16. 106–112; 36), *worst* (*messam*) (§§ 9; 18; 21–28; 33, 37), the *most lasting* (*búaine*, § 20), the *deafest* (*buidre* § 35), the excessive degree, with *ro-*, e.g. *rogáeth* 'too wise' § 29; How do you *distinguish (cia etergén?)* people § 13, women § 16, weathers § 17; How should I *be(have)? (Cindas (nom)beo?)* §§ 29, 30, cp. *Senbr. F.* §§ 7–8.

The *ways of folly* (*gabála báise*, § 14) and the Irish *code of ridicule* (*forus cuitbeda*, § 32) supplement each other. Together they offer a list of actions and of qualities which add variety to the constant play of the bad (unfitting, improper . . .) and the good (due, appropriate . . .) throughout the text. Finally, § 34—in similar vein—warns against qualities undesirable in an associate and supplements the list of *worst* types of man and *worst guarantor* in 27, 28, 33.

The themes of *Tec. Corm.*, then, fall under three closely-related heads which reveal a well-integrated gnomic pattern. I: what is meet, fitting, due (unfitting, improper), merging into II: how to behave (not to behave), and into III: the qualities of things (people), often with the superlative.[1]

---

[1] For the relation to Welsh gnomic classification and to the Irish concept of personal prerogative and taboo, cf. p. 130, f.n.1. Collocation in triads, tetrads, heptads, etc. is of course a related feature.

This text offers an insight into the psychological background of gnomic classification. In answer to the question: how do you distinguish weathers? the versatile Cormac declares: 'Ice is the *mother* of corn, snow is the *father* of fat, a shower is a *presage* of bloodshed, drought is a *presage* of pestilence, wind is *most troublesome* in a strait, the *best* of weathers is mist, *better* his brother rain; save for the sea, thunder is not *fruitful*'. Note the italicized epithets (criteria). In §22 he gives the 17 signs (*comartha*) of bad pleading, cp. *Senbr. F.* § 6. *Br. F. F.* § 4 contains 24 exx. with *descaid* 'sign, symptom', cp. § 4.6 *Descaid ēca uaman* 'fear is a presage of death'. Significant too is the term *airdena* 'signs, tokens' in *Senbr. F.* § 13, where 15 traits of good and of bad women are enumerated. Cp. the list with the catchword *eochair* 'key', Z C P 6, 270 f., beginning with *Eochair chéille coistecht, eochair seirce sāmud* 'the key of sense is listening, the key of love is associating'.

Basic to gnomic observation of this type is the affinity deemed to exist between the two members juxtaposed, which we find mirrored in *Tec. Mor.* in the *dligid* and *ad·mestar* series (A34, 39; B32), for instance; in the series recounting the blessings and dispensations which accompany a king's righteousness (*fír flathemon*), A 10a–26, B 12–28; and variously elsewhere. This affinity appears clearly from *Senbr. F.* § 2 (= *Br. F. F.* § 1) which is marked by the criterion (catchword) *adcota* 'begets', cf. § 2.3: *Adcota cīall cáinchruth* 'intelligence begets good looks', § 2.4 *Adcota báes burba* 'folly begets violence'.

One of the chief differences of a general type between *Tec. Mor.* and *Tec. Corm.* is that the element of inventory so pronounced a feature of the latter text seems subordinated in the former as a rule to the organic weight of the individual gnome or precept. This may partly account for differences in technique: in *Tec. Mor.* the structural unit is often compressed and highly structured; in *Tec. Corm.* the tendency is to weaken alliteration inside the line while often retaining it to bind successive lines of a series; cf. § 3, line 4 ff., § 4, line 5 ff., § 13 line 6 ff., § 14, line 4 ff. . . . Such lines are sometimes connected also by alliteration between their predicates, by an occasional rime, or by repetition of a keyword, all of which are illustrated in § 12.

In *Tec. Corm.* (as in *Tec. Mor.*) affinity is supplemented by *contrast*, which provides a conceptual basis for many gnomes and injunctions. The technical means employed to achieve this includes: (*a*) Opposition of concepts in nominal phrases or phrases with forms of the substantive verb (copula); cf. § 16.14–15: *feidle miscne,/dermatcha seirce* 'steadfast in hate, forgetful of love', or § 16.82–83; exx. with *ferr* 'better' § 16.106 ff. The simplest type with the copula is found in § 29: *Ní ba rogáeth, ní ba robáeth* 'Be not too wise, be not too foolish'; cf. also § 7.14–15. Other types include a qualifying phrase (§ 7.16–18; § 7.19–23; § 7.25–26), Exx.: § 7.18 *nírba ocus ar ná ba tromm* 'I was not close lest I should be burdensome'; 7.20 *nírba taircsinach ciarba trén* 'I was not given to promising though I was strong'; cf. *Senbr. F.* § 3, *Br. F. F.* § 2; the first ex. in each is: *Bat faitech ar nabat fíachach* 'Be cautious that you may not be in debt.'

(*b*) The subject is 'everyman' (*cách*) and the qualification follows with *co* 'to, till' in a nominal phrase: § 31.2–20, cf. *Senbr. F.* § 9. Ex. § 31.4: *cara cách co fíachu* 'everyone is a friend till (it comes) to debts'. For an ex. with *cach* 'every', cf. § 31.21.

(*c*) Related to the modes discussed is the use of *Dia* (*mba*) 'If (you are) + fut. of verb in the apodosis, § 29.10 ff. (= *Senbr. F.* 7.12 ff). Ex. 29.10 *Dia mba rogáeth, fritotsáilfider* 'If you be too wise, (too much) will be expected of you'. Two exx., § 29.13–14, have the verb 'to be' in the apodosis.

(*d*) Semantic opposition in verbal phrases; cf. § 16.85 ff.; type: *dorairngerat nád chomallat* 'they promise what they do not perform' (§ 16.90).

As the gnomes of a purer order are often marked by the nominal phrase, so the injunctions are often marked by the copula (*ba, bad, rop, nírba . . .*) or by the subj. or imperat. of other verbs. It is of interest to find that the fut. (of the cop.) is used (as in Tec. Mor. A 52) to express gnomic truths arising from given premises, cf. § 31.28 ff.: *Duine óc sochoisc umal erlataid bus léir cubus 7 cobais, bid cóem a óitiu, bid sruith a sentu, bid fír a briathar, bid cáid a forgnúis, bid úasal cid ísel, bid sen cid óc, bid maith a forcenn la Día 7 duine* 'A docile, humble, obedient young man of a nice conscience and confession, his youth will be lovable, his old age venerable, his word will be true, his countenance will be chaste, he will be exalted though low, he will be old though young, his end will be good with God and man'.

The collection of proverbs (and precepts) associated with the name of Fithal, Cormac's judge, are closely linked with those which bear the name of Flann Fína.—Only two of the seven sections of the latter are lacking in *Senbr. F.*: § 4 based on the criterion *descaid* 'sign, symptom, presage' (*Descaid drūisi dānatus* 'boldness is a sign of lust') and § 7 (not an original part of the text) which expatiates on the twin theses *maith dán ecna* 'wisdom is a good gift', *Doilig dán láechdacht* 'the layman's life is a troublesome gift'. Only 9 of the 139 maxims in *Senbr. F.* §§ 1–5 are lacking in the other text, which on the other hand shows a proliferation of exx.

The sections which the two texts have in common are marked by specific criteria (catchwords): *Tossach* 'beginning', *Senbr. F.* § 1, *Br. F. F.* § 5; Exx. *Senbr. F.* § 1, 18–19: *Br. F. F.* § 5, 20–21: *Tossach sodchaid dagben* 'the beginning of fortune is a good wife', *Tossach dodchaid drochben* 'the beginning of misfortune is a bad wife'. *Adcota* 'obtains, begets', *Senbr. F.* § 2, *Br. F. F.* § 1; Exx. § 2. 25, 27 (: 1.51, 33) *Adcota cath cóiniud* 'a battle begets keening', *Adcota imresain imned* 'wrangling begets misery'. The Imper. and Subj. sg. 2 *ba, bat* as in *Tec. Corm.* § 30: *Senbr. F.* §§ 3; 8.3–9; *Br. F. F.* § 2; Exx. § 3.1, 5 (:§ 2.1, 5) *Bat faitech arnabat fíachach* 'be cautious that you may not be in debt', *Bat gartaid corbat sochraid* 'be generous that you may be honourable'. Apart from these sections there are others—already signalled above—with still wider affiliations, particularly those marked by *cach* (*cách*) 'every(one)', *dligid* 'is entitled to, merits', *ferr* 'better'. This exhausts the repertoire of more common gnomic nuclei in *Br. F. F.*, while *Senbr. F.* has chiefly its superlatives left (*dech* 'best' § 11, and *messa(m)* 'worst' § 12); and its section (7) with forms of the copula (*nírbat* 'do not be', *diambat* 'if you are') which it shares with *Tec. Corm* § 29. *Senbr. F.* and *Br. F. F.* frequently show a tendency towards alliterative collocations.

In *Serglige Con Culainn* 'the Wasting Sickness of Cú Chulainn' §§ 21–23, it is recounted that the medium in the bull-feast ritual for divining who should succeed Conaire in the kingship of Ireland saw in a vision the form of Cú Chulainn's foster-son Lugaid. The latter was then found consoling his stricken foster-father at the bedside, who thereupon is made to voice the Instructions (*Bríatharthecosc*) to the young king elect (§§ 25–26).

The 41 precepts (ll. 263–301) are made up of (I) Eight (ll. 270–277) in Imper. or Subj. pl.3 on legal procedures connected with property, inheritance and the protection of strangers. All save one (l. 270) are in the positive; (II) Thirty-three direct injunctions in the Subj. sg. 2, of which eight only (ll. 286–289, 291, 296) are positive. Subj. forms of the copula, esp. *nírbat, níba(t)* are of frequent occurrence, as in the last three exx. borrowed from *Tec. Corm.* § 19: *Níbat comromach ar nábat miscnech* 'be not contentious lest you be hateful', *Nírbat lesc ar nárbat meirb* 'be not lazy lest you become enfeebled', *Nírbat róescid arnábat dóescair* 'be not too eager lest you become vulgar'.

Rhetorical features of the *Bríatharthecosc* are: alliteration as in l. 274 *Mrogatar genelaigi gésci úa genither gein* 'let the genealogical branches from which offspring is born be extended'; the position of attributive gen. before its noun, as here; and of adj. before its noun as in 276.

The prescriptive ideal is enshrined in terms such as *tēchtae, toich* (276) which as adjj. have overlapping meanings 'due, proper . . .'; *co fírinne fíu* (272) 'with worthy truth'; and in the precepts of 287–289. The negative pole—almost necessarily involved in the constant negative approach—is marked by the morphological variants *étechtae* (270), *antechtae* (296) 'unlawful, improper . . .'

Advice To A Prince is a Middle Ir. poem of 37 quatrains which (to judge from stanzas 6, 7) seems originally to have had some connections with Cashel. In one (of ten copies) it is entitled: *Fingin cecinit do Chormac mac Cuilennain. Advice,* which borrows from all the foregoing texts, makes in § 4 a specific reference to *Tec. Corm.*: *Tecosc Cormaic ba cor gāith*: *ar Coirpri Lifechair luath* 'Tec. Corm. was a wise contract to swift Coirpre Lifechair'.

The initial approach *Diambad messe bad rī réil* . . . 'If I were an illustrious king' is maintained throughout stt. 2–3. The most striking sententious observations here are: st. 2c *nī innisfind i fail ban: in scél bad áil dam do chleith*[1] 'that which I wished to conceal I would not relate where women are', and st. 3c *muire icnabít géill ingill: isé in lind i coire toll* 'the king who has not hostages in keeping is as ale in a leaky vessel'. St. 4 has *dech* 'best'; and one or other of the kindred *messu* 'worst', *maith* 'good', *ferr* 'better' occurs in 6, 8, 13, 18, 19, 26. In st. 5 we encounter the familiar and significant gnomic criterion: what is *proper, due,* here with *dlecht* in this meaning, from *dligid: Tairnem na diumsa ro dlecht* 'the humbling of pride is proper', cf. *Tec. Mor.* A 34c *dligid cach diumsach tairniud* 'every proud one deserves humbling'. The approximate synonyms *dúal* and *dú* 'meet, fitting, right' occur in 28d and 35b. Stanzas 9–12 detail triads relating to kingship. Stanzas 13, 16, 20, 21, 23, 24, 26, 35, are marked—some dominated—by the criterion *cach* (*cāch*) 'every(one)'; stt. 15 and 22c, d on truth in a prince and on tribes who have lost their king, respectively, contain striking similes conveyed by types of equative (*gilithir, samail*). St. 17 is an enumeration of four desiderata of a prince. St. 25 continues from 24c, d the listing of gnomes in the positive: A small herd is neglected; a prudent son obtains land; a promise made is a debt incurred; a king's word is the judgement of a district.

[1] Cf. Éigse III 67 f., and p. 118 *infra*.

Stanzas 27–33, with *mac* 'son' in nominal phrases, are a very interesting illustration of the gnomic ethos, particularly in view of the semantic development of *mac* in the direction 'one devoted to, addicted to, following (a calling or function), characterized by', cf. *mac ecailse* 'son of the church, cleric', *m. foglama* 'son of learning', 'student', *m. meda* 'son of mead, a heavy drinker'. St. 28, for instance, runs: *Mac in tsaír allus in táil: do chumma in chláir ina chirt/mac in goband cosin ṅgual: isé a dúal dechrad dia slicht.* 'The carpenter's son to the adze, to fashion the board aright; the smith's son to the coal;—it is fitting for him to follow his family'. *Isé a dúal* here in 28d is varied in 31b and 33d by *isé a bés (gním)* 'It is his custom (practice)'.

The related theme of youth's potential is the subject of 34c, d: 'It is from the fry the salmon comes forth: from the young man comes forth the king'. For the rest, stanzas 34–35 are either couched negatively (*ní suí nad athchain fa dí* 'he is no sage who does not repeat') or treat undesirable action (*Adaltras coilles cach clú* 'adultery ruins every good name').

c. *Icelandic*

The chief repository of gnomic lore in Icelandic is *Hávamál* (Sayings of the High One, i.e. *Óðinn*)—only a fraction of which justifies the name. It is chiefly made up of wise observations, maxims and magic-mystical lore, and has welded into it sequences in which Óðinn recounts experiences illustrative, heuristic and mystical. Its first main section (of 110 stanzas) contains the bulk of the poem's practical and gnomic wisdom: it offers a wide selection of observations and counsels on the requirements and behaviour of traveller, guest, and wise man;[1] on the evils of drunkenness and folly; on good and ill friends; on gift-giving, friendship and friendliness; on small blessings and the superiority of fame to riches. The theme of love and woman's falseness is considered in 84–102 in a context of things not to be trusted and against the background of an Óðinn parable. Stanzas 84 and 90 run thus: *Meyiar orðom skyli manngi trúa,/né því er kveðr kona;/þvíat á hverfanda hvéli vóro þeim hiǫrto skǫpoð,/brigð í bríóst um lagið* 'No man should trust a maiden's talk, nor any woman's word; for their

---

[1] Cf. st. 18: *Sá einn veit, er víða ratar/ok hefir fiǫlð um farit,/hverio geði stýrir gumna hverr -/sá er vitandi er vits* 'a man that travels far and has traversed many lands will know the mind (ways) of every kind of men, if he has his wits about him'; cf. ON *heimskr* 'foolish' (< 'homish'). For the text cf. G. Neckel, Edda³, I, Heidelberg 1936, and the further ed. by H. Kuhn, Heidelberg 1962.

hearts were wrought upon a whirling wheel, and fickleness planted in their bosoms': *Svá er friðr kvenna, þeira er flátt hyggia,/sem aki ió óbryddom á ísi hálom,/teitom, tvévetrom, ok sé tamr illa,/eða í byr óðom beiti stiórnlauso,/eða skyli haltr henda hrein í þáfialli* 'the love of a woman whose heart is false is like driving a slip-shod, wild, two-year old badly broken horse on slippery ice, or sailing rudderless in a furious gale; or like setting a lame man to catch a reindeer on the thawing hill-side'. Compare with this the gnomic and succinct verse of Pentadius (*c.* 290; cf. *Penguin Book of Latin Verse,* 1962, p. 68):

> Crede ratem ventis, animum ne crede puellis;
> Namque est feminea tutior unda fide.
> Femina nulla bona est, vel, si bona contigit una,
> Nescio quo fato est res mala facta bona.

'Trust your ship to the winds, but do not trust your heart to a maiden, for a wave of the sea is more trustworthy than a woman's word. There is no good woman anywhere; or, if one does happen to be good, I know not by what chance a bad thing has become a good one.'[1] In the course of a sustained and stylistically varied condemnation of women in the Irish *Tecosca Cormaic* it is said of them 'They are waves that drown you, they are fire that burns you, they are two-edged weapons that cut you . . . they are darkness in light, they are bad among the good, they are worse among the bad' (§ 16. 115–122). The manner of this is reminiscent of *Háv.* 90; but the cataloguing of woman's imperfections as in *Tec. Corm.* is also reminiscent of Greek literature (cf. Hesiod, ed. H. G. Evelyn-White, Loeb Classical Library, 1954: p. 123 (*Theogony*), p. 31 (*Works and Days*).

Stanza 103 takes up once more a recurrent and ever-relevant topic: the qualities of the accomplished, wise one: and Óðinn tells (104–109) how his ready tongue availed him to beguile Gunnlǫð and to drink the precious mead of wisdom and poetry. Features in this section which link it with Irish, English and Welsh gnomic poetry are the *sumr* passage in 69, the list of *best* (*and better*)[2] things, in 68, 70–72,

---

[1] Cf. *Sólarlióð,* st. 10 (F. Jónsson, *Sæmundar-Edda²*, Reykjavík (1926), p. 442): *Munaðar ríki/hefr margan tregat;/opt verðr kvalræði af konum;/meingar urðu,/þótt hinn mátki goð/skapaði skírliga* 'The might of love has brought grief upon many a man; torment often comes of women; they have become noxious, though Almighty God created them pure'.

[2] Cp. *Grímnismál* st. 44, *Beowulf* 1384b, *Guthlac* 1348a and our Ir. gnomic texts, pp. 111 ff.; also p. 93.

145, and of opportune acts and characteristic or appropriate uses in 81–83. The temper of the poem here is that of the well-wrought maxim, economical and pointed. Occasionally it transcends this, notably in the *deyr fé* sequence (76 f.). Striking too is the development of the heron of forgetfulness (*óminnis hegri*) as a symbol of intoxication in stanza 13; while the *lítilla sanda* sequence (st. 53), characteristic and impressive, is not developed in the sequel and falls away.

Stanza 111, which introduces the counsels to Loddfáfnir (112–137) in a ceremonial style marked by parallelism, is placed in the mouth of Óðinn, who had acquired rare and deep knowledge, he tells us, in the Hall of the High One at Urðarbrunnr, seat of the Gods. The counsels themselves, meanwhile, are not the exalted *rúnar* and *ráð* of the gods: they are precepts of conduct, mainly towards friends and acquaintances good and bad, women, and guests: they stress the need for caution in several respects, and warn against mockery. Of special interest are the more archaic injunctions in stanzas 113–114, 129, 136 and 137: against sleeping in a witch's arms; against looking up in battle and sharing the fate of Suibhne Geilt (*gialti glíkir verða gumna synir*); the counsel to place a gift on the door for the visiting wayfarer in order to avoid his curses; and the list of antidotes in 137 which includes invoking the moon against ill-will and runes against curses.

The pedestrian and insistent-familiar formula of direct address *Ráðomk þér, Loddfáfnir, en þú ráð nemir (nióta mundo, ef þú nemr, þér muno góð, ef þú getr)* which pervades the section marks it off from the first and belies the connection with divinity formulated in 111.

The third section (138–145) opens with a first-hand account of the wounded Óðinn on the gallows (whence the name Yggdrasil 'Óðinn's gallows') and of his subsequent progress in wisdom and knowledge. This is followed by a series of questions on the pattern: *Know you how to (carve runes)?* and a corresponding series: *Better not at all than (wrongly carved)* ... which springs from a sense of fitness or propriety fundamental to the gnome and widely exemplified in the Celtic material, and to a less extent in the English. It may be compared as well to Irish sequences with *better*.

The fourth section (146–164) contains an enumeration of charms unknown to others by the wise Óðinn (146: *Lióð ek þau kann, er kannat þióðans kona / né mannzkis mǫgr* 'I know songs (charms) such as no king's wife nor son of man knows'); he refuses to communicate the eighteenth and last, which accords with the injunction frequently repeated throughout the poem to keep one's own counsel.

The charms are various and include some against sickness and enmity, and for personal safety, and success in love; also one which prevents witches riding aloft from regaining their own shapes. Others too seem to derive from the same psychological background and milieu as the archaic injunctions to Loddfáfnir mentioned above.

The poem ends with a recapitulatory stanza (164) the opening of which (*Nú ero Háva mál kveðin, Háva hǫllo í*) harks back to 111 (*of rúnar heyrða ek dœma, né um ráðom þǫgðo,/Háva hǫllo at, Háva hǫllo í,/heyrða ek segia svá:*) This suggests that section 111–164—whatever its original content and shape—is to be thought of as a unit, for these two stanzas no doubt belong to its original nucleus.

The centre of unity of the diverse material in *Hávamál* is the concept of *wisdom* (*knowledge*), which can include *gnome* (1–110 mainly), maxim (112–137), mystic-heuristic experience (138–145) and spell (146–164). The emphasis on wisdom promotes the interrogative formula, as in 144: *Veitstu, hvé rísta . . . skal?* 'Know you how to carve (runes)?'; this can easily take on a superior tone as in the *Völospá* tease *vitoð ér enn, eða hvat?*; less so in *Hyndlolióð: varðar* (*vǫromz*), *at viti svá; viltu enn lengra?* (passim).

Closely allied to wisdom is experience, and so the account in the first person is an important illustration and prop for the sententious remark, cf. stt. 47, 78: *Ungr var ek forðom, fór ek einn saman;/þá varð ek villr vega;/auðigr þóttomz, er ek annan fann:/maðr er mannz gaman* 'Once I was young and travelled alone; then I went astray. I felt happy when I met another: man is man's pleasure'; st. 78: *Fullar grindr sá ek fyr Fitiungs sonom:/nú bera þeir vánar vǫl;/svá er auðr sem auga bragð:/hann er valtastr vina* 'I saw the full-stocked folds of the sons of Fitiung; now they bear the beggar's staff; riches are as it were the twinkling of an eye, the most unstable of friends'. Further exx. in stt. 14, 39, 52, 66–67, 70, 91, 111. The account in the 1st person is sometimes sustained as in the Óðinn narratives 96–102, 104–109, 138–143. It is noteworthy that while the gnomic part proper (I) is mainly and typically in the 3rd person, the didactic (II), mystic-heuristic (III) and necromantic (IV) are in first and second. The second person tends to creep into gnomic matter; cf. 76–77, 80, 102; the first is more common in the fact of experience on which the gnome is based; cf. 102 for both.

The more important stylistic characteristics of the poem, well illustrated in the final stanza, are economy, balance and repetition, frequently, as here, in a frame of parallelism:

Nú ero Háva mál	Now the Sayings of the High One
kveðin Háva hǫllo í,	have been spoken in the Hall of the High One,
allþǫrf ýta sonom,	most profitable to the sons of men,
óþǫrf iǫtna sonom;	most unprofitable to the sons of the giants.
heill, sá er kvað!	Hail to him that spoke them!
heill, sá er kann!	Hail to him that knows them!
nióti, sá er nam!	Profit to him that learnt them!
heilir, þeirs hlýddo.	Hail to those that have listened to them!

Beside certain ingenuous stanzas on behaviour (7, 33, 61 . . .) are others which—despite the differences in the metrical systems—are mannered and pointed like the Welsh englyn; cf. 21, 40, 47, 57, 58, 73, 74; also 49–50, which follow:

Váðir mínar	I gave my clothes
gaf ek velli at	to two men of wood
tveim trémǫnnom:	in the field:
rekkar þat þóttoz,	they felt gallant
er þeir ript hǫfðo;	when they were dressed;
neiss er nøkkviðr halr.	the naked man is ashamed.

Hrørnar þǫll,	The young fir withers
sú er stendr þorpi á,	in an open place;
hlýrat henni bǫrkr né barr;	Neither bark nor leaf shelters her:
svá er maðr,	so is the man
sá er manngi ann:	whom no one loves:
hvat skal hann lengi lifa?	why should he live long?

The resemblance in form and manner to the Welsh englyn appears clearly in 74 where the first three lines constitute a unit and appear as such in F. Jónsson's edition (i.e. as st. 73):

Nótt verðr feginn,	He who depends on his provisions
sás nesti trúir,	is glad when night sets in;
skammar ro skips ráar.	short are ship's berths.

Cf. also 73:

Tveir ro eins heriar,	Two prevail against one;
tunga er hǫfuðs bani,	the tongue works death to the head;
er mér í heðin hvern	a hand is to be expected
handar væni.	inside every cloak.

Another notable feature of *Hávamál* which links it with early Welsh poetry is the grouping of stanzas by identical or near-identical opening phrases, line, or lines. The counsels to Loddfáfnir (112–137) and the enumeration of spells (146–164) exemplify this, as also 8–9, 10–11, 23–27, 36–37, 42–43, 54–56, 58–59 and 76–77. Cp. *Canu Llywarch Hen, passim*.

Forms of the verb *skulu* occur commonly and with varying force throughout the poem: expressing an imperative (*fiǫlkunnigri kono skalattu í faðmi sofa*, 113), denoting obligation (*sá er at brǫndom skal/síns um freista frama*, 2), obligation and propriety (*hiarðir þat vito, nær þær heim skolo, 21*), propriety with future connotation (*hvar skal sitia siá?*, 2), reinforcing conditional *ef* (*ef ek skal þegn ungan/ verpa vatni á*, 158) . . .

The gnomic use of *skal/skyli* is quite frequent in the first 94 stanzas and it commonly expresses a recommendation ('should'). The first stanza is typical *Gáttir allar, áðr gangi fram,/um skoðaʒ skyli,/um skygnaʒ skyli;/þvíat óvíst er at vita, hvar óvinir/sitia á fleti fyrir* 'all ways should be viewed (spied) before advancing; one never knows where enemies may be sitting (in another man's house)'. The gnomes in this section are also frequently stated in the indicative of other verbs, and occasionally in the subjunctive (61).

Sigrdrífumál, the third of a trilogy which includes *Reginsmál* and *Fáfnismál*, is the next in importance to *Hávamál* for its gnomic content. Things *good, better,* or *best* find a place, typically, in each: cf. *Reg.* 19 ff., *Fáf.* 30, 31, and *Sig.* 36. The *magic runes* and *counsels* of *Sigrdrífumál* are directly communicated and are couched mainly in the second (and first) persons: *Sigrúnar þú skalt kunna . . . þat ræð ek þér it fyrsta . . .* But the application, i.e. the gnomic part proper, of the former (stt. 6 ff.) is on four occasions expressed by impersonal *skal* [*á horni (lófa, stafni, berki) skal (þær) rísta*], which also occurs in st. 8 (*Full skal signa . . .*)

The trilogy also contains quite a number of gnomes which can be placed beside the O E *oft, fela, monge* type of the Ex. and Cotton collections (p. 103); cf. *Reg.* st. 10.3 *mart er, þat er þorf þéar!* 'many are the woes of men!' = *Sig.* 30.6 *fiǫld er, þat er fíra tregr:* Sig. 2.3 *lǫng ero lýða læ!* 'the woes of men are long': *Helreið Brynh.* 14.1–4 *Muno við ofstríð allʒ til lengi/konor ok karlar kvikvir fœðaʒ!* 'Men and women will be born to live too long in great woe'!: *Sig.* 20.6 *ǫll ero mein of metin* 'all evils are meted out (by fate)': *Fáf.* 11.6 *allt er feigs forað* 'for the fey everything spells danger'. *Sig.* 24.4–6 (*þvíat ósviðr maðr lætr opt kveðin/verri orð, en viti* 'for a fool often speaks to worse effect than he thinks': *Sig.* 29.6 *margan stelr vín viti* 'wine steals the wits of many'. *Fáf.* 7.6 *æ kveða bandingia bifaʒ!* 'a prisoner is said to be ever fearful'; 6.4 ff. *Fár er hvatr, er hrøraʒ tekr,/ef í barnœsko er blauðr* 'an aging man is seldom valiant if he was cowardly in youth'. Of particular interest for their content and manner are stanzas 27 and 36 of *Sigrdrífumál. Skolo, þurfa,* and *vant* are used: *Forniósnar augo þurfo fira synir,/hvars skolo vreiðir vega:/opt bǫlvísar konor sitia brauto nær,/þær er deyfa sverð ok sefa* 'the sons of men need eyes of foresight where the wrathful do battle, for baleful women often sit near the way, blunting sword and mind'; *Sakar ok heiptir hyggiat svefngar vera,/ né harm in heldr;/vits ok vápna vant er iǫfri at fá,/þeim er skal fremstr með firom* 'Feuds and hates are not sleepy, nor malice either. The prince who is to be the chief among men must have intelligence and weapons'.

In theme and treatment *Hamðismál* reminds one of poems of the *Llywarch Hen* cycle. Guðrún, egging on her sons to avenge their sister Swanhild on the Gothic king Ermanarik, says of herself (stanza 5):

Einstœð em ek orðin sem ǫsp í holit,
fallin at frændom sem fura at kvisti,
vaðin at vilia sem viðr at laufi,
þá er in kvistskœða kømr um dag varman!

'I am left alone like an aspen in the wood; reft of my kinsmen like the fir of its branches; stripped of joy like a tree of its leaves when the branch-scather comes on a warm day'. Llywarch in his old age identifies himself with a withered leaf in the wind[1] (CLlH, 10):

Y deilen hon, neus kenniret gwynt.
Gwae hi o'e thynget!
Hi hen; eleni y ganet.

'this leaf, the wind drives it; alas for its destiny! It is old, this year it was born'. The theme of cowardice is to the fore in *Hamðismál* as in the Welsh poems. In the former Erp gives it proverbial expression (14.5): '*Illt er blauðom hal brautir kenna!*' 'it is ill work to show cowards the way' (with change of number!). In *Mechydd Ap Llywarch* (CLlH 27–28) one voice says: *meccid llvwyr llauer kyghor* 'a coward breeds many excuses', *dricweuet llyvrder ar gur* 'cowardice is an evil possession'.

---

[1] Cp. the *Aestuans Intrinsecus* of the 'Archpoet' (c. 1160), line 4: *Folio sum similis de quo ludunt venti* (Penguin Bk. of Lat. Verse, 1962, p. 206).

Cp. EWGP 21, st. 9c *Duw reen, py bereist lyvwr* 'Lord God, why hast thou made a coward?' and ibid. p. 25, st. 29c *meckyt llwuyr llawer adoet* 'the coward fosters many hurts'. In a parallel debate (CLlH, p. 3) Gwen answers his father's taunts with *ny bu eidyl hen yn was* 'no old man was ever a weakling young', which may be compared with *Fáf.* 6.4 ff. (*supra*). In spite of dodging death comes, says the voice in *Mechydd ap Llywarch* (ib., p. 27.7), or, in the final words of *Hamðismál* (30.6): *kveld lifir maðr ekki eptir kvið norna* 'no man lives through the evening after the word of the Fates (has been spoken)'. Cf. EWGP, p. 25, st. 33c *rybud y drwch ny weryt* 'warning avails not to the unfortunate'. Cp. the Ir. *Tec. Corm.* § 35, where to the question: 'whom do you deem the deafest you have heard?' the answer in triadic form has for its first term: 'a fey person (*trú*) who is being warned'. With this attitude to fate, reiterated throughout the Edda[1] and typical too of OE poetry, go aspirations to fame as in the preceding lines of *Hamðismál* (30.5): *Góðs hǫfom tírar fengit, þott skylim nú eða í gær deyia* 'We have got a good report though we die today or tomorrow', which illustrates the *deyr fé* sequence of *Hávamál*. Old Welsh offers a perfect parallel in the proverb *trengid golud, ni threing molud* 'wealth perishes, fame perishes not'. In the *Llywarch Hen* cycle the old concept of honour and fame clearly persists, but it is necessarily somewhat modified by tragic experience. Llywarch says (ib. p. 5):

> Pedwarmeib ar hugeint yg kenueint Lywarch
> O wyr glew galwytheint.
> Twll eu dyuot clot trameint.

> Pedwarmeib ar hugeint a ueithyeint vygknawt
> Drwy vyn tauawt lledesseint.
> Da dyuot vygcot colledeint.

'Twenty-four sons in Llywarch's household of brave fierce warriors; too great fame is grievous. Twenty-four sons, the offspring of my body—by my tongue they were slain; a little (fame) is good;—they were lost.'

d. *The Welsh Gnomic Manner (analytic, comparative and recapitulatory)*

While the Icelandic sources help *inter alia* to set the Germanic background of the English gnome in relief, and the Irish to show further possibilities in the way of approach and technique, the Welsh—as

---

[1] Cf. *Svipdagsmál* 4. 4–6, 47. 4–6, *Grípisspá* 53. 1–2, *Atlamál* 48. 3, *Fáf.* 11.6, *Sig.* 20. 6.

might well be expected—are of immediate and constant value as a criterion or standard of the English gnome and as a touchstone for its interpretation. That this is an empiric fact rather than a theory will appear from the evidence.

The two most common catchwords[1] of Welsh gnomic poetry are *bid* 3rd sg. Present-Future of *bod* 'to be' (cp. OE gnomic *bið*) and *gnawt* 'usual'. Either of these may dominate a poem. For an example of the *gnawt* type cf. EWGP, p. 26. Two examples of the other—called *Bidiau* from the prevalence in them of *bid*—may be found ibid. pp. 33–37. The two catchwords may occur together as in Bidiau I, st. 2c *bit gnawt aflwyd ar diryeit* 'usual is misfortune for the wretched'.

The whole tenor of the earlier Welsh sentimental poetry is in accordance with this: it is a poetry of observation (and feeling) in which the characteristics and concomitants of things are acutely listed and for the most part finely combined. The result is a true gnomic poem (cf. EWGP VI—IX), or—more characteristically—one in which the gnome seems to add a human application and a lyric depth to nature description: cf. EWGP I, stt. 10, 13, 15, 20, 7; II, st. 8; III, stt. 22, 28, 32. (I) shares with the purer gnomic type the characteristic that in the final lines of many *englynion* nature description is pointed or set off by a human reference. Cf. stt. 1, 2, 7, 8, 10, 13, 15, 20, 21, 24 . . . 35. A natural development is the human story or drama embedded in a sequence of final lines which this poem so strikingly illustrates (cf. pp. 71 ff.). Here the gnome is made to serve the specific case, to which it lends a cryptic, indefinite character. Precisely this happens in the *Wife's Lament* 42–50a, where it is followed (50b–52) by a specific reference to the loved one, which in turn is sententiously generalized in the closing lines (52–53). Cryptic in a similar way are the *Wanderer*, *Seafarer*, and final portion of the *Penitent's Prayer*, while the *Husband's Message* has the secretiveness of the riddle.

The main fields of observation in the Welsh gnomic poetry are external nature and man,—and human behaviour from an external angle and introspectively. These aspects are commonly made to mingle, and a favoured and attractive pattern is that of the englyn with its descriptive opening capped in the final line by a true gnome, i.e. a sententious saying about universals. (A further distinction between *particulars* and *universals* is not warranted by the poetry and may obstruct the study of it.)

---

[1] *Pob* (: Ir. *cach*) 'every' also occurs. Cf. EWGP II, 11c; III, 1a, 36c; VI, 2b, 13a, 14a, 15b, 17a; VIII, 8a.

What Welsh—and English—gnomic poetry lacks is that strong preoccupation with the precept which so characterizes the Icelandic and the Irish (cf. the titles *Hávamál* and particularly *Tecosca* 'Instructions')[1]. Welsh gnomic poetry, indeed—unlike English—seems to lack the maxim entirely. On the other hand, the combination of nature and human gnomes or sententious sayings (rendered often with deep lyrical feeling) so typical of Welsh, is no stranger to English poetry: cf. *Claf Abercuawc*, st. 2 and p. 75 ff. *supra*:

> Llem awel, llwm benedyr byw.
> Pan orwisc coet teglyw
> Haf, teryd glaf wyf hediw

'Keen the wind, bare the cattle-track when the wood puts on the fair colours of summer:—very ill am I today'. Cp. from the end of the *Penitent's Prayer* (103b–108a):

> . . . nu ic me sylf ne mæg
> fore minum wonæhtum willan adreogan.
> wudu mot him weaxan, wyrde bidan,
> tanum lædan; ic for tæle ne mæg
> ænigne moncynnes mode gelufian
> eorl on eþle . . .

'. . . now (that) I cannot, on account of my poverty, carry out my desire. The forest may grow, achieve its destiny, shoot forth its twigs; I, because of calumny, cannot love any one of mankind, any man in the land'. In both stanzas, Welsh and English, the miserable condition of man is delineated by contrasting it with the blossoming forest; and the technique employed is the same in both cases—comparable Icelandic examples (e.g. *Háv.* 50, 62 with *svá er*; *Hamðismál* 5 with *sem*, pp. 121, 123 *supra*) are rare, and are clearly less integrated than the Cymro-English: in the former, nature offers material for a simile, whereas in the Cymro-English it belongs to the texture of thought itself.

The whole first half of the *Seafarer* offers striking illustration of this spiritual symbiosis of nature and man. (—Here too the pilgrim theme broods in the Welsh manner beneath the storm-tossed surface—informing the tone of the whole poem, the poet's intent being well caught away in effective and sustained descriptions of nature.) A paraphrase of lines 12b–32 will serve to show how nature description

[1] Cf. p. 103, end of f.n.1.

is used to delineate a human condition: 'A man whose lot is cast most happily on land cannot know how I have passed the winter in paths of exile on the ice-cold sea, wretched and sorrowful, bereft of friends, and hung about with icicles, while hail flew in showers. There I heard nothing but the roar of the sea, of the icy wave. At times I had the song of the swan for my entertainment and the cry of the gannet and whaup in place of the laughter of men, the seagull singing instead of mead-drinking.[1] Storms buffeted the rocky cliffs, where the tern with icy feathers gave answer, and the dewy-plumed eagle very often took up the cry. I had no protecting kinsman who could comfort my desolate soul.[2] Wherefore he who—in splendour and elated with wine—has experienced a pleasant life with few hardships in the dwellings of men can hardly believe how I had often wearily to wait on the ocean path. Night-shadow(s) darkened; from the north came snow; frost fettered the earth; hail fell—coldest of grain . . .' The contrast with happiness which runs right through the passage is high-lighted on two separate occasions by the land-dweller references, while nature here is in tune with the poet. Further on, the joyous phenomena of early summer, the blossoming groves (as in the exx. above), the brightening fields (48–49) are juxtaposed to the brooding pre-occupation of the pilgrim (39–47) on the one hand, and to his urge to travel (50–53) on the other. Then the cuckoo's plaintive call becomes the true voice of his own soul (53–55a);—and here the poet splendidly seizes the opportunity to develop the figure of the bird-soul (58–66a). The corresponding passage of the *Wanderer* (45–57) offers an illustration of the use of nature in a human context comparable to 12b–32 of the *Seafarer*. In the opening of the former poem, too, epithets of nature are chosen to harmonize with and accentuate the effect of the psychological ones: e.g. 2b–5a . . . *þeah þe he modcearig | geond lagulade longe sceolde | hreran mid hondum hrimcealde sæ, | wadan wræclastas:* 23–25 *hrusan heolstre biwrah, ond ic hean þonan | wod wintercearig ofer waþema gebind, | sohte sele dreorig sinces bryttan.* Similarly in the *Wife's Lament* 27–41 her dreary life becomes identified with and expressed by the attributes of her meagre dwelling (*eorðsele* 29, *wic wynna leas* 32): gloomy depths, towering heights, and prickly thickets overgrown

---

[1] So too the Irish outcast Suibhne Geilt cries (ITS 12, 82–83): 'O woman, sad is it that you should take my watercress from me, if you but knew the plight in which I am, for neither tribesman nor kinsman pities me, nor do I visit as a guest the house of anyone on the ridge of the world. For kine I have my watercress, my water is my mead, my trees hard and bare or close-sheltering are my friends.'

[2] For another interpretation cf. p. 133 f.

with thorns. The briars motif is a constant in the Middle Ir. tale *Buile Shuibhne*, cf. ITS 12, 28: The hawthorn that is not soft-topped has subdued me, has pierced me; the brown thornbush has nigh caused my death'. Ibid., p. 30: 'Raw branches have wounded me, they have torn my hands; the briars have not left the making of a girdle for my feet'; p. 48: O toiling madman, 'tis my grief that thou art uncomely and dejected; I sorrow that thy skin has lost its colour, briars and thorns rending thee; p. 64: O briar, little arched one, you do not grant fair terms, you do not desist from tearing me till you have your fill of blood'. An early, (i.e. eighth century) instance is attributed to a Mac Samain or Mael Odrain, both of whom were hermits and shared the vicissitudes of the Wife and of Suibhne (Bruchst. p. 60): 'May the wood of Fuirmhe be unloved where it grows about Tuirbhe: its leaves wound me; its thicket does not shelter me.' Queen Gormflaith in her reduced state was later to make similar complaint.

Riddles 1–3 (Ex.) on different aspects of a storm offer a fine example of the man-nature synthesis.—Here the elements are personified and nature-poetry appears at its best; as in 3. 17–24a, 42b–52:

> hwilum ic sceal ufan yþa wregan,
> streamas styrgan ond to staþe þywan
> flintgrægne flod. Famig winneð
> 20 wæg wið wealle, wonn ariseð
> dun ofer dype; hyre deorc on last,
> eare geblonden, oþer fereð,
> þæt hy gemittað mearclonde neah
> hea hlincas . . .

'Sometimes from above I must rouse the waves, stir up the moving waters, and drive towards the shore the flint-gray flood. The foaming billow fights against the cliff. A mountainous wave rises wan above the deep; dark behind it, driven up by the sea, another follows, so that they strike against the high rocks near the boundary of sea and land'.

> earpan gesceafte
> fus ofer folcum fyre swætað,
> blacan lige, ond gebrecu ferað
> 45 deorc ofer dryhtum gedyne micle,
> farað feohtende, feallan lætað
> sweart sumsendu seaw of bosme,
> wætan of wombe. Winnende fareð
> atol eoredþreat, egsa astigeð,

50 micel modþrea monna cynne,
brogan on burgum, þonne blace
scotiað
scriþende scin scearpum wæpnum.

'Hastening over the peoples, the dusky creatures (i.e. the clouds) sweat fire, bright flame; and the dark thunder-clouds journey above men with a great din, advance fighting, and let fall black pattering rain from their breast, water from their womb. The fierce horsemen advance battling; there arises terror, great panic among mankind, fears in the cities, when the black gliding spectres shoot their sharp weapons' (M.)

Early Welsh has also its riddle on the wind (cf. J. G. Evans, *Llyfr Tal.* 36–37) which has a similar physical range as Riddle 1 (Ex.) but lacks its descriptive poetry and is more of an inventory. The 'creature strong, without flesh, without bone, without veins, without blood, without head and without feet' of this poem becomes (the fourteenth century) Dafydd Ap Gwilym's 'strange visitant', which in keeping with his treatment of nature he personifies—if vaguely. Even the negative elements in Dafydd's description, as in that of the earlier riddle, have of course an anthropomorphic basis. The Welsh poems also seem to stress the strange or marvellous, but then the personal standpoint ('I') of the OE riddle, though it familiarizes, does not otherwise diminish the marvellous in the actual description. Obviously related to riddling technique is the Welsh manner of making comparisons (*dyfalu*) in which Dafydd excelled and which—like the *kenning*—we find associated with word composition.

Dafydd's poem achieves descriptions of nature which are of an inspiration similar to that of Riddles 1–3. Compare with Riddle 3 the following excerpts:[1] 1–4 You nimble wind, come from on high, / With roar and bluster hastening by, / Strange visitant, with your hoarse din, / Footless, wingless paladin . . . 27–32 As you winnow the leaves no force of man / Can stay the sweep of your winnowing fan. / Though no eye see you in your lair, / Nest of the rain-storm, a thousand hear, / A God-sent thing, through earth's whole length / With sick roar rending the oak's strength . . . 39 Roaring in tempest o'er the sea, . . . 42 ff. Driving, scattering the leaves abroad, / Leaping in play from the hill's breast/'Mid surging seas to shatter the mast. . .' Riddle 30 (Ex.) reminds of Celtic metamorphic poems such as those associated with Amairgen and Taliesin (cf. *Voyage of Bran* II, 86 ff.).

In Welsh the riddle is rare, whereas in OE it is a flourishing genre,

[1] Dafydd Ap Gwilym: Fifty Poems, transs. H. I. and D. Bell, London 1942, pp. 189 ff.

in which description—including that of nature—is all, and the quiz element minimal and formulaic. It is the personal lyric building upon nature description and gnome which blossomed in Early Welsh, and compared with it the OE lyric, though it includes some notable poems, seems an embryonic category—showing indeed several marks of affinity with the more impressive Welsh and Irish lyric. The OE lyric is also a fragmentary category—as appears from B. J. Timmer's study, The Elegiac Mood in OE Poetry; Timmer convincingly re-establishes the old view of Christian influence behind the elegiac character of OE poetry, a theme fully in line with our own in this work.

From this comparative account of mixed genres we return to the point of our opening paragraph: the bearing of the Welsh gnome on the English. A survey of Welsh sententious sayings, gnomic and descriptive, will show that what they essentially do is to predicate the *characteristic*,[1] or the typical condition or situation: serried is the host, budding the ash, querulous is the feeble, there is clamour from the brave, an ill countenance hampers a man, the evening is good for enjoyment, want befalls in exile, the fickle is unfaithful, the one whom a bard loves is a handsome giver . . . This then is the centre from which subsidiary possibilities radiate: that which is *usual*, a large sub-type in Welsh: usual for theft to become manifest, usual with the wanton is excessive laughter. Things which go together, or agree (well agreed are the thief and long night; where there is no learning there will

---

[1] The attributes or characteristics (W. *cynneddf, angerdd* (sg.) . . .) of significant persons and things are a feature of the Mabinogi and cognate Welsh literature; cf. PKM pp. 9. 5, 34. 20, 68. 4 (121, 178, 254, 264); J. G. Evans, White Book Mab. p. 464, last line, 465. 1–11, 153. 17; M. Richards, Breudwyt Ronabwy (Caerdydd 1948), p. 11. 20 (cp. 7. 5 *Vn o rinwedeu y maen* . . . 'One of the virtues of the stone . . .').

To these correspond the Irish *ada* 'that which is fitting, appropriate, due; a customary due, a prerogative', *búaid* 'gift, lucky quality'; the semantic field here includes the important antonyms *airgart* 'prohibition', *geis, airmitiu* 'taboo': King Conaire of BDD had *teora búada* 'three gifts', namely, of hearing, eyesight, and judgement (§ 10); he had eight taboos (§ 16), the infraction of which formed the prelude to his death.

Cf. also the three faults (*lochta*) of Cú Chulainn ('he was too young, too brave, and too beautiful', van Hamel, Compert C. C. and Other Stories, 1933, p. 22); and p. 112, f.n.1, *supra*. For the prohibitions (taboos) and prescriptions (lucky things) of the Kings of Ireland cf. M. Dillon, Proceedings R. I. A., Vol 54, C 1, pp. 1–36, Dublin, 1951.

The Welsh terms *anghengaeth* 'injunction' (Evans, op. cit., 458), *tyngu tynghet* 'swear a destiny (upon)' (PKM 79, 81, 83, White Book Mab. 454 . . .), *torri tynghetfen* 'break a destiny' (PKM 83) will be seen to belong here; W. *tyngu*: Ir. *tong-* 'swear', W. *tynghet*: Ir. *tocad* 'fortune, luck'. In our view the Irish gnomic catchword *toich* (*toigh*) 'natural, due, proper' (cf. p. 116) belongs to *tong-* (otherwise Ped. II 666–7), and *dúthaig*, closely related in meaning, is a derivative of it; cf. Laws iv 152 Comm. *ani is toich no is duthaig bis orro*, Leb. Gab. 146. 22 *úair ro ba toich doibh ó a sinnseraibh rochtain innte*, Expugn. Hib. 16 *as toich dóibh a nduthaigh do cosnamh rind* . . .

be no mental facility) are offset by a greater number which don't, sometimes giving rise to negative recommendations: the misfortunate and the good do not agree, the misfortunate one is not willing to listen; do not confess your secret to a youth (maid, babbler). A condensed example such as: *the youth laughs when the old man stumbles* brings out the fact that stumbling is characteristic of the old and decrepit, but not of lively and gay youth. What is *fitting* finds expression (as such) less often than might be expected: *it is the part of the discerning man to love truly, . . . of the powerful to keep his pledge.* Cf. *the worst blemish is bad manners,* where the perspective is negative.

Other gnomes, which taken singly might not make sense, do so against this background. Cf. EWGP VIII, 8: The misfortunate one is disagreeable; the eager are wild; old age leads to poverty; there are pleasant men at a mead-feast (*bid addfwyn yn ancwyn medd*). The final line may seem at first somewhat ambiguous, and those which precede do not illuminate its precise application;—but they bring out what is *usual* and so help to suggest the social tone appropriate to a festive occasion (mead drinking).

A second example is (ECNP, p. 59, st. 14: EWGP, p. 23): Mountain snow, the stag is in the grove; very black is the raven, swift the roebuck; the healthy and free, it is strange that he complains (*iach ryd, ryuedawt pa gwyn*). The relation between this final gnome and the ones which precede is that it contemplates an actual situation which is the reverse of theirs, i.e. the reverse of the *usual.* This technique of paradox produces striking effects, cf. *Claf Abercuawc* 28 (*supra,* p. 77): 'Branching the tip of the oak, bitter the taste of the ash, sweet is cow-parsley, laughing the wave; the cheek does not hide the affliction of the heart'. It is not confined to the pure gnome, cf. EWGP III, 26: (Mountain snow; speckled is the breast of the goose; strong is my arm and my shoulder,) I pray I may not be a hundred years old.

A feature then of Welsh gnomic poems is that the sententious sayings of which they are composed are commonly quite disparate. What holds them together are considerations of an abstract kind, and these mainly two: gnomic classification of things, qualities, actions as *characteristic, usual, fitting, unfitting . . .;* distribution of these on grounds of poetic technique for greater effect. Hence the basis is *form* (rather than meaning) and this feature so characteristic of Celtic might seem to place the Welsh gnomic poems well apart from the OE material; but in fact we found it to apply there too (cf. pp. 69 ff., 125).

Furthermore, the Welsh gnome is dominated by the philosophical

notion of the peculiar or essential property of things, which we have
noted for the OE (cf. pp. 103–4) and which happily finds clear expression in EWGP II, 11c: (Rain outside, it wets the deep; the wind
whistles over the top of the reeds;) every achievement is lacking
without its talent (*gwedw pob camp heb y dawn*): relevant is (not the
deed but) the innate affinity of thing to thing, thing to quality, action
to result, cause to effect. It is this innate affinity which attracts the poet-
philosopher's eye and which in the last analysis generates the great
bulk of the gnomic corpus. The negative aspect too finds expression:
V, 4c: *lle ny bo dawn ny byd dysc* 'where there is no natural gift there will
be no learning', and III, 27c, where the terms *dawn, dysc* are inverted.
Cf. also VI, 30c: *gwnelyt agheluydyt annerth* 'want of skill makes want
of strength'. The point in these is of course that natural capacity,
learning, and skill condition affinity and through it achievement. The
link with OE is apparent from Ex. 120: *gód bið genge ond wiþ god
lenge* 'good prevails and has affinity with God', a philosophical gnome
similar to the Welsh. The idea of affinity also underlies gnomes such
as Ex. 66 *sceomiande man sceal in sceade hweorfan, scir in leohte gerised*
'a man who feels shame will walk in the shadow, an upright man has
his place in the light', Ex. 60 *þrym sceal mid wlenco, þriste mid cenum*
'majesty will go (i.e. goes) with pride; bold men with brave men',
18b–19 *þing sceal gehegan/frod wiþ frodne; biþ hyra ferð gelic* 'sage
will hold a meeting with sage; they are congenial spirits', 22–23a
*Ræd sceal mid snyttro, ryht mid wisum,/til sceal mid tilum. Tu beoð
gemæccan* 'good counsel will go with wisdom, justice with the wise,
a good man with good men. Two are consorts'. The notion of affinity
merges into that of the *fitting* (cf. Ex. 63b, 125–128, 165 . . .) or the
proper (45b–49, 166 . . .) or what is *proper to* something (57b–58, 152,
202–204, Cotton 1a, 3b–13, 16–54a).

Hence the conceptual basis of the Welsh and the English gnome is
in part the same, and this similarity is accentuated by the preference
shown in both for the spheres of nature and human conduct. Particularly the nature vignettes Ex. 50b–55 describing the violent and
the serene sea in illustration of human gnomes (50a *one should restrain
a violent mind,* 56 *so peoples are peaceful when they have settled their
disputes*) strike one as Welsh in manner.

For correspondences of detail between Welsh and OE gnomes of
the type EWGP VII, 16c: *bit wreic drwc ae mynych warth* 'a bad woman
has frequent scandals': Ex. 64 *widgongel wif word gespringeð* 'a gadding
wife causes talk to spread', cf. ECNP, pp. 129–131.

CHAPTER VI

THE *SEAFARER*:[1] INTERPRETATION OF TEXT

(with *excursus* on the *bird-soul*)

14a *earmcearig:* a dvandva compound meaning 'wretched and sorrowful'. Cp. I. L. Gordon, ed. p. 34.

20a *dyde ic me to gomene:* cf. Toller *dón* IV, 2. This semantic extension of *don*, as of *gedon* in 43b, is related to its grammatical extension as auxiliary verb.

26b MS. *feran*. Following Grein, all edd. save Sedgfield emend to *frefran*, which yields good enough sense in isolation, but bad context. The emendation is not very plausible paleographically, and it seems possible to justify the MS. reading in a sense different from Sedgfield's: 'Not one of the kinsmen, not a single wretched soul could travel (sail)'.

No firm clue to the motivation is offered, but the whole context would suggest that while the spirit may have been willing the flesh was weak. Furthermore, the boon companions of 21b and 22b were presumably the kinsmen of 16, and if these are further figured as enjoying life in 27 ff. the whole *forþon* crux of 27a gives way to a smooth transition in which this term has its normal meaning 'hence, therefore', the shift of thought occurring not with *forþon* of 27a but with *nænig* of 25b.

---

[1] For a survey of previous research cf. esp. O. S. Anderson 'The Seafarer: an Interpretation', K. Humanistiska Vetenskapssamfundets i Lund Årsberättelse I (1937–8); and I. L. Gordon, ed. Introduction.

On the dating (and place of composition) of *Seafarer* and *Wanderer* much has been written, but inconclusively. D. Grubl, op. cit. 178, considers the eighth century to be the most likely period of composition of all the 'elegies'; cf. also ibid. pp. 34, 60; and R. F. Leslie, ed. Three Old English Elegies, 34–36. I. L. Gordon (ed. *The Seafarer*, pp. 27–32) follows Sisam in taking c. 940 as a terminus ad quem for the composition of the Exeter Book.

On grounds of metrical form, diction and general treatment the *Penitent's Prayer* has been assigned to the later OE period. Cf. Sieper, op. cit. 253 ff., Krapp-Dobbie, Exeter Book, lx-lxi.

The description of the wintry, maritime scene in 17–25a would then be heralded in and out by the statement that the seafarer travelled alone, bereft of friends (16, 25b–26). From medieval Irish sources we learn that it was common practice for a small group of *peregrini* to travel together, as it also was to fare forth alone. Compare *Genesis* 2480–2482a *þu þas werðeode wræccan laste/freonda feasceaft feorran gesohtest,/wineþearfende* 'you sought this people on the track of an exile from afar, bereft of friends' where Lot is addressed, and *Gen.* 2822–2823 of Abraham: *siððan þu feasceaft feorran come/on þas werþeode wræccan laste.* The occurrence of *frefran* in a comparable context in *Wanderer* (28b) is not necessarily relevant to the *Seafarer* at all, the more so as here it tends to make the sequel unintelligible. Moreover the combination *ferð* and *feran* does occur in line 37. For the formulaic aspect of terms of exile such as *wræccan lastum* (*Seaf.* 15b), *wræclastas . . . lecgað* (57) cf. Greenfield, Speculum 30, pp. 200 ff. This aspect of verbal technique has no necessary bearing on the problem of the actual as against the figurative character of the *peregrinatio*.

38 *elþeodigra eard:* A vital crux examined in detail below pp. 195 ff. OE *el(e)land, el(l)þeod* 'foreign country' have the same formation as O. Ir. *ailithir* (*aili-* 'other', *tír* 'land') which occurs in this meaning. The meanings 'stranger', 'exile' are found too, but *ailithir* usually means 'pilgrim'. It is found on an Ogam inscription (Macal. Corp. I, p. 186). Its derivatives *ailithrech* 'pilgrim' and *ailithre* 'pilgrimage' occur in the Laws.

42–43: This anxiety about the voyage is elaborated in *Cormac's Choice*, stanzas 9–11. Cf. p. 59. Our interpretation of the OE poem as a whole is consistent with the view that not only here but throughout the whole preceding section (1–26 hardships afloat; 27–33a seafarer v. land-dweller; 33b–38 projected peregrination) a *second* religious and allegorical level may be and even must be assumed. It is implicit in the *peregrinatio* project which is in turn clearly and unambiguously set forth in lines 35, 37–38, 51–52, 57, 58 ff. There is absolutely no conflict between the two levels, actual and figurative. Rather do they sustain each other. Among English saints who lived on an island in a desert place were Cuthbert,[1] Hereberht and Guthlac. For (spiritual) life in terms of a voyage cf. *Christ* 850–866.

[1] Of Cuthbert B. Colgrave writes (Two Lives of Saint Cuthbert, Cambridge 1940, p. 5): '. . . it is clear that he belongs to the Celtic rather than to the Roman tradition, and that, in spite of his dying attacks upon the Celtic "heretics", he lived and died after the manner of the typical Irish monk'. Retiring to Farne for meditation was in the tradition of Aidan (ibid. p. 313).

47a *longunge:* the meaning is 'spiritual or emotional yearning or longing'. The idea is prominent throughout Irish and Welsh literature. In the latter it is expressed by *hiraeth,* a formation semantically identical with and formally close to *longung* (*hir* means 'long'). The Ir. equivalent of *hiraeth* is *sírecht* also in this meaning. Its derivative adjj. in *-ach, -ae, -aide* bring out our meaning clearly. Welsh *hiraeth, hiraethawc* (:Ir. *sírechtach*)[1] in the *Llywarch Hen* and *Heledd* cycles express a poignant grief and yearning, in one instance in connection with the cuckoo's call (CLlH p. 24; cf. also pp. 9, 39), which brings it into immediate relationship with our O E passage (cf. 74 ff.). These Welsh and English poems are all associated with outcast, wanderer, or bereft one. The *Wife's Lament* which also belongs here, has *longaþ* (41) and *mec longade* (14) with the same connotation of yearning. *Blickling Homm.* X, p. 113 (ed. Morris, E E T S 1880) has *þa ongan hine eft langian on his cyþþe* 'Then after a time he began to long for his native land again'; *for þære langunga* 'on account of the longing (grief) (which he felt at the death of his kinsman)'. In these instances we have the longing for a kinsman in connection with exile against a background of penitence which is precisely the context of *Seafarer* and *Wanderer*.[2]

A second Irish term for this is *eolchaire* which often has the specific meaning 'longing for home'. Cf. Meyer-Nutt, Voyage of Bran I, 41; Buile S., p. 64, 1. It is enumerated with *ailithre* 'peregrinatio' as one of the several sources of grief:[3] *Eolchaire .i. ima tír 7 cuma .i. a ndiaigh dáine 7 brón iar fuchacht 7 ailithre ar Día .i. ar mét a cinad 7 rl.* 'yearning for his homeland, and grief for (departed) persons and contrition for cuckoldry and pilgrimage for God's sake, namely, on account of his great sin' (A C L iii 139. 33). A third term occurs in a Mid. Ir. legend of Brendan of Clonfert: *romgabh imtholta andiaigh mu thigearna iarndul do curp Crist* 'a great longing for my Lord seized me when I had gone to

---

[1] In *Imr. Ua. C.* § 9, the music of bird flocks which represent human souls is described as *ceól sírechtach sírbinn* 'music plaintive and very sweet'.

[2] In *Guthlac* 353–360 the hermit's longing for human love and companionship is *sorg* (354) varied in 359 by *longaþ.* In 330 it is said that Guthlac had renounced desire of transient joys (*forlet longeþas lænra dreama*). In 316–317 *longaþ* and *sorg* are coupled once more: *Forþon mec longeþas lyt gegretað/sorge sealdun* 'wherefore longings visit me but little, sorrows seldom'.

[3] In the Old-Irish Penitential VI §§ 1–3 two forms of the vice *tristitia,* namely, worldly and godly sadness, are identified, described, and provided against. In §3 it is enjoined on the monk 'in grief and sadness so that he cannot be roused' to do penance in another place on bread and water and to return no more into the community of the brethren until he be joyful in body and soul (cf. L. Bieler, The Irish Penitentials, Dublin 1963, pp. 273–274).

Christ's Body (i.e. Communion)' (BLism. xiv, fo. 85d, 8–9). Here *imtholta,* O. Ir. *imtholtu* means basically 'great desire'.[1]

Hiraeth is still characteristic of the Welsh (cf. G. Rees, Encounter, March 1964, Vol. 22, No. 3, p. 45 f.) as *eolchaire* is of the Irish abroad.

The linking of springtime beauty with this yearning and with *woruld onetteð* (49b) in the sense of the world hastening to its end are justified by G. V. Smithers and J. Cross from homiletic and patristic sources (Medium Aevum 28, pp. 7, 104–105). Whether or not *onetteð* carries the symbolic meaning here, the ideas mentioned can be found fused in a comparable literary form nearer home, namely in the Welsh poem *Kintevin* (cf. p. 67).

53. For the sad cuckoo cf. p. 74.

58 ff. G. V. Smithers relates three important keywords in this passage to concepts characteristic of Norse (Med. Aev. 26, 137–153 (1957); 28, 1–22, 99–104 (1959)): *hyge* (:ON *hugr*), the spirit which is launched from the body in the form of an animal (op. cit., 28, p. 20 ff.); *anfloga* and *wælweg* for which see under 62b below. In spite of the learning and scholarly insight everywhere in evidence throughout these articles, the case for a survival here of old Germanic beliefs in the form adumbrated cannot be seriously entertained.[2]

V. Salmon also makes the point that *hyge* in line with ON *hugr* might bear the connotation 'free-ranging soul' (MLR 55, 1 ff., 1960). She lays O. Ir. and Christian Lat. sources under contribution and her interpretation of this passage tallies with ours.

In place of an absurd dichotomy splitting the mind of the seventh and eighth century Englishman into a Christian and a heathen half,

[1] The longing inspired by the chanting of *bird-souls* in *Imr. Sn.* iv 23 (p. 143 infra) is termed *lúth.*

[2] In particular we have to take into account instances in Plummer's Vitae Sanctorum Hiberniae of saints causing the souls of men to go forth from their bodies in sleep and visit distant scenes. 'The most interesting case of this' says Plummer, Introd., clxxii, f.n. 2 'is in the Acta SS Hib. ex cod. Sal. c. 310,§ 16: 'rogauit populus Finanum ut exirent uidere agonem. Quibus ait: "Maneant corpora uestra iuxta me, et exeant anime uestre" ... Dormientibus ... illis iuxta sanctum, exierunt anime eorum ad stagnum longe, ubi uiderunt agonem; ... et reuerse sunt ... ante uesperum anime ad corpora sua, et narrauerunt omnia que facta fuerant in agone, sicut erant.' In two other interesting cases the motif is represented as a vision seen in sleep: Cormac, monk and former king of Leinster, is consumed by a longing to revisit home, kinsmen and friends. These he sees in a vision from God through the agency of S. Comgall and turns from them back to the religious life (Vita S. Comgalli, § 42). In Vita S. Berachi § 25 the monk who without consulting his superior vowed that he would go on a pilgrimage *ad limina* fulfils his vow in a vision through the saint's agency. Cp. to Cormac's case that of the *Wanderer,* 39 ff.

what one really had was a Christian training and an outlook which incorporated many pre-Christian concepts and traditions. Cf. B. F. Huppé, The Wanderer: Theme and Structure, JEGP 42 (1943), p. 517.

60a *hwæles epel* 'home of the whale' a kenning for the sea, is matched by O. Ir. *adba rón (rebach)* 'home of the (sportive) seals (? or whales)'. Ir. *rón* 'seal' is mistakenly coupled with OE *hrán* (cf. Ped. i 21; R.I.A. Dict., Fasc. R). It may be from OE *hran, hron* ('small whale'). Cp. OE *mæwes epel, Husband's Message,* 26.

62b. *Anfloga,* usually analyzed *án-floga* 'lone-flier' is taken for the cuckoo by Sieper and Gordon. Ettmüller and Grein-Köhler render 'draco'. Smithers (*Med. Aev.* 28, 20 ff.) reads *ăn-floga* 'disease-bringing, malign influence', which may designate 'a creature of some such type as the valkyrie';—in conjunction with MS. *wælweg* (usually emended to *hwælweg* 'whale-road') 'way to the abode of the dead': *wæl* 'dead body' (ibid., 26, 137 ff.). N. Kershaw considers that *anfloga* 'merely carries on the metaphor which describes the speaker's imagination as a (solitary) seabird' and adds references to Psalms (10. 2, 123. 7) where the soul is likened to a sparrow (*Anglo-Saxon and Norse Poems,* Cambridge 1922, p. 170).

There can be no doubt that the key to passages 58–66 of The Seafarer and 45–55a of The Wanderer is the representation of the spirit or soul by the figure of a bird. Cf. Servati Lupi Vita S. Wigberhti, § 11: 'Verum hora exitus illius admirationis plena res obtigit. Circumstantibus fratribus, visa est avis quaedam specie pulcherrima supra ejus corpusculum ter advolasse, nusquamque post hac comparuisse'. Wigberht, abbot of Fritzlar, ob. c. 747, was a native of England and followed Boniface to Germany. His life, by Servatus Lupus, c. 836, is given by the Bollandists (Acta SS. August 13th, iii 132 ff.)

The bird-soul[1] is recorded widely in European and (particularly

---

[1] The material on the bird-soul surveyed in these pages is resumed and focussed in the following striking correspondence: the statue of Aristeas (seventh century BC) seen at Proconnesus by Pliny, represented his soul leaving his mouth in the form of a raven (Naturalis Historia VII 174. 8). On the Cross of the Scriptures at Clonmacnois a bird at the mouth of the recumbent figure symbolises the Resurrection. Cp. E. D. Phillips (to whom I am indebted for the Aristeas references), The Legend of Aristeas, Artibus Asiae XVIII 2 (1955), 161–177; J. D. P. Bolton, Aristeas of Proconnesus, Oxford 1962. Maximus of Tyre says that the soul of Aristeas left his body as it lay still breathing just enough to maintain life and wandered in the upper air like a bird, looking down on everything from above, land, sea, rivers, cities, races of men . . . It then entered his body again and raised it to its feet, using it like an instrument, and recited all that it had seen and heard (Phillips, 162, Bolton, 121). Cf. *Seafarer* 58 ff., *Wanderer* 56 f. Like the soul

North) African folklore. It is a characteristic of Coptic iconography which reappears in Early Irish (and Northumbrian) illuminated work beside other features of Egyptian origin. It occurs frequently in Early Ir. Literature and is found too in the Elder Edda. Moreover, the bird-soul (-tree) complex figures prominently in North Asiatic Shamanism. Some of this ground is covered by Grimm (Deutsche Mythologie, transl. J. S. Stallybrass, II, 828 f. (London 1883): '. . . popular imagination, childlike, pictures the soul as a *bird*, which comes flying out of the dying person's mouth. That is why old tombstones often have *doves* carved on them, and these the Christian faith brings into still closer proximity to spirit. A ship founders: the people on shore observe the souls of those who have sunk ascending from the wave toward heaven in the shape of *white doves* (Maerlant 2, 217 from a Latin source). The Romance legend of the tortured Eulalia says: 'in figure de *colomb* volat a ciel'. As a *bird* the little brother, when killed, flies out of the juniper-tree (machandelbom, Kinderm. 47). To the enigma of the green tree and the dry, each with a little bird sitting on it, the interpretation is added: 'ir *sêle* zen *vogelen* sî gezalt!' their (the christians') soul be numbered among birds, MS. 2, 248b. In the underworld there fly scorched *birds* who were souls (*sviðnir foglar es sálir váru*), like swarms of flies, Sólarljóð, St. 53. The heathen Bohemians thought the soul came out of the dying lips as a bird, and hovered among the trees, not knowing where to go till the body was buried; then it found rest. Finns and Lithuanians call the Milky Way the *path of birds* . . . i.e. of souls.

The Arabs till the time of Mahomet believed that the blood of a

of Aristeas, that of Hermotimus would leave his body, range abroad, and report distant happenings unknown save to an eye-witness . . . (Bolton, ibid.). Aristeas visited the Hyperborean regions in his travels, where he could have been in contact with shamanism. On the basis of impressive similarities, K. Meuli argued that Aristeas was a sort of Greek shaman, a view which has been accepted by many scholars (cf. Bolton, 125 ff.). The acquisition of wisdom is of outstanding importance for the journeys of Aristeas, as appears from a second passage in Maximus of Tyre (Bolton, p. 122). For Aristeas accompanying Apollo in the form of a raven cf. ibid., p. 120.

At the other end of the time scale and in connection with W. B. Yeats's use of the swan-soul symbol we have from T. R. Henn the comment: 'From time immemorial men have used many kinds of birds to symbolize the human soul or spirit; the hawk for the Egyptians, bats (since they live in the dark) for the ghosts in Homer; swallows or halcyons for the transformations of lovers in Ovid's *Metamorphoses*. The eagle is an emblem of strength, swiftness; it alone can gaze at the sun. In the folk-lore of Indonesia the souls go to their abode in the shape of geese, riding upon deer. In many parts of the West sea-gulls embody the ghosts of drowned sailors [cp. p. 145 infra]; and Yeats tells how the appearance of a sea-bird at the window portended death to a Pollexfen, his mother's family. . . .' (The Integrity of Yeats, ed. D. Donoghue, Cork, 1964, p. 40).

murdered man turns into an accusing bird, that flits about the grave till vengeance be taken for the dead.

According to a Polish folk-tale every member of the Herburt family turns into an *eagle* as soon as he dies. The first-born daughters of the house of Pileck were changed into *doves* if they died unmarried, but the married ones into *owls*. . . . When the robber Madej was confessing under an appletree, and getting quit of his sins, apple after apple flew up into the air, converted into a *white dove*: they were the souls of those he had murdered. One apple still remained, the soul of his father, whose murder he had suppressed; when at length he owned that heinous crime, the last apple changed into a *grey dove* and flew after the rest. (Woycicki's Klechdy 1, 180). This agrees with the un-resting birds of the Bohemian legend. In a Podolian folk-song, on the grave-mound there shoots up a little oak, and on it sits a snow-white dove (ibid. 1, 209).

. . . The popular opinion of Greece also regarded the soul as a winged being (ψυχὴ πνεῦμα καὶ ζωΰφιον πτηνόν says Hesychius), not bird, but butterfly, which is even more apt, for the insect is developed out of the chrysalis, as the soul is out of the body: hence ψυχή is also the word for butterfly. A Roman epitaph found in Spain has the words: M. Porcius M. haeredibus mando etiam cinere ut meo *volitet* ebrius *papilio*. In Basque, 'arima' is soul, . . . and 'astoaren arima' (ass's soul) butterfly . . .' Ibid. Vol. IV, 1548 (London 1888): 'The soul is *winged*', Plato's Phædr. 246–7–8; it loses and then recovers its wings 248–9, conf. Gerhard's Eros, tab. 1 and 5; . . . Il. 16, 856 . . . Od. 11, 222. Lucian's Encom. Demosth. c. 50 says of the dying orator: ἀπέπτη, evolavit.

The larva, the butterfly, is called ὁ νεκύδαλος. Swed. *käringsjäl*, old woman's soul = butterfly, Ihre 2, 529. Ir. *anamandé* anima dei = butterfly; . . . When a moth flutters round the candle, the Lithu. women say somebody's *dying*, and the *soul* is going hence. . . .'

W. G. Wood-Martin, Pagan Ireland, p. 141 (London 1895) adds: 'After death, the soul is supposed at first to remain in the form of a butterfly in the neighbourhood of the body, and then to follow it to the grave. The Bulgarians hold that it assumes the form of a bird or a butterfly, and remains on the nearest tree until the funeral is over. The Servians believe the soul of a witch often leaves her body while she is asleep, and flies abroad in the shape of a butterfly. The same idea prevails in some of the islands of the Pacific.'

Evidence of the bird-soul nexus from (S. and E.) Africa is as follows

(J. A. MacCulloch, The Childhood of Fiction, (London 1905), p. 112)' . . . the Basuto Zulu and Zanzibar versions (of the story of the murdered youngest brother) tell how the crime was discovered by a bird which, after the murder, denounced the brothers. The bird is a reincarnation of the victim, or possibly the soul of the deceased, in accordance with a widespread belief that the soul is a bird. In one Basuto version the heart tells the story; it is called a bird, and in the sequel the murdered man is restored to life; while in another the heart is a bird, and when its wings are pulled off, the girl who was killed steps out of the feathers.'

The Irish evidence for the bird-soul[1] is of particular importance, and it extends from the earliest Saints' Lives through elegiac, penitential and other religious literature, through the *Voyages*—themselves so largely penitential—down to Keating and to modern folklore. To take this last first: the swan on Irish lakes enjoys the immunity of a sacred bird, and indeed they are in some places believed to represent the souls of holy women slain by the Vikings of Lough Erne (W. G. Wood-Martin, Traces of the Elder Faiths of Ireland I, London 1902, p. 147). Cf. also the metamorphosis of the Children of Lir into swans.

In the second preface of Adamnan's Life of S. Columba (ed. of A. O. and M. O. Anderson, London 1961, p. 181) he relates his name to that of the prophet Jonah (Hebrew *Iona*, Greek *Peristera*, Latin *Columba*) and points to the scriptural figure of the Dove for the Holy Spirit.

In the Tripartite Life of S. Patrick (Stokes), p. 414, we are told . . . *irricht eoin ticed Victor aingel coPatraic intan roboi ic ingaire mucc Milcon* . . . 'in a bird's shape the angel Victor was wont to come to Patrick when he was herding the swine of Miliuc . . .' On p. 21, ibid., an angel appears to Patrick in the desert in the form of a bird; on p. 114 black birds are demons which torment him, while white birds sing melodies for him. The bird-flocks of the Land of Promise which came to welcome Patrick (*Dinds*. 68 (R C 15, 468) *Enlaithe Thire Tairrngire dodechadar [d]o failti fri Patraic*) are no doubt angels, as in *Imr. Ua C.* line 90.

In the life of S. Darerca (Monynna) we read: Cumque dormitorium intrassent, ipsa Briga virgo ad cubiculum ubi sancta Darerca orare solebat atque angelorum colloquium habere solebat accessit. Cum vero loco appropinquaret, quasi duos cignos inde volasse conspexit . . .

---

[1] In the present context we can make only passing reference to *Aislinge Óenguso*, *Tochmarc Étaíne* (changing to bird-shape) and BDD (bird-folk, bird-kin, bird-tabu) which belong to a discussion of the Irish antecedents of the feature.

duos cignos candidissimi coloris, de tua cellula ascendisse, conspexi, ex quorum visione mirabili pavere incepi . . . Tibi enim visionem suorum ministrorum, quam aliis abscondit, manifestare dignatus est . . . (Acta Sanctorum Hib. ex cod. Sal. edd. de Smedt et de Backer, Edinburgh, 1888, p. 182).

In Vita Prima Brendani (Plummer, *Vitae Sanctorum Hiberniae* (Oxford 1910) I, 98 ff.) § 26, the souls of angels only slightly involved with Satan in his rebellious designs are encountered on an island by the voyagers.—They appear in the form of white birds on a tree on Sundays and holidays. To Brendan, too, appears the archangel Michael in the form of a bird, and sings with great sweetness (Stokes, Lism. L., xiii; Rawl. B. 512, fo. 142a, b.) Keating's History of Ireland, iii (ed. P. S. Dinneen, London 1908), 220, tells how 'the company of Ui Coingheoidh appeared (from hell) in the air above, in the form of jet black birds, and they did not venture to light on the churchyard ground because of its having been blessed'.

An early eighth century elegy on King Aed MacColgen killed in battle in 738 and buried in (S. Ciarán's) Clonmacnois runs (Meyer, Bruchstücke, p. 44):

> int Āed isind ūir, in rī isind rūaim,
> int ēnān dil dēin la Cērān i Clūain.
> 'Aed (is) in the clay, the king (is) in the cemetery,
> the dear, pure little bird is with Ciarán in Clonmacnois'.

Énán, diminutive of *én* 'bird' can only mean 'soul', here.

In RC II, 200, W. Stokes offers some further instances of souls assuming the form of birds: '. . . in the Middle Ir. *Dá Brón Flatha Nime* (Two Sorrows of Heaven's Kingdom), L U p. 17, and the *Vision of Adamnán,* ib. p. 31b, the souls of the righteous come in 'shapes of pure white birds' (*i rrechtaib én nglégel*) to be taught by Eli under the Tree of Life. So the souls of Maelsuthain's three pupils come to him 'in shapes of three white doves' (*irechtaib tri colum ngeal*) O'Curry, Lectures 530. The souls of the wicked appear as ravens 'et extemplo precones toti combusti vitam finiunt; anime in speciebus corvinis alveum advolant'. Vita S. Paterni, Rees, Cambro-British Saints. Llandovery, 1853, p. 92'.

Similarly, in his vision of the 'Two Deaths' (Ed. C. Marstrander, Ériu 5, (1911), 120–125) a hermit recounts what happens to the souls of the evil and the good man, when they die. Here the soul of the sinful man, repulsed several times by Satan, is finally liberated in the form of a black raven (cf. also P H (Todd Lect. ii), ed. R. Atkinson, 1887, No. 36: On the Soul's Exit from the Body, lines 8158–8159). M. Schlauch (Journal of Celtic Studies I 159 (Baltimore 1950) comments: 'The scene, especially the presentation of the soul perched temporarily on the body's head, or crouching before the threatening demons, is characteristic of Christian iconography in Egypt. The soul as bird hovering over a man *in extremis* is . . . a symbol used in Irish and early Northumbrian iconography of the Crucifixion, which is traced by art historians to Egyptian sources.' Prof. Schlauch adds references from these to the soul (spirit) as a phoenix and as a hawk.

The references to the bird-soul in the *Immrama* are of particular significance as these are linked to *The Seafarer* by situation (voyage) and mood (penance). *Immram Ua Corra* offers several instances, of which the first (*infra*) really gives food for thought:

I. *Imr. Ua C.* § 3: Thereafter the jester died on board and they were sorrowful and dejected because of that. As they were there they saw the little bird on the gunwale of the coracle, and then the bird said: 'for God's sake, men, tell me the cause of your grief'. 'We had a little jester entertaining us, and he died a while ago in the coracle, and that's the cause of our sadness'. 'I am your jester', said the bird 'and do not grieve any more, for I shall go to heaven now'. Thereafter he bids them farewell.

§ 12 is also of great interest: Then they bid the woman farewell and row their coracle on the sea until there appeared to them large many-coloured bird-flocks in great numbers. One of the birds alighted on the gunwale of the coracle. 'It would be delightful', said they, 'if this were a messenger with tidings from the Lord'. Then the elder raises his face. 'God would be able (to do) that', he said. 'It is to speak to you, indeed, that I have come', said the bird . . . 'I am of Ireland' said the bird, 'and am the soul of a woman,—and a nun unto thee', said she to the elder. 'Tell me this', said he 'are we going to hell?' 'You will not go (there)' said the bird.

There are three further references to the bird-soul in this tale: In lines 90 ff. an angelic bird-flock makes music to the Creator in heaven, and the archangel Michael in the form of a bright bird is singled out for his sweet music (cf. Stokes, Lism. L., xiii, and Vita Brendani § 26, cited above). In § 23 a bright bird, capable of speech, acts as door-keeper of the hermit's church. In § 9 the pilgrims reach an island inhabited by beautiful bright bird-flocks which sing melodiously and plaintively, and by a disciple of Andreas who had been sent on *ailithre* in the ocean because of once forgetting his nocturns;—'and here I am awaiting Doomsday; and the birds that ye see are the souls of holy people'. With this compare *Immram Maíle Dúin*, § 19: '. . . And after that they saw in the island a man whose clothing was his hair. So they asked him who he was and whence his kindred. "Of the men of Ireland am I", said he. "I went on my pilgrimage in a little coracle, and when I had gone a short way from land my coracle spilt under me. I came again to land", said he, "and I put under my feet a sod from my country and on it I arose upon the sea, and the Lord established that sod for me in this place" said he, "and God adds a foot to its breadth every year from that to this, and a tree every year to grow in it. The birds which you see in the trees", said he, "are the souls of my children and of my kindred, both women and men, who are yonder awaiting Doomsday . . ."'

In the Voyage of Snédgus and Mac Riagla, Poetic version, IV, (Prose version § 4) we encounter the birds of the Plain of Heaven: (Poetic version, edd. van Hamel, Immrama; Thurneysen, Zwei Versionen der Mittelirischen Legende von Snédgus u. Mac Riagla, Halle, 1904, Corrigenda, ZCP 5, 418 ff. Cf. also E. J. Gwynn, Hermathena 44, 68):

22. The murmuring wind wafted them . . . to an elevated island on which there was a tree with a beautiful bird-flock.
23. They sang chants on the top of the tree—heart's longing!—a joyous strain—the exultant birds of Heaven's Plain.
24. Saintly the bird that led the choirs, without any envy, fair of shape and with head of gold and silver wings.
25. The worthy bird with the august secret preached to them the good God had done before creating creatures.
26. He preached the birth of Christ from the glorious virgin— sustained intoning—both baptism, resurrection and passion.
27. When he preached tidings of Doomsday to the festive bands, they beat their wings for long against themselves, until they were tired.
28. Healthy blood dripped from their sides, with a sound like the sea, for Christ's crucifixion, for the fame of the Doom of judgment.
29. Drops of blood poured from them—a wondrous course; it was kingly oil, it was wine, communion, a sacred relic.
30. There was thrown down on the clerics—(the Lord loved them!)— not secretly—a leaf as broad as the hide of a great team-ox.

31. 'Take it with you', said the beautiful bird. Fair renown, bright the great victory: it was on Colum Cille's altar.

32. Lovely (is) the tree whose trunk will not decay,—nor the colour of its leaves; it would fit the men of all Ireland under its crown.

33. Noble is the prayer of those birds, with firm words, bright pure psalms and sweet triumphant canticles.

From this long citation of evidence for the bird-soul symbol we return to relevant instances in OE literature[1], beginning with *Wanderer* 45–55a (cf. edd. of I. Gollancz, H. Sweet, N. Kershaw, Krapp-van Kirk Dobbie):

> 45 Đonne onwæcneð eft wineleas guma,
> gesihð him beforan fealwe wegas,
> baþian brimfuglas, brædan feþra,
> hreosan hrim ond snaw, hagle gemenged.
> þonne beoð þy hefigran heortan benne,
> 50 sare æfter swæsne. Sorg bið geniwad,
> þonne maga gemynd mod geondhweorfeð;
> greteð gliwstafum, georne geondsceawað.
> Secga geseldan swimmað eft on weg;
> fleotendra ferð no þær fela bringeð
> 55 cuþra cwidegiedda. Cearo bið geniwad
> þam þe sendan sceal swiþe geneahhe
> ofer waþema gebind werigne sefan.

'Then the friendless man awakes again and sees before him the grey waves—sees the sea-birds bathing and spreading their wings, hoar-frost falling and snow mingled with hail. Then are the wounds in his heart from the loss of his loved one the more grievous, and his sorrow is renewed when the memory of his kinsmen passes through his mind. He greets them with glad strains and scans them eagerly. Comrades of men swim away again—the spirits of the floating ones do not convey many familiar greetings. His grief is renewed, who must so often send his weary spirit over the frozen waves.'

As the friendless one is now awake, l. 52 is incomprehensible unless some concrete manifestation is intended. At all events the terms *greteð*, *geondsceawað* imply this. The following lines with *swimmað*, *fleotendra ferð* clarify it, the latter term ('the spirit (soul) of the floating ones') being decisive. Hence the passage develops (A) the picture of the sea-birds bathing and spreading their feathers (l.47), through (B) the *maga*

---

[1] The earliest instances of the bird-soul are in the Visions of Drythelm, H. E. v. 12, and the Monk of Wenlock (c. 717); cf. p. 206 below.

gemynd of l.51, to (AB) the composite *fleotendra ferð* of l.54, which comprises both aspects of the bird-soul. (The logical flaw in this term is perhaps inseparable from the literary development of the symbol). It would also seem—though this is difficult to say with certainty—that both aspects are comprized in l.53: where *secga geseldan* is best taken as a development of *maga gemynd* (51), a variation of *fleotendra ferð* (54), and in agreement with the drift of l. 52—particularly *geondsceawað; swimmað* (53) brings out the physical aspect, which is to the fore in N. Kershaw's rendering of *secga geseldan* as 'warrior comrades'. This phrase occurs where desire (l.52) has reached its zenith and is about to be disappointed (l.53), and it is on the whole inconceivable that at a point of such tension there should be a break of continuity or a deflection to the physical aspect (i.e. sea-birds). The more comprehensive meaning which we are urging here goes hand in hand with the etymological value of *geseldan* 'occupants of the same dwelling': *secga geseldan* 'occupants of man's dwelling'.

V. Salmon (MLR 55, 1–10) shares our view that the wanderer is communicating with spirits and points to O. Icel. *fylgjur manna* 'associates of men', 'guardian spirits capable of assuming the form of animals or birds'. Although there is no OE evidence for the heathen *fylgia* this comparison is of value, chiefly, I think, in helping to dispose of the unreal dichotomy between heathen and Christian thought processes. Cp. the striking and most relevant testimony by Mrs Emma Hardy, first wife of Thomas Hardy, that the gulls, puffins, rooks, and jackdaws which help to animate the wintry scene by the seaside cliffs which she describes, are sometimes called 'black souls and white'.[1] A partial interpretation is offered by G. Midgley (RES x 53–54) who argues that *secga geseldan* and *fleotendra ferð* are seagulls.

To clinch the matter for OE we have the decisive evidence from the *Phoenix*[2] 589 ff. which has not been cited hitherto in this regard, (Krapp-Dobbie, p. 110):

> Ðonne soðfæstum sawlum scineð
> heah ofer hrofas hælende Crist.
> Him folgiað fuglas scyne,
> beorhte gebredade, blissum hremige,
> in þam gladan ham, gæstas gecorene,
> ece to ealdre. þær him yfle ne mæg

[1] E. Hardy, Some Recollections, Oxford 1961; reviewed Sunday Times 22-10-1961, p. 30, coll. 6–7, where the passage is quoted.

[2] Cp. Christ II 635 ff. where the Saviour is named 'bird' and the figure then developed.

> fah feond gemah facne sceþþan,
> ac þær lifgað a leohte werede,
> swa se fugel fenix, in freoþu dryhtnes,
> wlitige in wuldre.

'Then o'er the righteous souls, high o'er the vaults of heaven, shineth the Saviour Christ: Him follow resplendent birds, radiantly restored, blissfully exulting in that glad home, spirits chosen unto all eternity; there the foul impious fiend may not basely injure them by guile, but they live there always, begirt with light, as the bird Phœnix in the Lord's peace, beauteous in glory.' Cp. Gollancz, ed. p. 237.

Of the disembodied soul's departure and return to the body, cf. Bede, H. E. III 19 on Fursa. A further O E example from the Whitby *Life of St. Gregory* is the ascent of the soul of Paulinus to heaven 'in the form of a white bird, great like a swan and very beautiful' (D. Whitelock, Engl. Hist. Documents I 689; V. Salmon, op. cit., p. 5, f.n. 3).

Lines 58–66 of *The Seafarer* open on the final note of the *Wanderer* passage (45–57) discussed above: the poet's spirit ranging over the expanse of waters.[1]

> Forþon nu min hyge hweorfeð ofer
>   hreþerlocan,
> min modsefa mid mereflode
> 60 ofer hwæles eþel hweorfeð wide,
> eorþan sceatas, cymeð eft to me
> gifre ond grædig, gielleð anfloga,
> hweteð on hwælweg hreþer unwear-
>   num
> ofer holma gelagu. Forþon me hatran
>   sind
> 65 dryhtnes dreamas þonne þis deade lif,
> læne on londe.

'So now my spirit soars beyond my breast, ranges widely along the course of the sea, over the home of the whale and the expanse of the world. Again it comes back to me, eager and hungry. It (i.e. 'the lone-flier') screams and impels my heart irresistibly to the path of the whale

---

[1] Cp. the lyrical ninth century Swan Sequence (The Penguin Book of Latin Verse, D60, 1962, pp. 152–154) which apparently pictures the soul in the form of a bird, buffeted by storms over the seas, and then helped to land by the breeze. It ends with an exhortation to the bird-flocks to sing the Glory of God. Cf. p. 142 ff. *supra*. For a similar invocation to birds cf. the Alleluyatic Sequence, ibid. p. 163.

over the expanse of waters; for the joys of the Lord are more alive for (mean more to) me than this dead, transitory life on land.'

The parallelism and vocalic harmony of l. 59 and the repetition of *hweorfeð* with *wide* contribute to the incantatory and almost soporific effect of ll. 58–61a.—Note that these lines also form a syntactic unit. In lines 61b–62 this effect is sharply dispelled. (*Gifre* and *grædig* are found in combination elsewhere (*Gen.* 793, *Soul and Body* I 74) and the collocation may have the weaker force of a semi-cliché).

The image employed in this passage is unmistakably that of the spirit (soul) as bird ranging over the ocean—anticipating, no doubt, the course of the voyage—and returning to egg on the voyager. In lines 64b–66a it is satisfyingly glossed. The image is well grounded and sustained: l. 58 expresses movement (*hweorfan*) of the spirit (*hyge*) from its seat (*hreþerloca*); 59–61a its progress over ocean and earth; 61b its return, and 62–64 its eagerness and loud incitement of the voyager (pilgrim) to *follow the course of the spirit.* This is an exceedingly apt and felicitous conception of the poet's, which enriches our understanding of the poem and reinforces our interpretation of its general character and *genre.*

Our reading is *fully sanctioned* by the text, and it implies an unbroken sequence of thought and one sustained image throughout, up to the motivation of ll. 64b–66a. The point of this is no longer apparent if *anfloga* be interpreted as 'cuckoo' or 'seagull'; for it is only by the pilgrim's *soul* (*spirit*) inciting him to his pilgrimage that the grounds for any motivation or spiritual rationalizing arises. It is apparent now, too, that *forþon* of l. 64 means 'because' and that 'the general sense of the passage (58–66a) . . . is that the Seafarer's spirit is impelled to traverse the ocean *because* the "joys of the Lord" mean more to him than "life on land" ' . . . (Gordon's ed., p. 41, f.n. to 58). But Mrs Gordon would like to have it both ways; she says (f.n. 62b) '*anfloga* is almost certainly, as Sieper suggests, the cuckoo. Some have understood it to be the spirit (*hyge*) sweeping over the sea like a bird; but the emphasis on the cries, which could have little or no metaphorical significance, would make such an image almost absurd . . .' But lines 58 ff. establish that the spirit (*hyge*) *has* gone forth, and 61–62a that it comes back *gifre ond grædig.*—Then it screams in order to incite (cf. *hweteð 63*) the pilgrim on to the goal he so desires (cf. *hatran, 64*). And in fact there is only one reference to cries (*gielleð 62*), explained by *hweteð* of the following line. Mrs Gordon says further (ib.): 'Probably the passage is intended to mark the return to reality: when his spirit comes back to him again the Seafarer awakes to consciousness of his surroundings and hears again the cuckoo's cry.' But this interpretation with cuckoo finds no support in the passage and rests solely on the reference in 53–55 to the cuckoo as a harbinger of ill. Its greatest weakness is that the text itself (58–61) has to be discounted to accommodate it. The sequel (64 ff.) then fails to yield good sense, and indeed the meaning of the whole passage becomes fragmented and obscure. In short, the 'cuckoo' interpretation belongs to the past.

Note that the word *hreþer* occurring in 58 and 63 links the spirit's departure with its return, and that OE *singan* and *galan*—but not *giellan*, are used of the cuckoo's call.

And finally an example open to some question. *Soul and Body* I, Verc. Bk. p. 56, 52–56 (cf. Ex. Bk. p. 176, 49–53) runs:

> Ne eart ðu þon leofra nænigum lifigendra
> men to gemæccan, ne meder ne fæder
> ne nænigum gesybban, þonne se swearta hrefen,
> 55 syððan ic ana of ðe ut siðode
> þurh þæs sylfes hand þe ic ær onsended wæs.

'You are not more dear as a mate to any living man, neither mother nor father nor any relative, than the dark raven, since I fared out from you alone by the hand of Him who formerly sent me'.

The raven here is either a bird of ill-omen and so a symbol of unsociability, or it represents the lost soul itself. *Beowulf* (ed. Klaeber, 1950) provides conflicting evidence on the first of these alternatives: ll. 3024–3025 refer to *se wonna hrefn fūs ofer fægum* 'the dark raven, eager after doomed men' and ll. 2447–2448 even more ominously, contemplates *þonne his sunu hangað hrefne tō hrōðre* 'when his son hangs as a sport for the raven'. But in *Beowulf* 1799–1803 the raven is harbinger of day:

> Reste hine þā rūmheort; reced hlīuade
> 1800 gēap ond goldfāh; gæst inne swæf,
> oþ þæt hrefn blaca heofones wynne
> blīðheort bodode. Ðā cōm beorht scacan
> [scīma ofer sceadwa];

'Then the noble-hearted man reposed; the chamber towered aloft, spacious and gold-adorned. The stranger slept within, until the swarthy raven, blithe of heart, announced the 'joy of heaven' (i.e. the sun). Then bright light of morning came hurrying after the shadows.'

It is quite in keeping with the context to take the dark raven of *Soul and Body* as symbol of the lost soul which addresses the body The passage is then much more closely knit: the body (ll. 52–53) is compared with the soul (l.54), and this by variation (. . . ic ana . . .) becomes the subject of ll. 55–56. The dark raven is immediately identified in the following line (55) as 'I (who) fared out from you alone'. Otherwise the juxtaposition of *se swearta hrefen* and *ic* is somewhat peculiar; besides, the idea of the body as *gemæcca* is better grounded in its conjunction with soul (*hrefen*). The meaning of ll. 52–54 then is that the body in question is no better a comrade to the living than its (lost) soul. The dark raven, which even as a symbol of unsociability is rather incongruous here, as such disappears.

69a MS. *tide ge.* Emended to *tiddæge, tiddege* 'final hour' by many edd.; to *ær his tid aga* 'before his life depart' by others. Others read *tidege* 'Zeitschrecken, Tod' (Schücking, Kluge). *Tiddege* in the meaning 'the end of the span of life' is preferred by Gordon, but the Gen. 1165 instance on which this is based does not sufficiently bring out the terminal notion, *tiddæg* commonly meaning 'period of a person's life', cf. Bosworth s.v. Krapp-Dobbie, Ex. Book p. 297 remark 'For either *tiddæge* or *tidege* we must assume that *tid-* means "death" and there are no other instances of the word used in this way.' But there are numerous instances in religious writing of *tíd* 'the time at which something occurs' in the specific application 'time of death, final hour' cf. *Ðá com his tíd ðæt hé sceolde of middangearde tó Drihtne féran* 'then his time came to depart from earth to the Lord' Bd. 4.3. Cf. Bosworth s.v., I. The MS. reading can be retained in the form *tidege* 'dread of the final hour, of death' or 'dread appertaining to the final hour, to death', the whole passage (68–71) conveying the meaning: before the dreaded time of death it is always in doubt which of three things, disease, old age, or violence will wrest life from the departing fey one.' The fear of death was an active religious concept and it fits well into the drastic context of *feorh oðþringeð,* 71b.

72–80. It has been commonly assumed that the syntax of this passage in the MS. version (with *þæt* in 72a and *fremman* in 75a) is not viable, and Gordon emends to *biþ, fremum* respectively. It may be said at once that the meaning of the passage is not much affected, but it seems doubtful that two emendations can be necessary. The MS. version can be rendered as follows:

'Therefore for every man the praise of those who live after him and commemorate him, (and) the best memorial that he may earn before he must depart, is to prevail (consists in prevailing) on earth against the wickedness of fiends, opposing the devil with noble deeds, so that the children of men may praise him afterwards and his glory live among the angels for ever (in the) blessedness of eternal life, bliss among the host of heaven'. In the opening, 'praise' (73a *lob*) may seem out of context with the second half of the sentence; but in 78a it means 'praise ascribed to one, glory', and in 79–80 it is parallel to *blæd* 'glory', *dream* 'bliss'; hence a similar nuance may be expected in 72 f.: 'Therefore every man's repute among those who live after him . . . .'

For the omission of the verb *to be* in 72a cf. *Beowulf* 811, 1559 and Klaeber's ed. sub *eom*. Syntactically, *fremman . . .* (75a) is complement of the adj. (subst.) *betst*[1] (73b) from which it is divided by a qualifying clause. For some exx. of the uninflected infinitive modifying an adj. cf. M. Callaway, The Infinitive in Anglo-Saxon, Washington, 1913, pp. 150 f.; cf. *Guthlac* 1077 ff.: Ic eom siþes *fus/* upeard *niman* edleana georn/ in þam ecan gefean, ærgewyrhtum/ *geseon* sigora frean. . . .

The insertion of *biþ* in 72a seems unnecessary, and, if our interpretation can stand, also the various emendations proposed for *fremman* in 75a.

Note the significance of struggling against demons[2] in the Lives of hermits such as Guthlac and Cuthbert and cf. pp. 61, 64 above for reff. in Irish poems; also *Gifts of Men* 89 f. (: *Guthlac* 961).

97–102. Gordon rightly takes the general sense of the passage to be that 'wealth, whether expended on his grave by his brother, or hoarded in his lifetime, cannot help the sinful man at the Final Judgement' (ed. p. 45). To her discussion of the difficulties (ibid.) cp. Krapp-Dobbie, Ex. Book, p. 297 f. As it stands, i.e. without the emendation *nille* for MS. *wille* in 99b, the text seems capable of the following interpretation: 'Though brother will strew with gold the grave for his brother born, bury by the dead one with (in the form of) various treasures that which he wishes (to go) with him, gold cannot help the soul that is full of sin in the presence of the terrible power of God, when he hoards (hides) it beforehand while he is still alive on earth.' The gold strewn would be that hoarded formerly by the dead one, and the logical nexus conveyed seems quite acceptable, though we should couch it differently nowadays. Our interpretation plausibly takes *geborenum* and *deadum* as parallel and does not require the addition of an object 'him' with *byrgan*. This verb is extended to cover the interment of objects asso-

---

[1] *Betst* refers to *þæt* (72a) . . . *þæt* (74a): cf. *Widsith* 132 ff. . . . *se biþ leofast . . . se þe him god syleð gumena rice to gehealdenne*. . . .

[2] It was part of the warfare carried on by the Christian soldier, cf. Colgrave, Lives of Cuthbert, p. 325.

ciable with the body, a use which seems possible even in early O E; cf. *þonne eal geador | bebyrgeð beaducræftig bān ond yslan* 'then the valiant (bird) buries all together, bones and ashes' (Phoenix 285 f.; ninth century?). The emendation may not, after all, be necessary.

111 ff. *healdan wiþ* 'to act towards, maintain terms with' is reminiscent of O. Icel. *halda (e-u) við*, and the thought expressed in these two lines (111–112) should be compared to *Háv.* 43, 64.

CHAPTER VII

THE *SEAFARER*: SUMMARY, ANALYSIS, SYNTHESIS

SUMMARY. The poem opens with an account of the hardships experienced on past voyages by the subject, as contrasted with the joys of a comfortable life on land (1–33). Then (33–64) the poet speaks of his craving to seek a distant place of exile. Whoever contemplates such a voyage is bound to be preoccupied about what the Lord has in store for him. His mind is not on ordinary human pleasures, but on the sea; and he yearns always. The promise and splendour of early summer strengthen his desire to set sail on his quest; and the cuckoo's sad voice adds its premonition of sorrow in store for him who 'prints his track of exile furthest' (–57). His soul is now eager for the self-imposed journey (–64), for indeed he loves the joys of the Lord more than the dead transitory life on land;—and it behoves every man by exerting himself manfully against the powers of evil to prove himself worthy of the bliss of heaven (64–80). Former glory has passed away; decay and death come to all;—and gold will not avail the soul against God's wrath (80–102). One should live in the fear of God, in humility and moderation, for God and fate rule mankind (102–116). We should (therefore) think of our real home and devise how to reach it. To God, who has honoured us for all time, we should give thanks (117–124).

ANALYSIS. The frequent occurrence of the vague and colourless link *forþon*—particularly at crucial points in the poem (33, 58, 64)—indicates the type of organization employed: a loose juxtaposition of ideas which the modern reader seeks—and is at a loss—to relate to one another. Hence the divergent views on such basic considerations as theme and structure.

The opening formula leads us quickly to the point of the first section (–33a): lines 2–4 *hu ic geswincdagum | earfoðhwile oft þrowade, | bitre breostceare gebiden hæbbe* 'how in days of hardship I have often endured times of stress, bitter anxiety of heart', 5 *cearselda fela* 'many abodes of care', 7 *nearo nihtwaco* 'a distressing vigil', 8b–12a *Calde*

*geþrungen/wæron mine fet, forste gebunden/caldum clommum, þær þa
ceare seofedun/hat' ymb heortan; hungor innan slat/merewerges mod*
'My feet have been numbed with cold, bound with chill fetters of
frost, while cares sighed hot round my heart and my spirit within me
was torn by hunger, wearied as I was by the sea'; 14 *earmcearig*
'wretched and sorrowful', 15 *wræccan lastum* 'on paths of (an) exile'.
The fortunate land-dweller, introduced in line 12, is a foil to symbolize
the pleasure and solace which the seafarer misses, and this implied
contrast underlies 16 *winemægum bidroren* 'bereft of kinsmen'. It also
underlies the terms 20 *to gomene* 'for (my) amusement', 21 *fore hleahtor
wera* 'in lieu of the laughter of men', 22 *fore medodrince* 'in lieu of
mead-drinking', 25–26 *nænig hleomæga/feasceaftig ferð frefran*[1] *meahte*
'no near kinsman could comfort my desolate soul'. In lines 27–29 (cf.
further 56, 65 f.) the land-dweller is resumed and the tale of privation
proceeds.

This first section is markedly introspective: we are not being told so
much about external phenomena as about their *effect on the subject.* The
detail from his seafaring experiences are immediately related to his
mood and feelings, and we get on the whole a quite subjective account
of the seafarer's *reaction* or *condition* (*earmcearig* 14, *wræccan lastum* 15,
winemægum bidroren 16, *bihongen hrimgicelum* 'hung about with
icicles' 17, *þær ic ne gehyrde* ... 18, ... *dyde ic me to gomene* ... 20–22).
Even the apparently objective lines 23–24 on storms and the answering
cries of seabirds are followed by the reflection of lines 25–26 that no
near kinsman could comfort his desolate soul. Similarly the point of
lines 27–30 is *how, often, I had wearily to remain on the ocean path,*
and the natural phenomena subsequently listed are obviously the ones
to illustrate his feelings of desolation (*feasceaftig ferð* 26) and privation
endured (*bealosiþa* 28).

The whole selection of detail in this section is of a piece with this
mood. And whereas seafaring has many moments of pleasure—none
of which are considered by the poet—there are others which are not
necessarily depressing. So for instance the noise of the sea, the song
of the swan, the cry of gannet, whaup, and seagull (18–22). But all
these are darkly coloured by the poet's recollection of misery endured.
They are set off against social pleasures to mark the environment of
the desolate soul, and both sides of this contrast are taken up and
elaborated in the sequel (23–30). The attitude of anxiety to seafaring
expressed here at such length and so insistently is maintained through-

[1] On p. 133 it is suggested that MS *feran* be retained.

out the poem.—Moving for a moment beyond line 34: no anticipation of pleasure lightens his unexpected resolve to fare forth once more (34–36). Indeed the *sorg* (line 42) of which we have already heard so much is further elaborated in a long passage there (39–47); and the references to *hean streamas,/sealtyþa gelac* (34–35), *yða gewealc* (46) have to be interpreted in this light and point back to the explicit *atol yþa gewealc* of line 6. It follows from this that the seafaring image, so prominent in the first half of the poem, is in reality subordinate to the poet's deeper intent. But here we anticipate.

The basis of the poem up to line 34, then, is clearly psychological, and this may supply us with the clue—and the criterion—we need in order to assess its 'transitions' and structure, and to arrive at the poet's intention.

The opening of the second section (33b–64) furnishes immediate evidence of this: And yet thoughts are now pressing upon my heart that of my own accord I shall venture on the deep seas, the tossing of the salt waves . . . The *object* of the journey is explicitly stated in 36–38: Heart's desire ever urges my soul to depart, that far from here I should visit the land of *peregrini*. Clues to the motive of the journey are given throughout the poem:—in the subsequent lines leading up to 43: that everyone worries about God's purpose regarding him when on his voyage; in lines 58–64, which also resume the intent of 34–38, and which state that the poet's thoughts and spirit range over the sea and return full of desire. The *lone-flier* which incites him on (62) can with confidence be taken for the seafarer's soul (cf. p. 137); then lines 62–64, which sustain the metaphor of flight, are a variation of lines 58–62. Lines 64–66 associate the projected voyage with the joys of the Lord (*dryhtnes dreamas*) and contrast it with the lifeless and transient existence on land. Then, too, life is so uncertain and problematical (68–71), and the best posthumous fame and hope of salvation for any-one comes from opposing the forces of evil with noble deeds (72–80). Lines 100–102 suggest that some special course prompted by the fear of God is necessary for the sinful soul, since gold will not help; and in the subsequent lines leading on to the conclusion, the fear of God is stressed among other beneficial qualities; and also the need to know what our true goal (i.e. eternal bliss) is, and to take thought how to attain it.

The conclusion from all this is inescapable; it is sanctioned by the text and supported by the whole poem: the projected journey is one of pilgrimage by sea to a distant place to atone for sin and to merit eternal reward. To arrive at this result we had to work forward from the resolve of lines 33–38, and we return now to pick up the other threads.

In lines 39–52 we find a triple elaboration of detail typical of OE poetry. The first concerns the types of man least likely to have forebodings of his destiny on sea, the second the pleasures one filled with longing might be slowest to forego, and the third the natural charms of Spring. Note how adroitly these are made to further the theme and are woven into the organism of the poem: the first explains away his anxiety, the second by its contrasts brings out his preoccupation with the sea-environment of his voyage and throws some light on the unworldly source of his *longung*, while the third urges him on to achieve his purpose. This the sad-voiced cuckoo also does and the premonition of anxiety which is mentioned here once more (*sorge* 54, *hwæt þa sume dreogað* . . . 56–57), and which is evoked by her call, is all the more real and relevant for the failure of the seafarer's foil (*esteadig secg,* 56) to apprehend anything of its source. Minor points to note are the triadic formula of lines 68 ff., the choice of posthumous fame as a criterion in lines 72 ff. and its fusion with the Christian idea of gaining heaven by good works here on earth. Following the reference to eternal life (79–80) comes the passage on our transitory life and the decay that goes with it (80 ff.). The aptness of this contrast assures us that there can be nothing fortuitous about the further sequence from decay and death through gilded grave to sinful soul and the fear of God (94–104 ff.). With the emphasis henceforth on the last end and the qualities and manner of life best calculated to prepare for it we are led back to the resolve of lines 37–38: *þæt ic feor heonan elþeodigra eard gesece* 'that I should seek the land of *peregrini* far away'.

The poet's intention is therefore clear and is established by a straightforward examination of the poem as a whole. To 'dismember' it is to substitute modern preconceptions for structural study. The poem has to be taken as a unit, since the so-called 'homiletic' second part (64 ff.) furnishes the moral background for the pilgrimage and motivates it for us. The second part of the poem, in fact, explains the first. Hence the view that at line 64 a not very obviously connected moralizing begins does not hold nor has it proved difficult to trace a connected theme throughout the whole. We have simply to accept the fact that an OE poet can compose a penitential poem as the author of *The Seafarer* has done: by concentrating at first on the perils and hardships of the sea (–34); then expressing his resolve—tempered by a natural anxiety—to fare forth (43); subsequently to consider what he intends to forego and to offset that by the stimuli offered (–57); then to find himself resolved (–64) and subsequently to offer the spiritual motives (64–124). From the evidence offered by the poem we should say that the pilgrimage is a real intent: real at least in point of poetic fact. That is to say, it belongs to the psychological basis of the poem.— Whether it was in fact subsequently undertaken it is almost outside our province to inquire.

The pronounced introspective character of the poem is accounted for proximately by its theme and basically by the character of its maker. The same might be said of *The Penitent's Prayer,* with the difference that there the penitential aspect is directly in the foreground and is not mediated by seafaring images, though the devices of contrast and ethopoeia do occur. *The Penitent's Prayer* has a poignant spiritual ring akin to that of our Irish penitential poem *Cormac's Choice;* but we have no grounds for considering its maker either an experienced seafarer or a resolute man of action;—and his proposed voyage is neither elaborated by any detail nor even in keeping with the realities of his situation. Our Seafarer too is inspired by religious motives— but quietly, and as it were, without tears or overmuch expostulation. His approach to religion is typically reflective and is enshrined in such phrases as *uton we hycgan* . . . (117), *ond þonne geþencan* (118); so too, his frequent references to the Lord are all in the less engaged, more contemplative third person. Pilgrimage was a common antidote to the critical human condition and the Seafarer's motivation of it does not break new ground. In fact this part of the poem is formalistic and can be matched in other OE poetry. It is impersonal, abstract, reflective-gnomic, and homiletic.

The seafaring image, as we have seen, is not treated for its own sake, nor is it accompanied by any joyful associations. Appropriate as it is for one to whom the circumstances of voyaging are second nature,— and particularly in view of his intended pilgrimage by sea—it is subordinated to the total intention and symbolizes the *sorg* (42) and *longung* (47) proper to this. To hold otherwise is to miss *the use made by the poet* of his experience and materials. The subject's preoccupation about the Lord's purpose with regard to him (42–43) is shared by the subject of our Irish penitential poem *Cormac's Choice* (stanzas 9–11), and his anxiety about the tossing of the waves (46) has an exact counterpart there (stanza 9).

The Seafarer's religious attitude is part and parcel of his reserved nature, and one of the manifestations of this common to most of the so-called 'lyric-elegiac' poems is the replacing of forthright personal communication and commitment by generalization (*gnomic, reflective, homiletic*), and by the adoption of a 'medium' or exemplar (*third person, impersonal, nameless, abstract*). *The Wanderer,* for instance, is chiefly based on this tendency,—which we have to invoke in order to understand the conclusion of *The Wife's Lament* (lines 42 ff.) and to appreciate the pessimistic generalization of *The Riming Poem* (44 ff.). The almost furtive secrecy of *The Husband's Message* is achieved by applying it, and it finds ready expression in riddle, gnome, and maxim.

The Seafarer, The Penitent's Prayer, and *Uga Corbmaic Meic Cuilendáin* belong to the sub-genre of penitential poetry (page 50). They may be compared to the related sub-genre of Hermit-nature poetry (Jackson, ECNP, I–X, pages 3–11; Murphy, EIL, pages 2, 4, 6, 10, 18, 28)[1]; but here the *retreat*—vaguely if at all visualized in the English poems—has become the subject (rather than the aspiration);—or if the aspiration (Jackson, No. III, page 4; Murphy, page 28) then visualized in concrete detail as the subject. Hermit-nature poetry may express the penitential motif (Jackson, III, Stanza 2; IV, 2; VI, 7; Murphy, page 20, Stanzas 3, 4, 5) or combine it with devotional exercise (Jackson, IV, 2). Many hermit poems have little more than the underlying intention to warrant their inclusion in the genre.—In substance they are nature poems built upon the phenomena of outdoor life. So Jackson Nos. I, II, V, VIII, IX. But selection is invidious: No. X (ECNP page 11), for instance, illustrates the concept of nature as second nature for the hermit:

> Ah, blackbird, it is well for thee
> where thy nest is in the brake;
> hermit that dost not clang a bell,
> melodious, soft, and peaceful is thy call.

No. IV, page 5, also shows the poet's dependence on the nature image:

> The skilled lark calls,
> I go outside to watch it
> that I may see its gaping beak
> above against the dappled cloudy sky.

[1] Chronology (cf. ECNP 35 ff., 93; G. Murphy, Studies 20 (1931), p. 102 (=GM), and EIL): I = EIL 112, c. 800; II = EIL 4, early 9th c.; III = EIL 28, tenth century; IV, VII: uncertain; V = EIL 10, 9th c.; VI, early 12th c. (GM); VIII–IX = EIL 6, 9th c.; X, 12th or 13th c. (GM).

> I will sing my psalms
> for holy bright heaven
> that I may be shielded from harm,
> for the purging of my sins.

Of the hundred lines in No. V (Jackson, page 5; cf. Murphy, No. 8), the first ninety deal solely with the form and environment of the hermit-poet's hut in the wood, and with his life there. They describe in great detail the trees and bushes around it, the animals which frequent it, and particularly the hermit's simple fare; also the music of birds and insects, the lowing of heifers, and the song of the wind, of the pines and of the swan . . . The following two references to God are the only suggestion of a religious motive in these ninety lines:

> 1 I have a hut in the wood,
>   none knows it but my Lord; . . .
> 13 A clutch of eggs, honey, mast, and heath-pease
>   (sent by God) . . .

But the last ten lines—with their sudden change of tone—place the whole in perspective:

> 23 Beautiful the pines that make music to me
>   unhired;
>   though I sing to Christ I fare no worse
>   than you do.
> 24 Though you delight in your own pleasures
>   greater than all wealth,
>   for my part I am thankful for what is given me
>   from my dear Christ.
> 25 Without a moment of strife, or din of combat
>   that disturbs you,
>   grateful to the Prince who gives every good
>   to me in my hut.

The message of the last ten lines, and its form, are basically that of the Seafarer, who compares *dryhtnes dreamas* with *þis deade lif, læne on londe* (65–66), and who operates for the sake of contrast with the foils of nobleman (56) and happy landsman (12–13, 27–28). But in attitude and manner of communication the two poems are poles apart: the forthright, direct communication of these final stanzas leaves the poet's intention in no doubt;—whereas the English poet, having stated his resolve, tends afterwards to disengage and to communicate by in-

ference from a distance. Nos. 8 and 9 (Jackson, pages 10, 11), com-
prizing one stanza each, though included in the genre of hermit
poetry, lack any religious reference of any kind. But the observation of
the blackbird's call which forms their substance is seen by comparison
to be characteristic of the solitary.

No. VI (page 9), attributed to Columba—though later than the
others—was composed by a lover of the sea. It begins

> 1 Delightful I think it to be in the bosom of an isle
> on the crest of a rock,
> that I may look there on the manifold
> face of the sea.
>
> 2 That I may see its heavy waves
> over the glittering ocean
> as they chant a melody to their Father
> on their eternal course.

The formula *That I may see* is continued for four further stanzas of
keen and zestful appreciation:

> 3 That I may see its smooth strand of clear head-
> lands, no gloomy thing;
> that I may hear the voice of the wondrous birds,
> a joyful course.
> 4 That I may hear the sound of the shallow waves
> against the rocks;
> that I may hear the cry beside the churchyard,
> the roar of the sea.
> 5 That I may see its splendid flocks of birds
> over the full-watered ocean;
> that I may see its mighty whales,
> greatest of wonders.

Then in the middle of stanza 6 a change of tone:

> 6 That I may see its ebb and its flood-tide
> in its flow;
> that this should be my name, a secret I declare,
> 'He who turned his back on Ireland'.
> 7 That contrition of heart should come upon me
> when I look on it;
> that I may bewail my many sins
> difficult to declare.

And in the following stanzas the devotional exercises contemplated are allied with and varied by references to earth, ebb, and flood tide, gathering dillisk from the rock, and fishing. The conclusion runs

> 12 The counsel which is best before God
>   may He confirm it to me,
>   may the King, whose servant I am, not desert me,
>   may He not deceive me.

The gloom and anxiety of the *Seafarer* give way here to brightness and to a kind of self-assertive, though prayerful, hope. For the Irish exile-penitent the sea is much more than a mere setting: it is part of his mood (stanza 2) and actively promotes his underlying intention. And because the latter has been made crystal clear to us it does not occur to us to cavil at his means.

Irish hermit-nature poetry, then, belongs to a different psychological climate, to a state of fulfilment rather than of aspiration, in which communication is unimpeded and direct, at times urgent and intense. But the Seafarer's spiritual involvement is none the less real for being cloaked in an oblique, reflective English (rather than Irish) manner. The chief distinction lies in the relation of manner to attitude.

Finally, we may mention a Latin poem by an Englishman which seems to embody the total Hiberno-English complex: Alcuin's *Farewell to his Cell* (cf. *The Penguin Book of Latin Verse*, pp. 137–138), over which broods the spirit of regret and nostalgia, recounts in its first section (1–22) the former joys of the hermitage (trees, herbs, streams, flowering gardens, birds singing praises to God, devout reading and prayer). Thence it passes over (23–38) to the transience of all earthly beauty and to a succession of familiar English themes: dark night, cold winter, bitter wind ruffling the sea, senescence, vain love of the fleeting world, exhortation to love God, prayer, and doxology.

CHAPTER VIII

THE *WANDERER*

A. *General.* The poem opens and closes on the theme of God's mercy, which in our view underlies the whole of it. Its subject is the wretched seafarer's progress from *dryhten* to *Dryhten* (as in *Seafarer* 41–43) which results from taking thought and acquiring wisdom by reflection and observation. Because the seafarer by traversing it has come to understand the whole human scene with its tale of disaster and continual change and has come to see where his only security lies, he is symbolized at the end by the wise man.

The recluse (*anhaga*) is represented in the opening lines as constantly seeking (living to experience) God's mercy in his long gloomy and trying seafaring life. The condition of the lonely wandering exile to which these opening lines introduce us is portrayed and developed in 8–29a and 29b–57. From 8 to 57 the account is personal and is marked by a detailed contrast between the wretched state of the sea-tossed exile and his previous happy state of retainer secure in his lord's friendship (cp. *Seafarer* 12 ff., 27 ff., 55 f., 64b ff.). There is a noticeable transition from the mainly general and objective bearing of the opening lines to the introspection of 8–29a, (continued in the third person from 29b) to the short-lived dream of wish-fulfilment in 39–44 and to the subsequent waking and disillusion of 45–57. In lines 58 to 110 this preoccupation (*cearo* 55, cf. also 59) is generalized as reflective experience or wisdom; that is to say, the wise (experienced) man observes the transitoriness of all things and notes that the Creator has brought former glory and splendour to nought. Lines 92–110 present the same theme with much feeling in rhetorical form. *Sub specie aeternitatis* all is ephemeral. Then (112–115) the wise, steadfast and self-reliant one communicates the lesson that God is security, only source of mercy and comfort, the one true Dryhten.

The seafarer's progress is worked out methodically and in detail. Exactly half of the poem (1–57) deals with his personal suffering in the wake of his fallen *dryhten* and his fruitless quest of another overlord; the second half combines reflection with observation until the mind is illumined and the solitary has become wise (l. 111 *swa cwæð snottor on mode, gesæt him sundor æt rune*). Because he has kept his faith his quest has been successful (inference from l.112): the Lord has become his patron. Because now experience has matured him he feels entitled to communicate his former grief; that is, his poem is now justified, as he proves by being able to mention the remedy (*þa bote*, l.113) which he has been able to apply, namely, prayer to the Father in heaven. Fate the ineluctable (lines 5, 15, 100, 107) is steered by God's hand, after all!

The bitter experiences and reflections of the homeless, friendless one are presented in the guise of reported monologues by the wise and self-reliant man who can keep his own counsel and who is clearly the subject's exemplar or better self.

Sweet's suggestion (Anglo-Saxon Reader[11], Oxford 1948, p. 148) that the poem should rather be entitled *The Exile* is a step in the right direction. It is supported by a heavy and sustained barrage of theme-words beginning with *anhaga* 'recluse', 'solitary' 1a (40a): *wadan wræclastas* 5a, *eardstapa* 6a, *earmcearig eðle bidæled,*/*freomægum feor* 20–21, *waráð hine wræclast* 32a, *wineleas* 45b . . .

The quality of reticence is highly prized (10 ff., 111 ff.) as in *Hávamál*. In 111 ff. reticence is considered a part of wisdom, and wisdom is undoubtedly a leading concept throughout. The poem is from one aspect a progress in *experiencing*, that is in *knowing*. Cf. 1b *gebideð* which fits perfectly in the meaning 'lives to experience'. The recluse finally experiences God's mercy after many years of hardship on the sea. The speaker of line 6 (*eardstapa, earfeþa gemyndig*) *knows* because he has made trial of the vicissitudes of exile and uses *ic to soþe wat* 'truly I know' in this sense in 11b. We are reminded of the relation of Norse *reyna* 'make trial of, experience, prove to be' to *raun* 'trial, test, grief. . . .' Cf. 29b *wat se þe cunnað* 'he who experiences it realizes', and similarly 37–38. Lines 64–65 herald in gnomes of wise behaviour with the observation 'no one can acquire wisdom till he has lived for many years in the world'. Cf. Cotton gnomes 11b–12: the old is wisest . . . who earlier experienced much. The section 64–72 is packed with terms reflecting the acquisition of knowledge: 64a *weorðan wis,* 65b–69b *Wita sceal geþyldig* . . . *ær he geare cunne,* 71b *cunne gearwe,* 73a *ongietan sceal gleaw hæle*. The same quickening of the facts of experience by reflective wisdom is mirrored in the terms *wise geþohte* . . . *deope geondþenceð,*/*frod in ferðe* of 88b–90a which punctuate two passages on the decline of the world. The second of these (92–110) is put into the mouth of the wise man communing with himself in solitude, and the denouement represents such a one as seeking comfort from his heavenly Father. Cp. Psalm 31. 8 *Intellectum tibi dabo, et instruam te in via hac qua gradieris* 'I will give thee understanding, and will instruct thee in this way wherein thou shalt go'.

A similar emphasis on reflection and wisdom is found throughout the lay of Guthlac, the 'wise of thought' (914): cf. lines 35 ff., 163 ff., 763 ff., 800 ff., 1001 ff. *et passim;* also in *Christ* (440 ff., 664 ff., 1327 ff.); it is a staple element in *Precepts* (Ex. Book, edd. Krapp-Dobbie, 140 ff.).

It is tempting to see in the *Wanderer* with its emphasis on the transitoriness of things a thematic prelude to the *Seafarer* in the sense that the former poem clears the way for the penitential design clearly expressed in the latter. Between them in the MS. are two poems devoutly rendered: *The Gifts of Men,* which contains such a striking passage as 86–90:

> Sum her geornlice gæstes þearfe
> mode bewindeþ, ond him metudes est
> ofer eorðwelan ealne geceoseð.
> Sum bið deormod deofles gewinnes,
> bið a wið firenum in gefeoht gearo.

'One diligently wraps here in his heart his spirit's need, and chooses his Maker's grace before all the wealth of the world. One is valiant in warfare with the devil; he is ever ready to fight against iniquity'. Like the *Wanderer* this poem reverts at its close (110 ff.) to its opening theme. The other poem is *Precepts,* which is entirely cognate, particularly in its final passage, with the religious intent of the two major lyrics.

In considering the many recent studies which relate the *Wanderer* to the *De Consolatione Philosophiae* one is reminded of Lawrence's dictum (JEGP 4,477) that 'the Saxon in misfortune found consolation in philosophy long before King Alfred translated Boethius'. Cf. also S. I. Tucker, *Return to the Wanderer* (Essays in Criticism 8, 229–237 (1958) pp. 231, 233, and I. L. Gordon, *Traditional Themes in the Wanderer and the Seafarer* RES 5 (1954), p. 1. In his *Der Wanderer, Eine Interpretation von Aufbau und Gehalt* (Festschrift T. Spira, Heidelberg 1961, 57 ff.) W. Erzgräber leans heavily on the *De Consolatione.* Previously R. M. Lumiansky (*The Dramatic Structure of the Old English Wanderer,* Neophilologus 34 (1950) 104–111) had made a case for the knowledge of this work in the O E period. In his *On the Genre of the Wanderer*, Neophilologus 45 (1961), 63–72, J. E. Cross has the *genre, consolatio* in mind. This interpretation is inconsistent with Smithers' view that both *Wanderer* and *Seafarer* are allegories, Med. Aev. 26 (1957), 28 (1959); so Cross will admit only *Seafarer* to that class on the grounds that the situation in the poems is different (op. cit., p. 72).

In one respect E. G. Stanley's position (Anglia 73, 414 ff., 452 ff.) is near to ours, namely in so far as he accepts that *Seafarer, Wanderer* and *Penitent's Prayer* are connected with penitential discipline. On the other hand, he sees in the Seafarer and the Wanderer merely *figurae* employed ethopoeically to mediate the rich linguistic resources of O E available for the theme of exile (as a penitential discipline). With Professor Whitelock (*The Interpretation of the Seafarer*, in The Early Cultures of North-West Europe = H. M. Chadwick Memorial Studies, edd. Fox, Dickins, Cambridge 1950, pp. 261–272) he rejects the allegorical, and against her, the literal, factual interpretation of the *Seafarer:* 'To understand the O E poets we must give up the attempt to distinguish precisely between fact and figure . . . A literal interpretation of these poems (i.e. *Wanderer, Seafarer,* and *Penitent's Prayer*) must fail, for they are not exercises in realism' (p. 452). But in the sequel he produces no refutation of Professor Whitelock's position (cf. p. 453 ibid.). Further 'The Wanderer and the Seafarer themselves are not the theme of the poems, but the best means of expressing it. O E poetic diction provides the key to an understanding of O E didactic poetry' (p. 466).

In our opinion the interpretation by *consolatio* and by *poetic diction* are both basically preconceived, in so far as they chiefly apply either a model from outside or a general consideration of linguistic resources to the particular problems of the individual poem. In fact Mr Stanley's position seems to involve the view that the closer reading on which we must depend for progress is foredoomed, if not quite out of place; whereas the main interpretative criterion behind the *consolatio* approach is so remote, abstract and general that neither full substantiation nor refutation of it seems possible.

We would still consider valid B. F. Huppé's statement (JEGP 42 (1943), p. 526) that 'the structure of the poem must be built around the themal contrast between earthly insecurity and heavenly security: a contrast stated at the beginning, developed in the body and summarized at the end of the poem.' S. B. Greenfield (*The Wanderer: A*

Reconsideration of Theme and Structure, JEGP 50, 1951, pp. 451–465)
disputed this and other conclusions of Huppé's, e.g. his ill-judged
distinction between the *personae* of *eardstapa* and *snottor,* and the extent of their respective speeches (8–62a; 92–110). Greenfield is intent
upon refutation, and some of his objections have already been answered by S. I. Tucker (op. cit., p. 235: God the destroyer, *Wanderer*
85, does not invalidate God the sustainer; p. 236: 'If, as Greenfield
complains, the poem says nothing about the Christian belief in Grace
and Salvation as an antidote to this transitory nature of the world, why
should it? Grace and Salvation are not antidotes; for the transitory
nature of the world is a fact . . . Cf. Greenfield, pp. 460, 454.). Greenfield speaks of lines 8–110 as 'part of the Wanderer's negative *de
consolatione*' (p. 462), but his conclusions (464–465) are nonetheless
quite close to ours: For *are gebideð* 1b he would accept 'experiences
grace or mercy' which we find to be in close correspondence with
are seceð 114: at the end of the poem the promise of future action is
entertained. Greenfield sees the unity of the poem to lie between the
introduction, which shows God's superiority to Fate, the body of the
poem as illustrating Fate's way, and the conclusion exhorting man to
respond and to seek God's mercy and help. With this we are in
agreement, understanding by Fate (*Wyrd*) simply 'the way of the
world, of life' illustrated in the life of man, coming from God and
leading back to Him. But Greenfield prefers the concept of a mono-
lithic, relentless *Wyrd* as pivot between God and man; his concept of
unity is a three-term one which does not really integrate; it is expressed in terms of power: Introduction: God greater than Fate;
Body: Fate greater than man; Conclusion: Man must seek God. But
such abstractions are far from the concrete realities of the poem, from
the *anhaga, eardstapa, snottor* . . . and the circumstances which give
it its real meaning. The Creator is represented in the middle of the
poem (85 ff.) as the author of all change and decay, and this in conjunction with the opening and conclusion point to the whole work
as a reflective and homiletic prelude to such remedial and penitential
activity as the *Seafarer* offers us.[1]

Mr Stanley's view that 'Like the Seafarer, the Wanderer is introduced because his experiences as an exile call for the very phrases

[1] Cp. *Wanderer* 55b ff. on sending forth the weary spirit constantly over the frozen
wave with *Seafarer* 58 ff. where the ranging of the spirit has become purposeful and
penitential. In the former case the spirit's goal is kinsman and fellow-man, in the latter
the quest is to God. The wise man who is patient (*Wanderer* 65b) finally finds the remedy
of his trouble (112–113) and seeks grace and solace of God (114–115).

which form the OE stock poetic expressions of misery: the loneliness of the morning, the icy sea, frost, snow and hail, all the ingredients of cold care' (op. cit., p. 463) seems to us to mingle effect with cause. It is further illustrated in Greenfield's *The Formulaic Expression of the Theme of 'Exile' in Anglo-Saxon Poetry* (Speculum 30, 1955, pp. 200–206) which derives from F. P. Magoun's *Oral-Formulaic Character of Anglo-Saxon Narrative Poetry* (Speculum 28, 1953, pp. 446–467). We are naturally interested to see what an approach so different from ours can offer for the interpretation of individual style (cf. Magoun, p. 461, Greenfield, p. 205). But tangible results are as yet inconsiderable. Of the *Wanderer* Greenfield (pp. 205–206) notes merely the use of conventional formulae belonging to all his four aspects of exile as detailed on p. 201. Apropos the *Seafarer* he considers the exile imagery to underline an ambivalence of attitude of the prospective *peregrinus* with which he deals in *Studies In Philology* 51, 1954, pp. 15–20. Turning to the latter article we agree that *dream* (65, 80, 86), *blæd* (79, 88), *duguð* (80, 86) have 'two distinct references: to heavenly joys and to departed social joys'; that *dryhten* (41b, 43a) refers to an earthly lord and to God; that *gemonian/monian* of 50a/53a may represent a subtle word-play and *cnossian/cnyssan* of 8a/33b perhaps also. The double reference of the first four terms is of course inherent in the comparative treatment of life and afterlife which forms the subject matter of 64–88. Mr Greenfield's main point is that the attitude of the seafarer towards his projected voyage in 39 ff. is not motivated by the ascetic desire to escape preoccupation in mundane things as Miss Whitelock (op. cit. p. 265) would have us believe, but that it is an attitude of hesitancy and trepidation, of anguish 'intensified now by the thought of a new and more irrevocable exile from earthly felicity' (p. 18). Our own interpretation of 39–43 is briefly that *everyman* is preoccupied by the thought of what God has ultimately in store for him when he undertakes a voyage of the kind. Miss Whitelock seems to us to press the ascetic purpose too far at this point; whereas Mr Greenfield sees the subject in 39–57 as casting 'envious or wistful glances at the fortunate on earth' (p. 17). This he fails to substantiate: the reference in 42–43 is to an ultimate outcome and not to the merely 'physical outcome of a physical voyage' (p. 17). Cf. Whitelock, p. 264, I. L. Gordon, ed. p. 39. The *longung* of unsatisfied desire is entirely in accord with the ascetic purpose, and the use of the fortunate man as a foil in 55 ff. is not invalidated by its use in 12b ff., 27 ff. before the pilgrim project unfolds. *Wlonc ond wingal* (29a) though a formula can hardly fail to be mildly deprecatory; even in *Ruin* 34a in the context *how the mighty are fallen* it surely retains some of its literal value.

B. *Manner of Presentation:* The *Seafarer,* as we have seen, conforms in its first section alone (1–38) to the basic formal requirement of the lyric: that the artist present his image in *immediate* relation to himself i.e. in the *persona* 'I'.

Apart from 58–66a where we observe a dichotomy between the *persona* and his ranging spirit, and the final exhortation with *we,* the epical form prevails, i.e. the image is presented in *mediate* relation to himself and to others and the centre of the stage is occupied by *anyman* (as in 38–57) and *everyman* (67–116). Note the keywords *mon ofer eorðan* 39b, *eorla gehwam* 72a, *monna gehwylc* 90a, 111; further, 47b, 50b. This applies even to a context of emotion personally experienced, as in 39–57.

The *Wanderer* is characterized rather by a dramatic use of (related) *personae* in which they are accoutred for a particular role and fulfil it by monologue. The *eardstapa* of 6a begins in the first person but evokes his touching picture of the solitary afloat (37–57) in the third. The wise, reflective man depicts the transitoriness of life directly and realistically in 92 ff. in the manner of the modern documentary film. Both *personae* are adequately described before or after their parts are played. The second instance is akin in technique and substance to the passage which includes the Elegy of the Last Survivor in Beowulf 2247 ff. Note the clear kinetic element in these examples.

To sum up, the interchange of first and third persons in the *Seafarer* (37–58 ff.) represents an alternation from the lyric to the epical method and back again; while the monologues of the *Wanderer* show an approach from the epical to the dramatic method which falls short of transcending the art-form or medium. Of such transitions James Joyce acutely observes: 'The simplest epical form is seen emerging out of lyrical literature when the artist prolongs and broods upon himself as the centre of an epical event and this form progresses till the centre of emotional gravity is equidistant from the artist himself and from others. The narrative is no longer purely personal. The personality of the artist passes into the narration itself, flowing round and round the persons and the action like a vital sea. This progress you will see in that old English ballad *Turpin Hero* which begins in the first person and ends in the third person.' (Portrait of The Artist, Jonathan Cape, 1954, p. 244). Cf. Wellek-Warren, Theory of Literature, Ch. 17.

The reverse movement is not uncommon in folk narrative where the narrator identifying himself with the actor in his story, shifts from the third person to the first. In essence the feature belongs to a wider complex of interchange: a levelling of persons is a natural feature of some North Eastern Asiatic linguistic systems, and in South American Indian the narrator himself (I, me) and his interlocutor (you) may be used for the actor (he), or may be combined (you-me) for purposes of vivid description to represent an otherwise unexpressed third person.[1] Such facts may seem somewhat remote, but the following well-known Alfredian instance brings them into focus and encourages us to refer shifts of person to a wider and more inclusive basis than that of literary rhetoric: *Ælfred kyning hāteð grētan Wærferð biscep his wordum luflīce ond frēondlīce; ond ðē cýðan hāte ðæt mē cōm swīðe oft on gemynd . . .* 'King Alfred bids greet bishop W. with his words lovingly and with friendship; and I let it be known to thee, that it has very often come into my mind . . .' (King Alfred's West-Saxon Version of Gregory's Pastoral Care, ed. H. Sweet, London 1871 (E.E.T.S. 45), p. 2.) Bearing this in mind we may return to the specific instance in the *Wanderer*, of which B. F. Huppé writes: 'following the lead of Margaret Schlauch in her discovery of a literary model for the *Dream of the Rood* in the rhetorical device known as *prosopopoeia*, we may find in the related rhetorical device of *ethopoeia*—imaginary monologue attributed to a fictitious human character—a similar model for the *Wanderer*. The purpose of such a rhetorical device is to render more forceful the conveying of some emotion or idea: as the emotion aroused by Christ's death is made more forceful by having the cross speak, so the idea of the instability of earthly fortune is enforced by means of the direct discourse of the wanderer who has had bitter experience of fortune's reversal. (The same holds true for the later monologue of the wiseman, lines 88–111). Thus the poet, in giving monologue form to the expression of a philosophical concept, might well have been utilizing a recognized literary form'. (JEGP 42. 517). E. G. Stanley adopts this view (Anglia 73, 450 ff.) and would deny any realistic basis to the poem.

The main weakness of this approach is that it tends to reduce the content of monologues in the first person to the role of rhetorical fictions serving philosophic notions found in the poems. To this extent it militates against full and proper analysis.

By ethopoeia the *fictitious human characters* of the Wanderer are

[1] From material kindly communicated by Professor Nils Holmer.

isolated and unrelated and are seen as media for conveying concepts; whereas in our interpretation they are organically related *personae* of the *ānhaga* representing different aspects or stages of him and combining to form a whole (poem). It seems to us therefore questionable whether the term *ethopoeia* justifies itself in relation to the *Wanderer*. It was already apparent that monologue through the mouth of another is a rhetorical device calculated to add force to the representation, and to explain the *Wanderer* instances as *ethopoeia* merely is to suggest that they are due to the application of a mechanical device. In fact the Wanderer identifies himself with the figures of the *anhaga*, *eardstapa*, *earmcearig*, *eðle bidæled* . . . which are placed before us and his reflective, moralizing bent produces an easy merging of first and third persons.

C. *Interpretation of Text:* The first problem concerns the points at which the speech referred to in line 6 opens (and closes). Gollancz and Mackie place lines 1–5 within quotation marks as the opening of the wanderer's soliloquy; more commonly the first speech is deemed to begin with line 8 (Kershaw, Krapp-Dobbie, Huppé, Greenfield . . .). It may be objected to the former view that such an opening is on the whole unlikely, that lines 1–5 contain nothing to suggest soliloquy or identify the *anhaga* with the speaker and that such identification can only be made retrospectively by correction from line 6, which would seem an artistic defect; also that the soliloquy continues in line 8 in the first person and not in the third. (Such a shift from third to first person at the beginning of the poem would hardly seem covered by the convergence of these persons discussed above). Besides, the opening lines read like a descriptive presentation of a theme in the third person. It ought however be conceded to Mackie that the *swa cwæð* of line 6 can have retrospective force—as it has in line 111.

Beginning the speech with line 8, on the other hand, involves a very abrupt transition between lines 5 and 6 and leaves the opening of the poem unintegrated and somewhat inconsistent.—The exclamation *wyrd bið ful aræd* which goes perfectly with what follows in 6–7 ff. but not at all convincingly with 1–5a is to my mind the opening of the first speech. This exclamation is completely out of harmony with lines 1–2a and disturbs the train of thought set out there and elaborated in 2b–5a; we wonder what *wyrd* has to do with the Lord's mercy solicited and finally experienced by the seafaring recluse. But in connection with the misery and affliction referred to in 6—7 and recounted thereafter, the reference to a seemingly immutable fate or fixed series of events is meaningful and apt. So 8–9a (*Oft ic sceolde ana . . . mine ceare cwiþan*) is rendered by Kershaw: 'Ever *it has been my lot* to bewail my sorrows in solitude . . .' Then again the immutability of fate is resumed in 15–16 and developed in 17–18, so that 5b really seems to form the opening and offer the theme of this whole section. By taking it thus we get a more consistent text and avoid difficulties and obscurities.

Our reading of the poem as a whole (p. 161) suggests that (*are*) *gebideð* (1b) means 'lives to experience (mercy)', as Grein, Thorpe and others have held rather than 'looks for (mercy)'. That a Christian recluse often prays to God for mercy is not a point which requires making.

In the second place that reading involves an unreal opposition— symbolized by the adversative conjunction *þeah þe* (2b)—between lines 1–2a and 2b–5a; whereas in fact God's mercy and the exile-seafarer's travail are complementary aspects of the one total experience which underlies the poem and which is presented to us as its theme in 1–5a: *though he has long had to experience hardship he finally reaches the haven of God's mercy.*

The question where the first speech commences has therefore a bearing on the meaning of the poem. Where it finishes is of less importance and many editors leave this unspecified. Kershaw prefers as terminal l. 29 to 62 or 87 (op. cit., p. 2). Greenfield (JEGP 50, 464) takes 8–110 'as one speech uttered by an *eardstapa* who has with the passage of time become a *snottor*.'

8b *uhtna gehwylce*. So also the Wife laments alone in the morning twilight (7b *hæfde ic uhtceare* . . . 35–36 *þonne ic on uhtan ana gonge*), and the father every morning for his son in *Beowulf* (2450). OE *uhte* meant 'nocturns; matins' and might refer to the middle of the night or to the time before daybreak. Cf. Anglia 73, 434, f.n.1. The same ambivalence is found with the Early Ir. term *iarmérge* lit. after-rising, 'midnight, daybreak; matins, nocturns' and with Welsh *deweint* 'midnight, dead of night, time before dawn; nocturns'. With *iarmérge* 'the confusion . . . is due to the fact that Matins, though properly the midnight office, came in the late Middle Ages to be celebrated immediately before lauds, the first of the day-hours of the Church' according to Contribb. I, s.v. where a reference to Gougaud, Christianity in Celtic Lands, is given. In Early Ir. and Welsh sources waking before dawn is recommended as a form of repentance, cf. *iarmērge ūar lethrannach fri mōidmuigi mōir* 'cold harsh nocturns against great boasting' ZCP 6, 271. 4; *O kyuodi pilgeint adeueint duhunau. ac ymeitunav. ar seint. id keiff. pop cristaun. kyrreiueint.* 'By rising to matins and nocturns, awaking and interceding with the saints shall every Christian obtain forgiveness' BBC 85. 3–6; also BBC 70. 4–7: *Daearaul pechodaul imyoel a duv. a deweint. duhuned. a gothuy crist nachisced. Nachisced mab. din. yr dioteiveint mab duv. a duhuned pilgeint. ew keiff new a chirreiveint.* 'let sinful mortal entreat God and wake at dead of night; let him who offends Christ sleep not. For the sake of the passion of the Son of God let the son of man not sleep but wake up at dawn; he will obtain heaven and forgiveness.' Similarly BBC 71. 8–11 prays the protection of God and the saints for his diligence at matins. The word for matins is *pylgeint* from Lat. *pulicantio* and it also means 'dawn'. The nocturnal singing of psalms as a penitential exercise is prescribed in Penitentials connected with St. David (*Excerpta,* canons 8, 9) and St. Gildas (*Praefatio,* can. 22); also in the *Regula Coenobialis* of Columban.

This liturgical background undoubtedly plays a part in the OE instances and suggests a close connection with monastic life. Note that in the *Penitent's Prayer* 96a, just before the abortive pilgrimage is mentioned, the poet's spirit is *morgenseoc* 'distressed at morning time'.

23a MS. *heolstre* is often emended to *heolstor,* but *heolstre* yields perfectly good sense when *ic* is construed with *biwrah;* cf. B. T. 98a 'I covered my bounteous patron in a cave of the earth' and *Wanderer* 83b–84: one was buried in a hole in the earth by a knight of sad countenance.

29a MS. *weman* 'allure, entice . . .' (often emended to *wenian* 'entertain') seems assured. Cf. Krapp-Dobbie, p. 289.

32 ff. *waraδ hine wræclast . . .* 'thoughts of his exile and of his chilled body occupy him, not twisted gold or aught of earth's bliss' as in *Seafarer* 44 ff. Similarly *Seafarer* 54 ff, prior to the forward movement of the mind in eager anticipation (58 ff.). This parallel seems to strengthen our case for the *Wanderer* as introductory and exploratory prelude to the other poem. Note the latent happy retainer/wandering exile antithesis in *Wanderer* also. The passing of all former joy (*Wanderer* 36b *wyn eal gedreas*) sums up the detail of *Seafarer* 44–46.

45–55. This passage is discussed above p. 144 f. in connection with the bird-soul symbol.

55b–57. It appears from this passage and from *Seafarer* 58 ff. that the concept of sending the spirit abroad offered no difficulty. Cf. p. 136, f.n.2 *supra* for instances from Plummer where saints cause the souls of men to go forth from their bodies in sleep and visit distant scenes; especially the case of Cormac, consumed by longing to visit his home and friends (Vita S. Comgalli, § 42); also that of the monk in Vita S. Berachi, § 25. For a discussion of the heathen background and for Icelandic and Latin exx cf. Smithers, Med. Aev. 28, 14 ff.; cf. also Salmon MLR 55, 1 ff. In the *Seafarer* passage there is a sense of purpose and an eager anticipation in sharp contrast to the frustration evident here in *Wanderer*. Cf. under 32 ff. *supra*.

58b. N. Kershaw refers to the extensive or exhaustive use of the prefix *geond-* throughout the poem (ed., p. 164) and to the non-literal employment of *geond þas woruld* here. In *Deor* 31b this collocation still retains a rather literal force: 'throughout this world'. The word *geond* however is not essential to the expression of the extensive notion which is achieved in Celtic, English and Anglo-Irish on the basis of the concept 'world' alone: all the Celtic languages have an idiom corresponding to Ir. *ar bith* lit. on the world 'at all'; Welsh *yn y byd*, Breton *ebed*, Sc. G. *'s am bith*, Anglo-Irish and English *in the world* 'at all'.

At a certain point the extensive notion becomes an intensive one and the burden of expression is then carried by *world* alone, cf. *Husband's Message* 30 *worulde willa* 'a wish in the world' where the meaning 'at all' is already reached, similarly in Beowulf 1079 f. *þær heo ær mæste heold/worolde wynne* 'where she formerly possessed the greatest pleasure of the world'. *Piers Plowman* has *al the wo of the worlde* (Passus vii, C. Text, l. 415 (Skeat's ed.), Gawain and the Green Knight *alle þe wele of þe worlde* (50), *al þe wonder of þe worlde* (238); and with *molde* 'earth': *on þe most on þe molde* (137). *The Cornish Death of Pilate* (Everyman and Medieval Miracle Plays, ed. A. C. Cawley, London 1958, p. 253) has *whatever pain is in the world* where the extensive and intensive commingle, and *the cruellest death in the world* (ibid.) where the intensive value is paramount.

In Anglo-Irish *I'm not dead at all in the world* (J. M. Synge, Plays, Poems and Prose, Everyman No. 968, p. 262), we observe the coupling of two intensives, the one inspired by English, the other at least partly by Irish idiom.

65a *wintra dæl*. This partitive idiom like *wælsleahta worn* of 91a bears witness to the development of the substantival system in OE. Cf. ZCP 28, 19 ff., and Anglia 27, 228. Nouns such as *dæl* 'share', *worn* 'crowd' are attracted into the important partitive construction and adopt the new grammatical meaning 'much, many' and the function of a pronoun. The idiom is common in OE: a) of *number:* cf. *Deor* 34, *Beowulf* 1150 *weana dæl* 'many woes', B. 1752 *weorðmynda dæl* 'the many honours', B. 2028 *wælfæhða dæl* 'many deadly feuds', 2843 *dryhtmaðma dæl* 'the many splendid treasures', *Deor* 30 *earfoða dæl* 'his many trials'; b) of *quantity:* B. 1740 *oferhygða dæl* 'great arrogance', B. 2068 *dryhtsibbe dæl* 'much friendship'.

111 ff. Here we are brought into contact with the exemplar (*snottor on mode*) who has learnt through experience how to live. He is represented, typically, as being alone (111b). The maxims which follow (112–115) represent the quintessence of good living: one should keep (his) faith; one should not communicate his distress (*torn*) unless one has learnt to apply the remedy, make reparation (*bot:* German *Busse*) and seek mercy and comfort where alone it can be found. Here the theme of reticence is resumed from lines 11 ff. and coupled with solitariness and a religious outlook, so that we are tempted to relate lines 11 ff., too, directly with the religious opening of the poem.

Both of the meanings we suggest here for *bote* (113): 'remedy' and 'reparation', occur in the *Penitent's Prayer,* 20, 110.

The final lines express the Christian faith in a central security in spite of harsh experience and the decline and decay of the world.

D. *The Homiletic Pattern.* Blickling Homily No. X (ed. Morris, E. E. T. S. 1880, p. 106 ff.) on the theme *middangeardes ende neah is* and on the urgency of repentance, offers in its second part a sequence of thoughts and a mode of expression which relate it immediately to the second parts of *Wanderer* and *Seafarer* and in a general way to the whole of these poems. The main lines of this treatment will be apparent from the following abridged version (p. 111) . . . no man hath so much wealth or such magnificent treasures here in the world but that he shall soon meet his end . . . (*Seafarer* 66b–71; *Wanderer* 60–63) . . . Where shall be then his riches and his feasts? Where his pride and his arrogance? Where shall be his vain garments? Where the ornaments and the expensive attire with which he previously decked his body? Where then his will and the lusts that he followed here in the world? (*S.* 80b ff., *W.* 92–104). (Exemplum:) A certain rich and influential man died; and one of his loving kinsmen for grief and longing departed for many years to another land (*W.* 19–29a); his longing never diminished (*W.* 29–36); so he returned to his native land (cp. *W.*

37–44) and to the tomb of his kinsman, whose bones spoke to him thus: my garment of purple and gold is turned to dust and my limbs once fair to dry bones; my riches are vanished, my dwellings decayed (*S.* 80b–102, *W.* 73–109). So turn aside from the world to your own spiritual needs. May we, similarly, learn not to overvalue this decrepit, unstable and transitory world. (Excursus:) In the beginning the world was fair, delightful and serene; it drew men's hearts from God, but Christ's holy people valued it not (cp. *S.* 64b–66a). Now the world is filled with lamentation and evil (*W.* 106–110; *S.* 86 ff.) and we love it though bitter and fleeting. Let us remember that it is illusory and transitory and press on to what is good. Let us diligently obey our Lord and thank Him for everything (*S.* 122b–124; *W.* 114b–115).

We learn from the following Homily (No. XI) that the world was shortly to come to an end[1] as its sixth and final age was now well advanced (ibid. 117, 119). That this concept derives from the life of man and its stages appears from *Seafarer* 86 ff. where the juxtaposition is made; so that lyric and homily serve to illuminate each other, cf. *Seafarer* 89–90: 'All that is noble on earth grows old and fades away— just as every man now does throughout the world.' The concept of the six ages helps to explain why the world is represented in the lyrics as deteriorating. Cf. also Smithers, Medium Aevum 26, 144 (1957).

The *uton we* . . . of Seafarer 117a is of course the form of final admonitions in the homilies (cf. Blickl. Hom. pp. 97, 115, 131 . . .). The negative sequence expressing *degree* in *Seaf.* 39–43 (For there is no man on earth so high-spirited or so generous . . . or so active . . . or so brave . . . that is not in his voyage on the sea always fearful of what the Lord has in store for him) with *to þæs* is paralleled in a sustained sequence with comparable ideas in Blickling Hom. X, p. 111: *Geseo we nu . . . þæt nænig man on worlde toðæs mycelne welan nafað, ne toðon modelico gestreon her on worlde þæt se on medmycclum fyrste to ende ne cume . . . & se man næfre toðon leof ne bið his nehmagum & his world- freondum, ne heora nán hine to þæs swiþe ne lufað þæt he sona syþþan ne sý onscungend, seoþþan se lichoma & se gast gedælde beoþ,* . . . 'Let us then consider . . . that no man in the world has so much wealth or so much splendid riches but that he shall in a brief interval come to an end . . . and be the man ever so dear to his kinsmen and friends and let any of them love him ever so much, nevertheless he shall soon afterwards shun him when body and soul shall be separated'.

[1] This belief was current in the tenth century; cf. the O. Ir. *Calendar of Oengus* (Fél.²) p. 17.

E. *Seafarer*, *Wanderer* and *Guthlac* and the relation of literature to life: The *Life of Guthlac* by Felix (ed. B. Colgrave, Cambridge 1956), composed probably between 730 and 740 (ibid., p. 19) might readily serve as quarry for our two lyrics. Cf. the following excerpted account from the English translation: Ch. 18 (p. 81) 'And so when this same man of blessed memory, Guthlac, was being storm-tossed amid the uncertain events of passing years, amid the gloomy clouds of life's darkness, and amid the whirling waves of the world, he abandoned his weary limbs one night to their accustomed rest; his wandering thoughts were as usual anxiously contemplating mortal affairs in earnest meditation, when suddenly, marvellous to tell, a spiritual flame, as though it had pierced his breast, began to burn in this man's heart. For when, with wakeful mind, he contemplated the wretched deaths and the shameful ends of the ancient kings of his race in the course of the past ages, and also the fleeting riches of this world and the contemptible glory of this temporal life, then in imagination the form of his own death revealed itself to him; and, trembling with anxiety at the inevitable finish of this brief life, he perceived that its course daily moved to that end . . . As he thought over these and similar things, suddenly by the prompting of the divine majesty, he vowed that, if he lived until the next day, he himself would become a servant of Christ (famulum Christi) . . . Ch. XIX (p. 83) . . . when he had completed the twenty-fourth year of his age, he renounced the pomps of this world, and kept his unwavering faith and trust fixed in Christ. Ch. XX (p. 85) Then he began his journey, and, leaving everything he possessed, he came to the monastery of Repton . . . and, assuming the dress of a cleric, he strove to make expiation for his past sins . . . Ch. XXI (p. 85) . . . He was endowed with wisdom and prudence . . . strong with inward strength, steadfast in his judgement of what was right, abundant in forbearance, firm in patience . . . Ch. XXIV (p. 87) And so when four and twenty months had run their course during which he lived a life of the greatest self-restraint in the habit of a cleric, he planned to seek the desert with the greatest diligence and the utmost earnestness of mind . . . he started out on the path to eternal bliss and proceeded to look for a solitary place . . .' Chapters 29–34 tell of his struggles with devils (cf. *Seafarer* 75 ff.); the other thematic parallels of this account with our two lyrics are obvious.

CHAPTER IX

THE *PENITENT'S PRAYER*

This poem, found in the *Exeter Book* 117b–119b, has also been called *Gebet* (Wülker), *A Prayer* (Chambers), *Gebet des Vertriebenen* (Brandl), *Klage Eines Vertriebenen* (Sieper, Schücking), *The Exile's Prayer* (Mackie) and *Resignation* (Dobbie, ed. Ex. Book, cf. p. lx). The various titles reflect a certain indecision about the poem's meaning, purpose and *genre* although they do form one semantic group. The apt title which we owe to E. G. Stanley (op. cit., Anglia 73, 414) seems to us to be justified by the whole poem and to offer the key to a solution of it. Of this poem Stanley writes: 'Three things relevant to the interpretation of *The Wanderer* and *The Seafarer* are to be found in *The Penitent's Prayer*, and all three have a direct bearing on O E poetic diction and rhetorical devices. First, there is mention of a journey or journeys, perhaps an example of O E symbolic poetic diction; secondly, it shows confusion of the first and third person singular, perhaps the result of the rhetorical device of ethopoeia; and thirdly it is penitential, and therefore perhaps governed by the traditions of penitential prayer'. . . (op. cit., 414). And again: '*The Penitent's Prayer* is closely related to *The Seafarer* both in manner of expression and in subject-matter. The greater part of the poem is in the form of a penitential prayer, beginning with an informal confession. Then it introduces the theme of exile, and finally there is a message of resignation. Unlike *The Seafarer*, the manner of exposition in *The Penitent's Prayer* is confused.' (Ibid., 456–7). 'The value of *The Penitent's Prayer* for the interpretation of *The Seafarer* lies in the combination of confession and exile' (ibid., 461).

With the factual part of these statements most will readily agree. As regards the interpretative part it will be remembered that Mr Stanley considered it impossible to separate fact from figure (allegory) in O E poetry (op. cit., 454, 461), a view which inevitably leads to stressing the formal (formulaic, conventional) at the expense of the (f)actual, and perhaps ultimately to a mechanical theory of literary origins. But Mr Stanley's remark on the tradition of penitential prayer[1] in our poem

---

[1] Cf. also Sieper (op. cit. p. 256), Dobbie (ed. Ex. Book, p. lx).

can be fully substantiated, and we are in agreement with many of his observations of detail (ibid., 456–461).

In the first nine lines of the poem the penitent commits himself in body and soul, word and deed utterly to God. In lines 10–15a he prays God to indicate to him where he might best observe His will. The meaning of this becomes clear from lines 29–33 where another way of life (*lif æfter oþrum*, 31b) is envisaged which would lead to eternal salvation (similarly Stanley, op. cit. p. 457); also from 72–74 and 97, where a specific reference is made to what is obviously a journey of pilgrimage (*ferðweg*, 72a) cf. *gæst gearwian* 'prepare my soul' 74a, and Stanley, op. cit. p. 458. The point of view is that of *Guthlac* 26–29

> Hwider sceal þæs monnes mod astigan
> ær oþþe æfter þonne he his ænne her
> gæst bigonge þæt se gode mote
> womma clæne in geweald cuman.

'Whither must a man's mood aspire sooner or later, if he would cherish his one soul here that it may come to God's dominion free of blemish?'.[1] In lines 15–36a the penitent's purpose of atonement for sin is stressed. The repetitive section 36b–67b is chiefly a prayer for spiritual comfort and help. Lines 67b–75 offer thanks for favours received and for help in bracing himself for his pilgrimage. In lines 75–96 his plight as a friendless exile (rendered from 90 to 96 in the third person!) is attributed to his sins which are previously referred to in lines 20, 35, 48–49, 51 and 65. In 96b he reverts to his present situation (in the first person!) and to the now abortive journey which he had not the means nor the backing to undertake. In the concluding section (105–118) he contrasts the forest which achieves its destiny with his own thwarted situation, an exile without means or friends, a recipient of carping charity. Only in the next world can he hope for a remedy, as in this he has always found hardship and sorrow to wait upon comfort and love. So he resigns himself to enduring what he cannot alter (117–118).

TEXT. 15a *ræd arære:* Mackie (The Exeter Book II, E.E.T.S. 194 (1934), p. 165) translates 'build up benefit for myself'; but it may rather mean 'set up, determine upon a (proper) course of action', which would link up with the pilgrimage project. The *þe geþeo* of line 13a means 'develop towards Thee; increase in virtue'. Mackie renders 'prosper in Thy sight'.

---

[1] Otherwise Krapp-Dobbie, Ex. Book, p. 262.

21b *cume to gif ic mot:* (This is preceded by *ic þa bote gemon/cyninga wuldor* (20b–21a) 'I am mindful of atonement, glorious King'). Mackie translates '. . . and shall come to Thee, if I may'. But the meaning rather is 'and shall achieve it, i.e. reparation (*þa bote,* 20b) if I may (can)'. Cf. Toller, *Cuman* III (1).

28a *grimra gylta.* The emphasis on sins committed belongs to the penitential genre as such. Cf. also the early sinful epoch in the lives of saints such as Guthlac (*Guthlac,* 108–110) who later became anchorites.

39b–40 *onstép minne hige/gæsta god cyning in gearone ræd* 'Raise up my soul, good King of spirits to the benefit prepared' (Mackie). But *ræd* may have the meaning of 'plan' here, as in 15a: 'Raise up (confirm; initiate) my soul . . . in the plan prepared'.

41a *fundige:* The etymological meaning 'endeavour to find, direct one's course to' is to be preferred to Mackie's '(now that) I hasten (to thee, Father of mankind)'.

46b–47 *þonne is gromra to fela/æfestum eaden* 'When too many foes are intent upon malice, (I have then aid from the Lord . . .) (Mackie). This reading depends on taking *æfest* 'malice' rather that *æfest* 'pious' (Klaeber, Archiv 167, 37) and may be right.

82b ff. 'I am not a sage judge wise before the assembly; therefore I speak these words with a sad heart . . .' There seems to be a relation between the outspokenness of the destitute exile and the reticence prescribed by the wise man in the *Wanderer.* The penitent, in fact, did not quite reach his goal (cf. 103–106) and according to the standard of the other poem was not quite justified in 'giving vent to the grief in his heart'. Note that the passage is framed by references to God's anger with the penitent (78–79, 91). Mackie's interpretation of *fus on ferþe* 'with a sad heart' can hardly be right. Translate rather 'readily' and compare with *afysed* in 88b. The text continues (84b–85) *swa me on frymðe gelomp/yrmþu ofer eorþan* 'since long ago poverty befell me on earth' (Mackie). *On frymðe* here is clarified by 92 *on his geoguþe* 'in his youth'.

85b. ff. *þæt ic á þolade/geara gehwylce gode ealles þonc/modearfoþa ma þonne on oþrum.* The obvious rendering is 'so that every year (God be thanked for everything!) I suffered hardships of mind more than in previous years'. This reading depends on taking *mod* with *earfoþa* (Klaeber, Archiv 167, 37, Dobbie ed., page 355) rather than with *þonc* (Mackie, who renders otherwise). 88b *afysed eom* 'have been driven' Mackie, but 'impelled from within' (rather than from outside) seems preferable. Cf. N. F. Blake, ed. *The Phoenix*, Manchester 1964, p. 86, sub 654b.

95a *sarcwide secga* 'men's bitter reproach' can accompany their cold charity. But reproach and calumny (cf. *tæle* 106b) are stock trials in the penitential psalms; cf. p. 180 and Stanley, op. cit. p. 460.

96a *mod morgenseoc.* Cf. p. 171 and Penitential Psalm 142. 8: *Auditam fac mihi mane misericordiam tuam, quia in te speravi* 'Make me to hear Thy mercy in the morning: for in Thee have I hoped'.

96b *bi me:* translate: 'about myself' forming a natural return from the figure of the exile to his own case. In this Stanley (op. cit., 458) sees a possible anacoluthic use of ethopoeia, to avoid which he prefers the meaning 'for my own sake'.

98a *longunge fus* 'sad with longing' (Mackie). Rather 'impelled by longing' (Similarly Stanley, op. cit., 459). Cf. the Celtic analogues of this expression, p. 135.

105 ff. *Wudu mot him weaxan wyrde bidan | tanum lædan* ... 'The forest may grow, await its destiny, shoot forth its twigs ... I, because of calumny, cannot love in my heart anyone of mankind, any man in the land.' (Mackie). *Wyrde bidan* is rather to be construed 'achieves its destiny' as illustrated by *tanum lædan*. A sharp contrast with the frustration of the poet is clearly intended. The remainder of the poem is the working out of similar antitheses; cf. for example 115b–116 where *alifde* means rather 'experienced' than 'proved' (Mackie).

The Penitential Tradition: it is clear that in the *Penitent's Prayer* the project of pilgrimage is conceived realistically even though the intent of the subject to undertake it may be open to question. The treatment of the project seems to show that the actual journey of pilgrimage has become an important symbol of the penitent as such. Compare *Christ* 850 ff. where life is rendered in terms of a voyage; *Guthlac* 800 ff. where those with wise thoughts overcome the fiend and lead a life of holy meditation and mortification; *Juliana* 696 ff. which represent the soul journeying forth from the body; and *Fates of the Apostles* where the speaking subject 'weary of wandering, sad in spirit' (1–2 *siðgeomor, on seocum sefan*) contemplates his exemplars who were 'bold in journeying (*siðfrome* 77a; cf. also 33, 34–35) and contemplates his own journey to the next world (91 ff., 109 ff.) and his need of help (91 ff.). The actual and the figurative journeys complement each other: their ultimate goal is the same. In *Penitent's Prayer* pilgrimage is not a practical possibility, but its mere envisaging is meritorious, cf. page 31 (713) *supra*.

To the penitent is accorded 'pilgrimage'. But he is also invested in a manner reminiscent of the penitential psalms with sins and iniquities (20, 26, 28, 51, 65), God's wrath, blame, and punishment (76, 78, 80), fear for his soul (66), misery and exile (88 ff., 111 ff.); with reproachful neighbours (95) and with carping enemies (106). Psalm 50. 3–5 runs: 'Have mercy upon me, O God ... Wash me yet more from my iniquity: and cleanse me from my sin. For I know my iniquity: and my sin is always before me.' Psalm 37. 2–5: 'O Lord rebuke me not in Thy indignation: nor chastise me in Thy wrath. For Thine arrows stick fast in me: and Thou hast laid Thy hand heavily upon me . . . there is no peace in my bones because of my sins. For my iniquities are gone over my head: and like a heavy burden press sorely upon me.' Psalm 37. 10: 'Lord, all my desire is before Thee: and my groaning is not hidden from Thee' (cp. *Penitent's Prayer* 96 ff.). Psalm 37. 12–13: 'My friends and my neighbours drew near, and stood up against me. And they that were once nigh me stood afar off ... And they that sought to do me evil talked vanities: and imagined deceits all day long' (cp. our poem, 106 ff. *tæle* 'calumny' and 95a *sarcwide secga* 'men's bitter reproach'); further Psalm 37. 17: . . . 'and when my feet slip, they (i.e. my enemies) have spoken great things against me.' Similarly Psalm 101. 9: 'My enemies reproached me all the day long: and they that praised me have sworn together against me' (cf. *Penitent's Prayer* 114 ff.: 'When I gained affection from strangers and a pleasant home, sorrow was ever the requital of love . . .'). For the environment of enemies and tribulation cf. also Psalm 6. 8, 11; Psalm 31. 7; and Psalm 142. 3, 11, 12.

The central strand of the *Penitent's Prayer* is expressed as follows in 10–13: *getacna me tungla hyrde | þær selast sy sawle minre | to gemearcenne meotudes willan* 'Signify to me, Shepherd of the stars, where it may be best for my soul to observe God's will'. Cf. Psalm 142. 8 ... 'Make me to know the way wherein I should walk: for to Thee have I lifted up my soul.'

The foregoing seems to indicate that the penitent of our poem is a composite figure deriving from the central penitential tradition. The human references, so puzzling biographically, fit into this tradition, and the poem as a whole has the structure of a prayer. It is based then on mood (prayer) and emotion (intensity), and it uses repetition as an emotive means. Logical (as against lyrical) coherence belongs to a different climate and category of poetic production.

CHAPTER X

THE PENITENTIAL MOTIF
AND THE BACKGROUND OF THE
EXILIC AND SEAFARING IMAGES

With the *Seafarer*, the *Penitent's Prayer* belongs to the *genre* of penitential poetry. Lines 96b–104 of this poem tell that the repentant one is thinking of a journey on the ocean but has not the means to buy a boat for this purpose nor a friend to provide one:

> ic bi me tylgust
> secge þis sarspel ond ymb siþ spræce,
> longunge fus, ond on lagu þence,
> nat min . . . .
> hwy ic gebycge bat on sæwe,
> fleot on faroðe; nah ic fela goldes
> ne huru þæs freondes, þe me gefylste
> to þam siðfate, nu ic me sylf ne mæg
> fore minum wonæhtum willan adreogan . . .

'I relate this tale of woe mainly about myself, and, impelled by longing, I speak about a journey and think of the ocean. My . . . does not know with what I may buy a boat on the sea, a ship on the wave; I have little gold and indeed no friend who may help me upon my voyage. I myself now cannot, on account of my poverty, carry out my desire.' What is behind the desire of the repentant man to travel on the ocean? A hint is given in the (Early) OE Genesis 927 ff. God speaks to Adam: *þu scealt oðerne eðel secean/wynleasran wic, and on wræc hweorfan/nacod niedwædla, neorxnawanges/dugeðum bedæled.* 'You shall seek another land, a joyless abode and live in exile, a destitute wretch, deprived of the happiness of heaven.' A tenth century OE Penitential prescribes as a means to obtain forgiveness for sins that one should leave home and family for God's sake and go on lifelong pilgrimage: *þæt gehwa his æhta 7 his bearn 7 his eard forlæte for godes lufan, 7 on ælþeodignysse fare, 7 þær hys lif geendige* (B. Thorpe, Ancient Laws and Institutes of England II 224; R. Spindler, Das altenglische

Bussbuch, p. 175). D. Whitelock adds (op. cit., p. 263) that there is nothing to correspond to this passage in the Latin sources of this penitential. On the other hand lifelong *peregrinatio* is characteristically Celtic and Irish. The fuller motivation of pilgrimage is offered in a Middle Ir. homily on Repentance in the *Leabhar Breac* (Atkinson, p. 221): Atat din dí ernail fors-in fhúisitin .i. fuisitiu doníther do Dia, 7 fúisitiu doniter do dainib. Uair is s-ed dlegar do neoch cloechlod inaid do denum in tan do-s-gní aithrige ńdíchra i n-a phecdaib, amal do-rigne Adam ar sen-athair, 7 Petur apstal ar forcetlaid. Ar is a parrdus do-s-gni Adam immarbus, 7 ro-dichuirthea as in lucc i n-a r-pecdaig dochumm inaid aile .i. hi talmain, do denam aithrige. Petur apstal din, i n-Ierusalem do-s-gní imarbus in tan ro-díult Ísu Crist fo thri, aidche a chesta, 7 fo hill-tuathaib in domain do-rígne aithrige is-in peccad-sin. Is for a slicht-side is dénta do neoch aithrige indíu .i. dia pecdaige nech il-locc airithe, is s-ed is techta dó imgabail in luic-sin, 7 dul il-locc aile do aithrige índ, co fhuisitiu a chinad for tús .i. in fáth im a nderna peccad, 7 in t-inad 7 in aimser i nderna, 7 aithrige ndíchra do dénam iar-sin. 'There are also two kinds of confession: that which is made to God, and that which is made to men. Further it is required of everyone to make a change in place when he does earnest penance for his sins, as did our forefather Adam, and our teacher the Apostle Peter. For it was in Paradise that Adam committed his transgression; and he was cast out of the place in which he had sinned into another place, the earth, to do penance. As to the Apostle Peter, it was in Jerusalem that he sinned, viz., when he denied Christ thrice on the night of the passion; so it was in the many nations of the world that he did penance for that sin. Everyone today who does penance should follow in their footsteps; and if he commits sin in one particular place he should avoid that place, and go elsewhere to repent therein, with confession of his fault first, confessing the cause and the place and the time of his sinning, and should earnestly repent thereafter'. Compare with this the account of *peregrinatio* from the Book of Lismore pp. 29 ff. *supra*.

It is clear from the discussion on pp. 35 ff. above that the basic attitude of the Irish and the English towards *peregrinatio* was at first one and the same: as Watkins puts it '. . . the going forth into an unknown land seemed to them desirable in the first instance as being a further grade of mortification' (op. cit., Vol. II, p. 613). Hiberno-English spiritual commerce also extended to the patterning of penitential codes destined to affect the whole of Western Christendom. When St. Columbanus and others introduced the Celtic type of monastery into the Frankish lands, to Annegrai, Fontaine, Luxeuil, Bobbio and elsewhere, the Celtic system of *private* penitence was also introduced in these areas. Celtic monasteries multiplied in the Frankish lands in the seventh century and the penitential system of Columbanus would be used in all of them (Cf. Watkins, op. cit., Vol. II, pp. 621 ff.).

Theodore of Tarsus who became Archbishop of Canterbury in 668, based his O E Penitential on the Celtic system, represented notably by the sixth century penitentials associated with the Welshman David, and by those of the Irish Finnian and Columbanus. In the two latter and in the Welsh *Lucus Victoriae* banishment from home and country is prescribed for certain sins. Theodore's Penitential was later introduced in the Frankish regions; it was spread by English missionaries such as Boniface, Willibald and Willibrord in the Germanic countries and by Alcuin and his band at the Court of Charlemagne. Gradually this Hiberno-English system laid hold on the rest of Western Christendom (Watkins, II, pp. 762–3).

An important linguistic criterion for the Irish leaven in the penitential practice of Western Christendom is the late Latin word *arreum* attested in the Canones Hibernenses (cf. L. Bieler, ed. The Irish Penitentials, Dublin 1963, p. 8; D. A. Binchy ibid., 49 ff., and *Ériu* 19, 47 ff.). It may be defined as 'the substitution of a shorter, and usually more intensive, discipline for the normal penance prescribed by canonical or monastic rules' (*Ériu* 19, 52), and it is now accepted as a latinization of an Ir. word *arre*, verbal noun of *ar·ren* 'pays on behalf of another; pays over in place of something else' (cf. Vendryes, Lexique Étymologique de L'Irlandais Ancien, A, s. v.; Binchy, op. cit., 47 ff.) The word *arreum* is found only in section II of the *Canones Hibernenses*, while *arre* in our meaning occurs only in Early Ir. penitential sources connected with Tallaght and Culdee reform.

It is now established that the *libellus Scottorum* mentioned in the preface of the *Penitential of Theodore* and used as a basis for that work contained part if not all of the *Canones Hibernenses* (cf. Kenney, Sources, I, 229; J. T. McNeill, R C 39, 293 ff.) McNeill writes: 'Theodore's recognition of composition (by money settlement) and commutation in penance is based upon Irish penitential practice, and taken directly from Irish written sources, not, be it observed, from Anglo-Saxon national custom' (R C 39, 295). For Theodore public penance must have been the normal type and the Hiberno-British system new and strange. 'Either because he was persuaded of the superiority of the Celtic usage, or because the latter had already, through the Scottic missionaries, obtained recognition in the English Church, he was brought to a conscious departure from the older penance to that of the Celts. This appears not only in his approval of commutations and compositions . . . It appears also in his adoption of private and formal rejection of public penance. 'Public reconciliation' says Theodore 'is not authorized in this province, since there is no public penance (Poenit. Theod. lib. I, xiii, 4)' (McNeill, RC 40, 81–82). So that Theodore, arch-enemy of the Irish ecclesiastical system, accepted the Irish penitential system *in toto* (Kenney, Sources I, p. 229; Watkins, Vol. II, pp. 649–653).

This tutelary relationship of the English to the Irish Church in penitential matters seems to be confirmed by a series of religious terms adopted into OE. But before considering these (Chapter XI) it is convenient to deal with the background of the related *exilic* and *seafaring* images.

A feature of the Celtic Penitentials referred to above is the sentence of exile for certain offences including homicide.[1] In the Lives of the saints also we can see how exile merges with penance. Columba, excommunicated at the Synod of Teltown, probably in 562, is represented by his biographer Adomnan as *pro Christo peregrinari volens* (4b). He was held in later times to have instigated the battle of Culdrebene and his pilgrimage to Britain was interpreted as a penance

---

[1] Sinodus Aquilonalis Britaniae 1, 3–4; Sinodus Luci Victoriae 6 (perpetual pilgrimage); Penitential of Finnian 23; Pen. Col. B 1–2, 13; Tres Canones Hibernici 1–3; The Old-Irish Pen. I 9; V 2, 11 (a life of exile in destitution). In Pen. Col. B 1 it is said of a cleric who has committed homicide 'But if he does not make satisfaction to his relatives, let him never be restored to his native land, but like Cain let him be a wanderer and fugitive upon the earth.' (Bieler-Binchy, op. cit.).

Similar provisions are found in OE Laws and Penitentials (cf. Liebermann, op. cit., II sub *Verbannung, Pilgerfahrt, Pabst* . . .) A priest guilty of homicide or other serious crime is deprived of religious and social status and of home *7 wræcnige swa wide swa papa him scrife 7 dædbete georne* 'and let him travel as a pilgrim (in exile and misery) as far as the Pope prescribes for him and let him atone zealously' (VIII Atr 26). He who kills a minister of the altar becomes 'an outlaw with God and men' unless he make redress to the kin of the slain man and go upon his pilgrimage within thirty days (II Cn 39). Ps-Theod. Poenit. 3, 11 prescribes seven years exile . . . for this crime. If the land is to be thoroughly cleansed, all those who persist in evil and do not make atonement to God are to be sought out and forced to change their ways, otherwise banished (VIII Atr 40). He who kills a cleric or a kinsman, commits adultery or violates a nun has to seek absolution from the Pope (i.e. go on pilgrimage to Rome) (Bussbuch 73, 6, 6a). The priest who discloses secrets of the confessional is degraded and condemned to perpetual exile (Hn 5, 17). In the case of an unbaptized child who dies, the relative responsible loses his residence right and has to go abroad in exile (Homil. n. Wulfstan 120. 300). Related to exile is the transplanting of local magnates who represent a threat to the régime (sub *Verbannung* 7 ff., *Verpflanzung*).

(of perpetual exile) undertaken by him or imposed by his confessor Laisran (Cf. A. O. and M. O. Anderson, Adomnan's Life of Columba, London 1961, pp. 71 ff.). Columba himself administers the penance of exile to one who has perpetrated fratricide and incest: 'If you do penance among the Britons with wailing and weeping for twelve years, and do not return to Ireland until your death, perhaps God will condone your sin' (I 22); also to the Irishman Libran who had made the laborious journey from the West of Ireland to expiate his sins in pilgrimage; in this case he prescribes a penance of seven years in Campus Lunge in Tiree, place of a monastery to which penitents were sent (II 39). So too Brendan, whose negligence had caused the death of a youth by drowning, is commanded by St. Ita to visit the land of pilgrims, teach others and bring souls to Christ ('Terram peregrinam debes uisitare, ut alios doceas, et animas Christo lucrifacias', Vita Prima Sancti Brendani, in Plummer, Vitae SS. Hib., I 141). Cp. *elþeodigra eard, Seafarer* 38. For other exx. of pilgrimage enjoined as a penance cf. Vita Sancti Coemgeni § 38, Declani § 6, Mochoemog § 18 sub fin. Added testimony is found in the Laws. The *anmchara's* or confessor's rights are implied in the wording 'if it be pilgrimage that his *anmchara* has enjoined upon him', Laws III, p. 72. Laws I 204. 22 refer to the remains of a *deoruidh dé ro dilsiud don muir ocus do gaith* 'a hermit (pilgrim) abandoned to the sea and the wind': the right to them belonged to the people of the land where he happened to be cast ashore. In Laws III 30 pilgrimage and penance are equated: The unfree are freed by receiving church grades and by performing penitential service to God: *tre fognam naithirge .i. tre fognam do denam do dia ac aithrighi, .i. in nailithre* 'by penitential service, i.e. by doing service to God in penitence, i.e. in pilgrimage'.

This feature of ecclesiastical discipline is mirrored in old Celtic custom.[1] It was a common practice in Gaul. Nicholas of Damascus (b. 64 B C) tells us that exile, φυγή, was the resource of the Celt who murdered a compatriot (H. d'Arbois de Jubainville, Cours de Littérature Celtique 7, 83). On two occasions these fugitives supplied strong contingents to armies levied against the Romans (Caesar, De Bello Gallico V 55, VIII 30). In Welsh law the murderer of a kinsman is outlawed, cf. Gwentian Code II xxxix 54[2]: 'Three persons hated by a kindred: a thief; and a deceiver; since they cannot be depended

---

[1] For a comparison with Greek and Mosaic law cf. de Jubainville, op. cit. pp. 84–87.
[2] For a striking parallel to this triad in Early Irish Law (Senchas Mār: Bretha Im Gatta) cf. V. Hull, ZCP 25 (1956), p. 216, § 1.

upon; and a person who shall kill another of his own kindred; since the living kin is not killed for the sake of the dead kin, everybody will hate to see him'. (A. Owen, *Ancient Laws and Institutes of Wales*, 1841, p. 385). The manner in which a murderer or other serious offender is banished appears from Welsh Laws I xiii 26: 'for it is required of everybody of every sex and age within hearing of the horn in the direction taken to accompany the progress of that exile; and keep up the barking of dogs to the period of putting to sea, and until the one banished shall have gone three score hours out of sight' (ibid., p. 632). In the Ir. Laws III, p. 72, mention is made of pilgrimage enjoined by the transgressor's confessor for the murder of a kinsman.

The Irish material on voluntary and involuntary exile, on its various motivation and its rich literary fruit is considerable. It will be recollected that List A of Irish medieval tales includes a (new) section headed *Immrama* 'Voyages' (cf. p. 46 above) which subsumes tales of *Longes* 'exile' such as *Longes Labrada* 'The Exile of Labraid'. *Longes*, a derivative of *long* 'ship' originally meant 'a voyage of exile' and concretely 'a band of exiles'. By a secondary development *longes* was applied to exile inside Ireland; so, for instance in TBC, of Fergus *fri Ultu ammuig ar longais* 'away from Ulster in exile (in Connacht)' (Windisch 465); also in the concrete sense 'a band of exiles' ibid. 2792. In the tale on the expulsion of the Déssi reference is made to gathering all the exiled bands of Ireland under the banner of the Déssi (cf. Ériu 3, 138, line 103: *Nach loinges rofitir Eithne . . .* 'Every exiled band known to Eithne' . . .) These are then enumerated over the next fifty lines, which reminds us of the situation in Gaul referred to above.

The longer title *Immram Curaigh (Maíle Dúin*, etc.) 'the Voyage of the Curragh of Mael Dúin . . .' indicates the essence of the Immram, or 'Voyage'; it is the *navigatio* with its attendant wonders which is the centre of interest, as for example in the marvellous *Navigatio Brendani*.[1] The *longes*, however, is in the first instance an involuntary exile representing a voyage of compulsion or propulsion rather than one of attraction. It is here that the *Echtrae* (<*echtar* 'outside') 'Adventure', with the Promised Land as its goal, comes in. The earliest *Immram*, that of Bran son of Febal (cf. p. 46 *supra*) shares with the *Echtrae* the motifs of fairy visitant and voyage to the Happy Otherworld. So that an overlapping of genres and of titles is to be expected. Indeed in

---

[1] Cf. H. Zimmer, Zeitschrift für Deutsches Altertum und Deutsche Literatur 33, 1889, p. 145.

YBL the tale is entitled 'The Voyage (*Immram*) of Bran son of Febal and his Adventure (*Echtra*)'.

In the *Immram Snédgusa & Maic Riagla* (cf. pp. 48, 143 *supra*) we find the motif of voluntary pilgrimage on the ocean combined with that of punishing wrongdoers by casting them adrift. So that the Christian hermit seeking Christ on the ocean, or the Christian penitent in exile (both portrayed in Adamnan's Life of Columba, I 6, 20, II 42; II 39) are but two figures on the maritime scene; beside them we have that of the wrongdoer cast adrift, as well as that of the voyager seeking the Celtic Elysium in the western seas, portrayed in the *Echtrai*.

An early Irish reference to the punishment of sending adrift[1] occurs in the Life of Patrick by Muirchú moccu Machthéni (fl. end of seventh century). Cf. Lib. Ardm. 6a, 2; Trip. i 222. 10, ii 288. 18. In the words of M. E. Byrne, On the Punishment of Sending Adrift, Ériu 11, 97: 'The wicked scoffer, unbeliever, and tyrant Maccuill, being converted by a miracle of Patrick's, confesses to the saint that he had tried to murder him and asks him to pass judgement. Patrick answers: 'non possum iudicare sed Deus iudicabit.' He orders Maccuill to go to the sea-shore scantily clad and bearing no food or drink, and that there, his feet having been fettered and the key of the fetter thrown into the sea, he is to be sent adrift in a boat of a single hide without oar or rudder, to go wherever (to whatever land) Providence brings him (and to dwell in that land according to the divine commands)'. In the event Maccuill's coracle reaches an island, and he is rescued by two saintly men who had converted the islanders; 'and he learnt the divine rule with them, and he spent the whole time of his life with them, until he took the bishopric after them' (Trip. i 223).

This instance anticipates the scheme of the penitential voyage which we find later for instance in the *Immram Ua Corra* (pp. 50, 142 supra). The life of sin is followed by penitence and the desire to make amends; the sinner confesses and prepares for the voyage of pilgrimage imposed or undertaken; the pilgrim embarks, and as soon as the high sea is reached the oars are thrown overboard. Then comes the visitation of marvellous islands, several of which are inhabited by hermits. The further course of the voyage is foretold by one of these holy men and the conclusion follows with an account of the transmission of the story. The long and detailed Pilgrims' Litany (ed. Plummer, Irish

---

[1] Stokes, Trip. i, clxxiv writes that a punishment somewhat similar to that described here existed in Iceland, but that the felon there was given oars, flint, steel, and a supply of victuals.

Litanies, London 1925, pp. 60 ff.) invokes the sons of Ua Corra as well as the *semper viventes* encountered by them on an island, and 'twelve men who went with Ailbe to death'.

Muirchú's account, then, which undoubtedly represents the consciousness of the fifth—seventh centuries, contains the germ of the later penitential *immram*, just as the story of Bran anticipates the *genre* in general. What is characteristic of the penitential variety is its organic use of religious themes;—as early as *Bran* Christian themes appear, without as yet being integrated in the structure of the tale.

Casting adrift is the penalty prescribed in the 'Law of the Innocents' (Cáin Adamnáin, promulgated according to the Annals of Ulster in 697) for some slayers of women; and also for women who commit certain grievous crimes. In the second case 'she is to be put out in a boat of one paddle at a certain distance on the sea to go with the wind from land. A vessel of meal and water to be given with her. Judgement upon her as God deems fit' (Cáin Adamnáin, ed. K. Meyer, Oxford 1905, § 45).

The Law texts contain similar provisions. Cf. H. 3. 18, p. 227a 23 et seq. (O'C. 413): 'In the case of a *mac scrīne,* that is a boy who has been begotten on a kinswoman in her own guise (i.e. without mistaking her for another) he shall be put in a leather box out to sea as far as a white shield is visible . . . If it be a man in a wicker boat of a single paddle, that is, a man who is put in a boat of a single paddle on the sea for his crimes of negligence as far out as a white shield is visible; enough meal and water for one night with him and a . . . sledge-hammer . . . in his hand for keeping off the beasts of the sea.' Cf. *Ériu* 11, 98–99; *Cáin Ad.* pp. 43, 44; Laws I, pp. 14–15.

Comparable instances are not far to seek in English mythology, legend, history and literature. An obvious parallel is the coming of Scyld-Sceaf; cf. Beowulf 4 ff. and Klaeber's ed.[3], p. 121 ff. J. A. Giles (ed. of William of Malmesbury, Chronicle of the Kings of England, London 1847) writes (p. 109): 'Sceaf . . . as some affirm, was driven on a certain island in Germany called Scamphta, (of which Jornandes, the historian of the Goths, speaks), a little boy in a skiff, without any attendant, asleep, with a handful of corn at his head, whence he was called Sceaf'. A second Beowulf example is the Offa-þrýð story (cf. Beowulf 1931b ff., and Klaeber's ed., p. 195 ff.). This is a legend of the Constance type: the innocently suffering, patient heroine marries a foreign prince, is banished with her child (or children), but in the end happily rejoins her husband. It becomes attached to Offa II—

Cyneþrȳð and is told by an anonymous writer as follows (Vita Offae Secundi, in Wats' ed. of Matthew Paris, 1640, p. 12): Diebus itaque sub eisdem Regnante in Francia Karolo rege magno ac victoriosissimo, quaedam puella facie venusta, sed mente nimis inhonesta, ipsi Regi consanguinea, pro quodam quod patraverat crimine flagitiosissimo, addicta est judicialiter morti ignominiosae, verum ob Regiae dignitatis reverentiam, *igni vel ferro tradenda non judicatur, sed in navicula armamentis carente apposita, victu tenui, ventis & mari eorumque ambiguis casibus exponitur condemnata* . . . For long at the mercy of storms on the sea, she is finally driven on to the British coast, is presented to the king, who is deceived by her beauty and later marries her. Further Klaeber, p. 197.

The earliest Middle English romance, that of Horn-Rimenhild, with its pronounced Irish connections, affords another interesting parallel in the exposure of Horn and his companions 'without sail and rudder' (cf. J. Hall, King Horn, Oxford 1901, pp. liv-lv, 7–9, 12–13, 101–103). The editor finds (p. lv) 'that the story is originally a British tradition, arising out of some temporary success in which the Cornish, aided by the Irish, checked the westward progress of the English invader. It was annexed by some English poet, and recast to suit the similar position of his countrymen resisting the attacks of the Danes. Finally, it emerged at a much later date in the shape of the extant versions under the impulse of the rising spirit of the English people recovering from the Norman Conquest, which found its peculiar literary expression in a whole cycle of outlaw and exile stories in verse and prose, such as the Gesta Herwardi, Fulk Fitz-Warine, Wistasse le Moine, the Robin Hood ballads'. Further instances of exposure in a boat in the romances are given by Hall, p. 102: 'Emare is thus sent to sea twice, ll. 265–79, 637–84, and Crystabelle with her son in Eglamour, 802–825. The sorrows of Desonelle (Torrent of Portyngale, 1813–42) are imitated from those of Crystabelle. Custance in Chaucer's Man of Lawe's Tale has the same hard fate as Emare (ll. 439–45, 865–9). S. Gregory was, when an infant, enclosed in a tun and sent adrift in a boat with the consolation that "Al þat God wil haue, don þan schal be," Gregorlegende, 262'.

Another instance of punitive casting adrift is the punishment inflicted at the instance of King Edmund on Berno for the murder of Regnar Lodbrog in 870: Tunc rex Eadmundus, diligenti de morte Lothebroci facta inquisitione, Bernum venatorem de opere nefando convicit, et jussit a militibus de curia sua adjudicari ac legis peritis, quid de homicida foret agendum; at omnes in hoc pariter consenserunt, *ut venator in illa navicula*, in qua saepe dictus Lothebrocus in Angliam applicuit, *poneretur, et in medio maris solus sine omni instrumento navali dimissus, probetur si illum Deus velit a periculo liberare.* Itaque venator, juxta quod sententiatum fuerat, in profunditatem maris dismissus, post dies paucos in Daciam est projectus; (Luard's ed. of M. Paris, *Chronica Majora*, 1872, I 395). Similarly the criminal Rainer who has been marked out by providence is placed in a boat with his wife and ill-gotten gains (AD 1144), but under the weight of sin the boat sinks and he perishes (*Historia Rerum Anglicarum*, Vol. I, ed. R. Howlett, London 1884, p. 46). In William of Malmesbury we find the legend of Edwin's exposure at the hands of his suspicious brother King Athelstan: 'The mode adopted too was cruel in the extreme: he was compelled to go on board a vessel, with a single attendant, without a rower, without even an oar, and the bark crazy with age. Fortune laboured for a long time to restore the innocent youth to land, but when at length he was far out at sea, and sails could not endure the violence of the wind, the young man, delicate, and weary of life under such circumstances, put an end to his existence by a voluntary plunge into the waters. . .' (Giles, Chronicle, pp. 139–140). This case corresponds closely to that of the Irish Mothla, King of Ciarraige, who had a nephew Ciar Cuircheach (Ciar of the Coracle) cast adrift because his claims were dangerous to him: *docuired a curach œnshluaisti for muir* 'he was put to sea in a coracle with a single paddle', Lism. L., p. 95.

The casting adrift of S. Kentigern's mother (A. P. Forbes, *Lives of S. Ninian and S. Kentigern*, Edinburgh 1874, pp. 167, 249, 250) is an interesting case of the *ordeal by water* as a test of chastity, and it has clear and close affinity with the practice of the Continental Celts. In fourth century Gaul the new-born babe was exposed on the Rhine in the hollow of a buckler and the sceptical father awaited the verdict of the veracious and jealous river: the true-born babe was sustained, the illegitimate sank. (D'Arbois de Jubainville, *Études sur le Droit Celtique*, pp. 26 ff.) The power of the elements which constitute the material world and their place in the ordering of human life is reflected in the Gaulish and Irish custom of invoking them as guarantees with powers of retribution. King Loegaire when defeated and captured by the Leinstermen renounced the tribute, giving as his guarantors *sun and moon, water and air, day and night, sea and land*. He was released then. But later he ignored his pledge and invaded Leinster once more. When he reached the place appointed for him *he died there by sun and wind and the other guarantors* (LU 9794 ff.). In *Cáin Adamnáin* §§ 22–23 we read: 'Adamnan did not rest satisfied until securities and bonds were given to him for the emancipation of women. These are the securities: sun and moon and all other elements of God; Peter, Paul, Andrew and the other apostles; Gregory, the two Patricks, the two Ciarans, the two Cronans, the four Fintans . . . (Here further Irish saints are listed). Those guarantors gave three shouts of malediction on every male who would kill a woman with his right hand or left, by a kick, or by his tongue, so that his heirs are elder and nettle and the corncake. The same guarantors gave three shouts of blessing on every female who would do something for the community of Adamnan, however often his reliquaries would come . . .'

Here we have the fusion of the old Celtic custom with Christianity. M. E. Byrne seems to invert the actual historical development when she writes 'From the earlier allusions to this punishment (of sending adrift) it seems clear that it was originally a penalty inflicted by ecclesiastics, and that it is post-Christian in origin . . . Afterwards it appears to have become a part of ordinary law to punish offences where there was not full criminal intent, or as in the case of a child of an incestuous union to remove from the community the guiltless fruit of another's sin . . .' (*Ériu* 11, p. 100).

The attitude of mind behind the casting adrift of malefactors appears from the material on record. It was applied in Ireland as in Wales to one who committed *fingal* i.e. who slew a member of his *fine*, which shows a reluctance to take a kinsman's life and an abhorrence of one who does so. The matter was referred to the arbitration of the element water. Incontinent women were liable to death by burning, cf. RC 2, 90; LL 287 b 7. In the *Adventures of Art Son of Conn* (*Ériu* 3, 150 ff.) it is told that Bécuma of the Land of Promise, a married woman who had sinned with Manannan's son, was banished in a coracle without oars, which was wafted by the wind to Ireland. Here the sentence of burning was waived in favour of banishment: *Ocus adbert Manannan gan a losgudh do denamh nach lenadh a cin don tir na dibh fein* 'And Manannan said not to burn her lest her guilt should cleave to the land or to themselves' (§ 3).[1] In the sequel the beautiful transgressor, like Cyneþrȳð, became attached for a time at least to the king.

---

[1] So too in OE Law those who commit grievous offences are banished, in order to turn away God's wrath from the people as a whole, and to cleanse the land (Liebermann, op. cit. II, sub *Strafe*, 10e: EGu 11 = VI Atr 7 = VIII 40 = II Cn 4. 7, 1; *Verbannung* 1c, 4: cf. Hom. nach Wulfstan 310. 266).

Exposure, then, was a convenient way of getting rid of troublesome persons without becoming involved in unpleasant consequences. The *elements* (*na dúli*) can play the part of *arbiter* here as they do of *guarantor* elsewhere. Later they are seen as *dúli Dé* 'the elements of God', and finally it is God Himself who decides the fate of the foundling on the high sea as He does that of His pilgrims. The three stages are represented in the death of Loegaire, the securities of Adamnan, and the Maccuill episode in the life of Patrick, respectively. Meanwhile voluntary exposure becomes an important penitential discipline and literary motif and we find it in *Snedgus and Mc.R.* as a variant to the punitive measure.

Note: Elemental Guarantors and the Runes of *Husband's Message* (50 ff.): Cf. Lines 48–53 (Krapp-Dobbie numeration; for text cf. Mackie, Exeter Book II 196; Krapp-Dobbie, Ex. Book p. 227; R. F. Leslie, Three Old English Elegies, Manchester 1961, p. 50; we insert letters for runes where possible):

> Ofer eald gebeot incer twega
> gehyre ic ætsomne. S.R. geador
> 50 .EA. W. ond. ⋈ aþe benemnan
> þæt he þa wære ond þa winetreowe
> be him lifgendum læstan wolde,
> þe git on ærdagum oft gespræconn.

The reading *gehyre* (49): *gehyran* 'hear' is based on Mackie, p. 196, and on Schipper's note (*Germania* 19, 335) that in the scratched and stained MS. at this point it is *n* or the bottom of *h*, not *c*, which appears faintly in the verb (cf. Leslie, op. cit., p. 66). So also Trautmann, Holthausen, Sieper and Bradley (cf. Krapp-Dobbie, Exeter Book, p. 364). Kock and Krapp-Dobbie read *gecyre: gecyrran* 'turn' but the collocation *gecyre . . . ætsomne* 'place together' (Kock, Blackburn) remains dubious.

Taking *gehyre* in 49, line 48 now goes contextually and grammatically better with what follows than with what precedes (cf. Leslie op. cit., 65–66). The meaning of the runes is the next important point at issue (cf. Leslie 15–18, and Krapp-Dobbie 363–364). S(*sigel*) and R(*rad*) according to the wording of line 49 are meant to be read as a compound, *sigelrad*; EA (*ear*) and W(*wyn*) to combine similarly in *earwyn*. The final rune is ambiguous and may stand for D(*dæg*) or for M(*mon*). It looks like the D-rune and has been so taken by many edd. including Mackie; but it has the same form as the rune in *Ruin* 23, which stands for M. Kock, Anglia 45, 122 takes *sigelrad* for 'the sun's road' i.e. 'heaven' and EAW for *earwyn* 'earth's joy', i.e. 'earth', and translates 'I place together (*gecyre* . . .) Heaven, Earth and Man, confirming by an oath that he would keep, throughout his life, the compact and the faith . . .' Leslie interprets *sigelrad* 'sun's road' as 'sky' and *earwyn* as 'the lovely earth' on the analogy of compounds such as *eðelwyn*, *eardlufu* and of *eorðan wyn*; Kock had previously taken *earwynn* as 'the lovely earth'; Leslie also takes M for *mon* and translates: 'I hear heaven, earth and the man declare together by oath that he would implement those pledges and those vows of love which you two often voiced in days gone by'. Leslie continues (p. 17) 'He uses the present tense for vividness, in recalling an event at which he himself has been present. The husband's actual words had probably been put in such a traditional form as 'I call upon heaven and earth to witness that I shall remain true to my vows . . .' These are the sacred elemental names (cf. ZCP 11, 58 (1917)) which may be coupled with his own on the rune-stave and names by which they had in all probability both sworn their *eald gebēot* (49) *þe git on ǣrdagum oft gesprǣconn* (54). The last line is an exact repetition of line 16, where the *wordbēotunga* of husband and wife are recalled in the same passage as the only direct reference to the rune-stave, a passage containing the text of the message which the husband had commanded his messenger to relate. The repetition of line 16 is not accidental or fortuitous; it underlines the reciprocal nature of their vows, twice mentioned in connection with the rune-stave, whose contents when disclosed at the end serve by their runic form to underline the sacred and solemn nature of the vows which the husband has now reaffirmed.'

The ZCP passage cited by Leslie is from an old Irish poem basic to the prose legends of the rise of the *Aithechthuatha* or subject non-Goidelic peoples against their masters. The exiled Goidelic princes were invited back by the insurgents, as crops and produce had failed these owing to the lack of a righteous and legitimate ruler. The *Aithechthuatha* gave the princes the following guarantees (§ 10): 'the sky, the earth, the moon, the bright sun that they (the princes) would have their will from height to height as long as the sea encompasses Ireland.'

Leslie's discerning interpretation of the runic passage 48–53 requires correction in one particular. Lines 48 (*ofer eald gebeot incer twega*) and 53 (*þe git on ærdagum oft gespræconn*) fully and adequately refer to the plighted couple. The inclusion of one of them among the guarantors is quite incongruous here and finds no support from Irish sources. In lines 49–50 the rune-stave is in fact listing the *elements* which were invoked by the Husband in the first instance as guarantors that (51–52) he would implement his vows.[1] The final rune has to represent one of the elements and cannot stand for *mon*. The outraged guarantors which caused the death of King Loegaire (p. 190 *supra*) were *sun and moon, water and air, day and night, sea and land*. This supplies the answer to our problem. In *Husband's Message* the final rune is for D (*dæg*) ('Day is the Lord's messenger, dear to men, the splendid light of the Creator, joy and hope of rich and poor, useful to all' as the *Rune Poem* 74–76 has it.) Lines 48–53 now run 'Concerning the ancient vow of you both, I hear heaven (sky), earth, and day declare together by oath that he (i.e. the Husband, who is the central subject throughout from 13 ff.) would be true while he lives to the compact and pledge of fidelity that both of you often voiced in days gone by'.

[1] On the relation between the Elements and Truth (in Hindu tradition) cf. M. Dillon, The Archaism of Irish Tradition, Sir J. Rhŷs Mem. Lecture 1947, p. 6.

CHAPTER XI

SOME OLD ENGLISH RELIGIOUS TERMS

Professor D. Whitelock (*Interpretation of the Seafarer*, 1950) was the first to argue that *Seafarer* 38 *elþeodigra eard gesece* should be taken in the sense of an actual *peregrinatio* in the tradition of Irish and British *peregrini*, cf. pp. 35 ff. *supra*. Before her, Ehrismann, Schücking and Anderson, and after her Smithers argued for the allegorical interpretation of the seafaring theme, for which cf. Whitelock, op. cit., pp. 262–263 and I. L. Gordon, ed., pp. 4–10. In the course of a paper entitled *Saxons and Celts in South-West Britain*[1] Professor C. L. Wrenn remarked 'One wonders if the OE phrase (*on elþiodignesse*) might owe its origin to the need to render the notion of the Irish *ailithre* ("peregrinatio")'.

OE *elþeod* is recorded in the meanings 'gens peregrina, exilium', and *elþeodig* adj. and subst. in the meanings 'foreign, peregrinus, living in another land; exile, foreigner (also figuratively cf. Blickling Homilies 23. 1 ff.: *Forþon we habbaþ nedþearfe þæt we ongyton þa blindnesse ure ælþeodignesse; we send on þisse worlde ælþeodignesse; we synd on þisse worlde ælþeodige, & swa wæron siþþon se æresta ealdor þisses menniscan cynnes Godes bebodu abræc; & forþon gýlte we wæron on þysne wræc-síþ sende, & nu eft sceolon operne eþel secan, swa wíte, swa wuldor, swe we nu geearnian willaþ*. 'Therefore it is needful for us to perceive the blindness of our pilgrimage; we are in the foreign land of this world— we are exiles in this world, and so have been ever since the progenitor of the human race broke God's behests, and for that sin we have been sent into this banishment, and now we must seek hereafter another kingdom, either in misery or in glory, as we may now choose to merit.'). Beside these terms we have OE *elland, eleland* 'foreign country, strange land', cf. Beowulf 3016 ff. *mægð . . . sceal geomormod . . . elland tredan* 'a woman . . . sad of mind . . . shall traverse a foreign land'; and *ellende, elelende* 'foreign; foreign parts'.

In the OE translation of Bede's H. E. (cf. T. Miller, E.E.T.S. 95,

---

[1] *The Transactions of the Honourable Society of Cymmrodorion*, London 1959, p. 47 ff.

London 1890) *peregrinam ducere vitam* and its equivalents are commonly rendered by *in elþeodignesse lifian (awunian)*.[2] Cf. H. E. III 19, of Furseus . . . cupiens pro Domino, ubicumque sibi oportunum inueniret, peregrinam ducere uitam: *Wilnade he, þætte he swa hwær swa he gelimplice stowe findan meahte, þæt he wolde for Godes noman in elþeodignisse lifian* 'He desired, wherever he might find a suitable place, to live in a foreign country for God's name'; III 27 of Egbert in Ireland: Uouit etiam uotum, quia adeo peregrinus uiuere uellet, et numquam in insulam, in qua natus est, id est Brittaniam, rediret: *Swelce he eac gehat geheht, þæt he á wolde for Gode his liif in elþeodignesse lifigan 7 næfre to Breotone ealonde hweorfan, þær he acenned wæs* 'And he also made a vow, that he would for God's sake live all his life in a foreign land, and never return to the island of Britain, where he was born'; ibid. exulabat: *in ellþeodignesse lifde* 'lived in exile'; IV 3 of Chad and Egbert: Sed illo postmodum patriam reuerso, ipse peregrinus pro Domino usque ad finem uitae permansit: *Ac he Ceadda eft æfter fæce in his eðel hwyrfde in Breotone: se Ecgberht þær in elþeodignesse fore Godes noman awunode oð his lifes ende* 'But Chad after a time returned to his native land in Britain; but Egbert abode there in exile for God's name up to his life's end.'; similarly of Egbert V. 9; IV 23: of Hild who had 'left the world' to serve God alone in East Anglia . . . desiderans exinde, siquo modo posset, derelicta patria et omnibus, quaecumque habuerat, Galliam peruenire, atque in monasterio Cale peregrinam pro Domino uitam ducere . . .: *willade þonon, gif heo meahte, þæt heo wolde hire eðel forlætan 7 eal, þæt heo for worulde hæfde, 7 wolde cuman in Gallia ríce 7 in Caale þæm mynstre in elþeodignesse fore Drihtne lifigean* . . . 'from this she desired, if possible, relinquishing her home and all she had in the world, to pass into Gaul and to live in exile for the Lord at the monastery of Chelles . . .; III 13 of Wilbrord in Ireland: Sed et in Hibernia cum presbyter adhuc peregrinam pro aeterna patria duceret uitam . . .: . . . *mid þy he ða gena mæssepreost wæs in Hibernia 7 þær for heofona rices lufan in elþeodignesse lifde. . . . '. . .* when he was still a priest in Ireland, living there in a foreign land for love of the heavenly kingdom . . .'; V 9 of Wihtberht . . . ipse contemtu mundi ac doctrinae scientia insignis, (nam multos annos in Hibernia peregrinus anchoreticam in magna perfectione uitam egerat . . .: *(Wihtbriht)* . . . *se wæs middangeard forhycgende, 7 he wæs on wiisdome codcundre láre mære, 7 monig gear he in Hibernia ellþeodig áncorliif dede in micelre fullfremednesse* . . .' (Wihtberht) . . . he

[2] Cf. Whitelock, op. cit., pp. 267 ff.

196

had renounced the world, and was celebrated for his knowledge of the word of God, and had lived as an exile and hermit for many years in Ireland a life of great perfection . . .'; V 10 of the two Hewalds qui in Hibernia multo tempore pro aeterna patria exulauerant: *þa in Hibernia þem ealonde micelre tiide for hiofana riices lufan in ellðeodinesse liifdan* 'who had long lived in exile in Ireland for love of the kingdom of heaven'.

OE *in elþeodignesse* of these examples corresponds exactly to O. Ir. *i n-ailithre*, cf. Ml. 137 b 7 *is sunt bia sa in eilithri collae messa* 'here shall I be in pilgrimage till the Day of Doom'; *dul i n-ailithre (ailithri)* 'to go on pilgrimage' Laws III 72. 6; V 124. 4, 7; V 296. 16 . . .; *ina ailithri* 'on (his) pilgrimage' EIL, p. 82.

Ailithre is a jā-stem derived from *ailithir* 'peregrinus'. This is a Bahuvrīhi formation from *aili-* 'other' and *tír* 'land' with the original meaning 'having another land; exile'; it is found on an Ogam inscription (Macal. Corp. I, p. 186). The same formation is found in the ja-stems OE *ellende, elelende* 'foreign', O.Sax. *elilendi* OHG *elilenti* (Mod.G. *elend*); cp. Lat. *misericors*, Gothic *armahaírts*: OE *earmheort;* also Gothic *aljakuns* 'belonging to another race, foreign'. The first element of *ailithir, ellende* and cognates reflects an Indo-European compositional **ali-*. As the formation corresponding to *ellende* is absent in North and East Gmc it seems probable that this term was transmitted by the English to the West Germans in the course of their missionary labours on the continent. The same distribution holds for OE *elþeodig;* cf. O.Sax. *elithiodig* 'alienigena', OHG *alidiotig, elidiotic*. Here it is rare, beside the common *elilenti;* the precise distribution of both words in OHG sources is a desideratum.

The development suggested here may be illustrated by another word associated with *elþeodig* in H.E. V 9 (quoted *supra*). The relevant passage is *7 monig gear he in Hibernia ellþeodig áncorliif dede in micelre fullfremednesse* 'and he had lived as an exile and hermit for many years in Ireland a life of great perfection'. The word in question is *ancor:* in V 12 *solitarius* is rendered *in ancorsetle* 'as a hermit', with reference to Hamgels; cf. also (ibid.) of a householder who had renounced the world: *locum secretae mansionis . . . intrauit: in dygle aáncorstowe eode* 'proceeded to a retired hermitage'. Latin anachoreta (Gk. ἀναχωρητής) yielded O. Ir. *anchara;* this in turn was taken over into OE as *ancor, ancra* and transmitted to O.Sax. in the form *ēnkoro*, and to OHG as *einchora(n)*.

For the literal interpretation of *elþeodigra eard* cf. *terram peregrinam* (*debes uisitare*), Plummer, Vitae SS.Hib., I 141, quoted above, p. 185.

OE *gylt, gelt*, Mod.E. *guilt*, lacks an etymology. Its semantic field is defined by Toller thus: I a failure of duty, a sin, crime, an offence; II a debt; IIa a penalty, payment on account of crime; III responsibility for an offence, a (person's) fault; IV desert of a penalty; V state of being guilty, criminality, culpability. Its Gmc synonym *scyld* is defined by Bosworth as I guilt, sin, crime, fault; II a debt, due; here the semantic value is brought out by *sculan* 'owe, should, ought . . .'; the base is **skel-:* Lith. *skolà* 'debt'. The Gmc word dies out in English.

Examples of the use of *gylt* relevant to our discussion are as follows: Blickling Homilies X, lines 1–13 (Morris, p. 107): . . . nú anra manna gehwylcne ic myngie and lære . . . þæt anra gehwylc hine sylfne sceawige & ongyte, & swa hwæt swa he *on mycclum gyltum oþþe on medmycclum gefremede*, þæt he þonne hrædlice gecyrre to þam selran & to þon soþan læcedome; þonne magon we us God ælmihtigne mildne habban; forþon þe Drihten wile þæt ealle men sýn hale & gesunde . . . swa Dauid cwæþ, 'þa eaðmodan heortan & þa forhtgendan & þa bifigendan & þa cwacigendan & þa ondrædendan heora Scyppend, ne forhogaþ þa næfre God ne ne forsyhþ; ah heora bena he gehyreð, þonne hie to him cleopiað & him are biddaþ'. 'I now admonish and exhort every man . . . everyone to behold and understand himself, and, whatsoever he hath committed *in great sins or in venial ones,* forthwith to turn to the better and to the true medicine, then may we have God almighty merciful (to us), because the Lord desires all men to be whole and sound . . . as David said, "The humble and fearing and trembling and quaking hearts and those fearing their Creator, God will never despise nor disregard, but will hear their prayers when they cry to him and pray to him for mercy." ' The aspect of guilt underlined here is the psychological state of *fear* which ought to go with true repentance; the larger context is that the end of the world is nigh and that one should contemplate one's own end and act accordingly. Our second example from Hom. II (ibid., p. 23) associates guilt with the state of exile: we synd on þisse worlde ælþeodige, & swa wæron siþþon se æresta ealdor þisses menniscan cynnes Godes bebodu abræc; & forþon gýlte we wæron on þysne wræc-síþ sende, & nu eft sceolon oþerne eþel secan, swa wíte, swa wuldor, swe we nu geearnian willaþ. 'We are exiles in this world, and so have been ever since the progenitor of the human race broke God's behests, and for that sin we have been sent into this banishment, and now we must seek hereafter another kingdom, either in misery or in glory, as we may now choose to merit.' Similarly Hom. I, p. 9. 5 where Adam's guilt and sin has caused exclusion from Paradise. A final example associates guilt with flight (H. Sweet, Orosius, London 1883, p. 140. 12 ff.): Fabius had ignominiously fled before the Samnites with his army in his train:—*þa bæd his fæder . . . þæt þa senatum forgeafen þæm suna þone gylt . . .* 'then his father . . . besought the senate to forgive his son's delict . . .'

A very close parallel to the aspects of *gylt* illustrated in the foregoing OE examples is offered by Irish and Sc. Gaelic *geilt*. In Sc. Gaelic the word has the following meanings 'terror, fear, dread, cowardice, timidity; a wild man or woman; one who dwells in woods or deserts;...' Cf. A. MacBain, An Etymological Dictionary of the Gaelic Language, Stirling 1911; E. Dwelly, The Illustrated Gaelic Dictionary, Fleet, Hants., 1918. Contribb. G s.v. defines it thus: 'one who goes mad from terror; a panic-stricken fugitive from battle; a crazy person living in the woods and supposed to be endowed with the power of levitation; a lunatic'. Its earliest occurrence is in a poem ascribed by K. Meyer to the early seventh century (Ält. Ir. Dicht. I, p. 26 ff.): *Caur gaile Gelt Gáith, / grīan nime nīamdai nāir* 'Valorous champion . . . Sun of heaven, splendid and noble'. Here the epithet *Gelt* parallel to *caur* (*gaile*) is probably to be taken in the meaning 'Champion, Hero'. The *Laws* take no account of the *geilt* though they do deal with the following range of related types: the madman (*dásachtach, fulla*), the absconder, wanderer (*fóindledach*), the half-witted person (*óinmit*), the proclaimed person (*airfhócrach*), the outlaw, outcast, exile (*deora(i)d*), the hermit, anchorite (*deora(i)d, deora(i)d Dé* lit. God's outcast—in the opposite sense to OE *Godes útlaga*).

For the characterization of the *geilt* as a type we have the adequate account of Suibhne Geilt in *Buile Shuibhne* (cf. pp. 25 ff. *supra*). The main features are: he sins against the Church; he suffers metamorphosis to a reduced physical and mental state and takes to a solitary life in a natural environment; there he lives a life of penitence and vicissitude, subsisting on a vegetable and berry diet; he develops in sanctity and as poet and prophet; associates with the Church; dies miserably as foretold, but withal a holy death. In the tale of Suibhne all the ingredients listed above for the OE examples are found together: crime, flight, exile, terror, expiation; the element of metamorphosis in the spiritual sense (as in the physical condition of outlawry) is involved in the OE examples too, and the sense of culpability ('guilt-complex') is very important. The semantic range of Sc. Gaelic *geilt*[1] covers much of this ground, and here we find the abstract meaning of the word which we require as an immediate source for the OE meaning of *gylt*. The objection that Early Irish does not seem to offer the abstract connotation is readily answered: it is a feature of the language that nomina agentis derive semantically from nomina actionis: cf. *gein* 'birth; infant', *flaith* 'sovereignty, kingdom; ruler', *longes* 'exile; exiled band', *techt* 'going; messenger' ... cp. O. Icel. *bani* 'death; slayer'; OE *scop* 'poet', O. Icel. *skop* 'railing, mocking' ... Further Ped. II 837, 64, 611, 641.

This brings us to the etymology of *geilt*. The case for its being a borrowing from Welsh *gwyllt*, mentioned Ped. I 96 as a possibility, was taken up by J. Carney, Studies in Irish Literature and History, Dublin 1955, pp. 150 ff. and 385 ff., and criticized on phonological grounds by K. Jackson (*Éigse* 7, pp. 113 ff.). W. Stokes referred the word to a root **ghel-* 'fly': Gk. χελιδών 'swallow'. B. Benes (ZCP 28, 1961, p. 327) takes **ghel-* in the meaning 'call, cry, sing' related inside Irish to *gol* 'weeping, wailing', *goltar* (:ON *galdr*), *goltraige* 'sad musical strain' ... and outside Irish to ON *gala*, OE, OHG, O. Sax. *galan* 'call, sing ...' For these I.E. etymologies of *geilt* there is no convincing evidence. Both support the bird-metaphor; at the same time the levitation of Suibhne appears from §§ 39–41 to be more in the nature of leaping or bounding than of flying, cf. also §§ 12, 33 (as against §§ 17, 15, 20 which support flight). Further evidence of this is supplied in the Norse account of Irish Mirabilia in the 'Speculum Regale' (K. Meyer, *Ériu* 4, 1–16) which Meyer believed to be based on oral information obtained in Ireland. The account is worth quoting in full for the light it throws on *geilt* as a secular concept: 'There is also one thing, which will seem very wonderful, about men who are called *gelt*. It happens that when two hosts meet and are arranged in battle-array, and when the battle-cry is raised loudly on both sides, that cowardly men run wild, and lose their wits from the dread and fear which seize them. And then they run into a wood away from other men, and live there like beasts, and shun the meeting of men like wild beasts. And it is said of these men that when they have lived in the woods in that condition for twenty years, then feathers grow on their bodies as on birds,[2] whereby their bodies are protected against frost

---

[1] The equation *geilt*: E. *guilt* was found by Professor Wagner in a Sc. source which I cannot trace.

[2] For a similar description of the anchorite encountered by S. Brendan in the Land of Promise cf. Lism. L. pp. 260, 354; also *Buile S.* § 60.

or cold; but the feathers are not so large that they may fly like birds. Yet their swiftness is said to be so great that other men cannot approach them. . . . For these people run along the trees almost as swiftly as monkeys or squirrels.' This account is in substantial agreement with *Buile Shuibhne*. Less to our present purpose is the subsidiary account of a *geilt*, this time a *sea-geilt* (*muirgeilt*) in the tale *Aided Echach Meic Maireda* (LU 39a–41b). Here underseas wandering in salmon shape is the chief feature (cf. LU 2965 ff.) Neither levitation nor criminality appear, but the *geilt*, a mermaid, is saintly and associated with saints and is accompanied by the significant[1] otter; for which motif cf. N. K. Chadwick, Scottish Gaelic Studies 5, 1942, p. 124.

B. Benes's etymology of *geilt* furthers her thesis of shamanistic influence in *Buile Shuibhne*, a theme already mooted by others, which she has richly illustrated. But the contribution of the Mediterranean area and Middle East to Irish and British Christianity has been considerable. We need only mention two features central to shamanism borrowed from this area: the *Tree of Life* in Paradise (on which the souls of the righteous in the form of white birds perch while listening to the discourse of Elijah, cf. p. 49 *supra*); and the tree and nest of the Phoenix (*Phoenix* 447 ff.). In connection with *geilt* we have the following vital testimony (Mrs Chadwick, The Age of the Saints in the Early Celtic Church, London 1963, p. 109:) 'A close analogy to these *gealta* of the Irish Christian Church, who shun the society of men and live alone with wild nature under the open heavens or even in the trees, is found in the recluses of the Syrian desert, referred to by Greek writers as βοσκοί 'Grazers' and δενδρῖται 'Tree-dwellers'. The βοσκοί are so described, because they had no houses, ate neither bread nor meat, and drank no wine; but dwelt constantly on the mountains, and passed their time in praising God by prayers and hymns. . . . At the usual hour of meals they each took a sickle and went to the mountain to cut some grass as though they were flocks in pasture; and this served for their repast. . . . (Sozomen, H. E. vi.33.2).

In connexion with Suibhne reference has also been made to the δενδρῖται or 'tree-dwellers' (Leclercq, Dictionnaire, s.v. Dendrites, and the references there cited), a small number of ascetics related to the pillar-saints. John Moschus speaks of a monk Adolas who came from Mesopotamia and dwelt in a large plane tree and made a window

---

[1] For the anecdote of Dobarchú ('Otter') who kills S. Brénainn's oxen, is cursed by the saint, falls into Loch Lir, and is turned into an otter, cf. Lism. L., p. xvii.

through which he used to talk to visitors . . . (here follow other examples) . . . Suibhne Geilt is at no very distant remove from the Syrian 'grazers' and 'tree-saints', whether we suppose that the more severe forms of penitential discipline of the Celtic Anchorites received a direct impetus from Syria, or whether, as is perhaps more probable, stories of these more extreme forms of Eastern asceticism have made their way to western Europe and formed the nucleus of the story of Suibhne's fanatical austerities. . . .'

In *Buile Shuibhne* § 17 it is told that when their year in madness was complete the *gealta* of Ireland used to go to delightful Glen Bolcain. Its many amenities there listed include watercress and brooklime, sorrels and herbs of all kinds, berries, sloes, brown acorns . . . 'The madmen moreover used to smite each other for the pick of watercress of that glen. . . .' Gleann na nGealt 'the glen of the *gealta*' in West Kerry was also a resort of madmen, according to folk tradition.

Obviously then *geilt* in our meaning is nomen actoris to the abstract *geilt* 'grazing'. The *geilt* is originally the 'grazer'; cf. Greek βοσκός lit. 'a herdsman', 'one who feeds', 'used in patristic writing in the sense of a "grazer", one who lives on grass like cattle and avoids human company' (Chadwick op. cit., p. 109, f.n. 2.) His condition (*geltacht*) is in the first instance the result of a voice from Heaven accusing him of the sin of bloodshed (Chadwick, Sc. G. Studies 5, p. 131: of the *geilt* in Ireland and Wales). The Christian *geilt*, subsisting on the diet of birds and animals, is like Suibhne an outcast, culpable, living in fear and expiating sin. This new meaning is imprinted on the associated abstractum which comes to connote what we understand by *guilt*: O E *gelt, gylt* is born. *Egylt* (=*ǣgylt*, cf. *āgyltan*) 'excessus, (culpa, delictum)', Corpus Glossary 808 (eighth century), suggests that this development may be as early as the seventh century and refers us back to the earliest Irish occurrences of the term (cf. Chadwick, Geilt, pp. 106 ff.).

Alone among the Gmc languages O E has the term *neorxnawang* for 'Paradise': cf. Hexam. 16 *Paradisum ðæt wé hátaþ on Englisc neorxna wang*. Beside the meaning 'Paradise' of Genesis and the early poetry, the meaning 'abode of the blessed after death' is found in New Testament sources (Luc. 23, 43; II Cor. 12, 4); the term is never used for *heofon* 'coelum'. In the West Saxon Gospels *paradisus* is used, but *neorxnawang* is frequent in prose, especially in Ælfric. In the twelfth century, *paradis(us)* 'the Garden of Eden' supersedes it, cf. Cotton

Hom. 221 (before 1175) *God þa hine brohte into paradis* and the twelfth century gloss *paradis(us)* for *Elisia* (Englische Studien 11, 65. 25; Anglistische Forschungen 56, p. 226). The English word *paradise* rests ultimately on Old Persian *pairidaēẓa* 'enclosure, park' whence it was transmitted to English via Greek, Latin and French. Greek *parádeisos* is used '. . . (first by Xenophon) for a (Persian) enclosed park, orchard or pleasure ground; by the LXX for the garden of Eden, and in N.T. and Christian writers for the abode of the blessed, which is the earliest sense recorded in English' (OED s.v.).

It is generally agreed that the second element in our word is *wang* 'field'. The main forms recorded for the first element are: North. *nerxna-, neirxna-, nercsna-, erexna-*. West Sax. usually *neorxna-, nerxena-;* less usual: *neorxne-, neorcxna-, neorxene-, nearxne-* (and seven further variants.)

The OE *Phoenix* offers a variety of terms with *wang* or equivalents for 'Paradise': cf. *se wong* 7, 19; *se æþela wong* 43; *se halga wong* 418, *se sigewong* 33; *wynsum wong* 13; *þone wlitigan wong* 439; *willwong* 89; *þæt torhte lond* 28, *þæt æpele lond* 20. . . . The designation 'field, plain' recurring in Wulfila's *vagg* is widespread for 'paradise'. The Phoenix terms *wynlond* 'blissful land' (82) *willwong* 'delightful plain', *wynsum wong* 'pleasant plain' are reminiscent of Otfrid's *wunnisamaẓ feld* and Notker's *wunnigarto, ẓartgarto;* also of O. Ir. *Mag Meld* 'plain of sports', name of the Irish Elysium in *Im. Brain* §§ 34, 39 (cf. K. Meyer, A. Nutt, The Voyage of Bran I, London 1895, pp. 18, 20).

Of the many suggestions put forward to explain *neorxnawang* none has found favour; as most of them seem highly implausible, a brief summary may suffice: (Cf. especially A. Leitzmann, PBB 32, 60 ff., and R. Jente, Anglistische Forschungen 56, 230–232):

1. (a) E. Lye (Dict. 1772): Neorcsen . . . Adj. Formatum ex Ne negativo et Veorc 'opus, labor' . . . Neorxena-wang . . . 'Labore vacuus campus, Elysium, Paradisus'.
   (b) J. Grimm (Gramm. 2, 267; 3. 726): Neorc-sa 'otium', eine s-Ableitung.

2. Ettmüller (Lex. Anglos. 239): neorcsen from ne + Adj. *ricsen (cf. Gothic riqizeins 'dark') by metathesis to *ircsen, *eorcsen. Neorxnawang 'hortus splendidus'.

3. Neorxnawang 'nympharum pratum', from the name of the Nornir:
   (a) Weinhold (Zeitschrift für deutsches Altertum 6, 460): *neorxu, the OE name of the Nornir.
   (b) Grein (Sprachschatz): Neirxena by metathesis from *neriscena,

*nericsena, Nom. *nerisce. Cf. ON Nari 'brother of Hel' and Neri 'brother or father of a Norn'. *Nerisce formed like mennisca from Mann.

4. Bradley (The Academy, 19th October, 1889): Neorxna from *nēorōhsna- (cp. Gothic naus and rōhsns) 'field of the palaces of the dead'.

5. Leo (Ags. Gloss. 491, 604): Neorxna(wang) from Latin narcissus, Greek nárkissos 'narcissorum campus'.

6. Leitzmann (PBB 32, 60 ff.): I.E. *nert->Prim. Gmc nerþ- (cp. O.Icel. Njörðr) + suffix *(i)ska, yielding *nerþska, *nerska. Neorxnawang 'Wiese der zur Nerthus gehörigen'.

7. Uhlenbeck (PBB 33, 185) relates OE *neorh to Sanscrit *nárka- from which he derives Sanscrit náraka-'Underworld, hell'. OE neorh-suna 'sons of the Underworld' with semantic shift of 'Underworld' to 'paradise' as in 6.

8. Ritter (Anglia 33, 467 ff.): Neorxnawang from n- + eorxnawang. *eorxna from *ercsena<*Ercsuna: Erce 'Mother Earth'. *Ercansuna 'children or sons of Mother Earth', eorxna-wang 'Gefilde der Erce-Söhne'.

9. Krogmann (Anglia 53, 337 ff.): Neorxena, gen. pl. of *nerhsa < *nerh- + suffix -isa-. *Nerhsa 'Fessler', Neorxnawang 'die Wiese der Nerxen, der Todesdämonen' > 'Paradies'(!).

10. Langenfelt (Anglia 55, 250 ff.): *eorc(n)an- 'glänzend', n- from a preposition; Neorxnawang 'the Glittering Plain, the Holy Plain'.

In general these suggestions are characterized by impossible or unlikely concepts and/or by hypothetical forms. *Neorxnawang* is best explained from Irish: beside O. Ir. *nem*[1] we find the word *erc* for 'heaven'; in Z C P 8, 197. 11 it is said that S. Colum Cille traverses the 'plains of Heaven', *maighne Erca* (cf. K. Meyer, *Wortk.* 205; otherwise rendered, Contribb. M, sub *maigen*). *Maigen,* acc. pl. *maigne,* is derived from *mag* 'plain', which we have noted in *Mag Meld*, the designation of the Irish elysium. A common Early Ir. designation of the 'blessed in heaven' is *muinter nime* lit. community of heaven, to which *fer nime*[2] lit. man of heaven, can serve as singular. The term *mac nime* lit. son of heaven 'one of the blessed in heaven' does not seem to occur, though many comparable collocations with *mac* 'son'

[1] The compound *nimiath* lit. heaven-land occurs in *Amra Choluim Chille* (composed shortly after AD 597) §§ 5, 92. Cf. § 5 *Dia firién firfocus cluines mo donúaill do nimiath nél* 'God the righteous, the truly near, who from the heavenland of clouds hears my sad wail' (cf. ZCP 28, 243). Cf. *maige* 'plains (of Heaven)' § 36.

[2] Cf. *Ísu co feraib nime* 'Jesus with Heaven's inhabitants' EIL, no. 11, st. 2c, p. 26.

are found: *mac eclaise*, lit. son of the church, 'a cleric', *mac báis* lit. son of death 'a wicked man', *mac bethad* lit. son of life 'a righteous man' . . .

OE *neorxnawang* in the form **erc-suna-wang* 'plain of the sons of heaven' would correspond to Ir. *mag muinntire nime* 'plain of the blessed' of FA 7; cp. *Fél.* 7th November *i mmaig nime* 'in heaven's plain'. The basis for **erc-suna-wang* is given in the North. form *erexna-*. It has been commonly assumed that the *n-* of *neorxnawang* derives from the agglutination of a preceding preposition *in* or *on*; in O. Ir. the neuter *mag* requires an *n-* before a following vowel: *mag nErca* 'heaven's plain', as against *maigen Erca* (above); *maigen* is fem.

The borrowing of O. Ir. *erc* 'heaven' into OE could arise from the Irish mission in Northumbria. To the same mediation may be attributed those features in the description of the paradisiacal land where the Phoenix dwells (*Phoenix* 1–85) which differ from the Latin source, while corresponding to the Irish vision of heaven or the great Pleasant Plain (cf. Meyer-Nutt, op. cit., Vol. I, p. 245); further we may refer to the bird-souls of heaven, *Phoenix* 589 ff., a commonplace in Early Ir. literature, cf. Ch. VI. On the fourfold division of the human race after death common to early Irish and English eschatology cf. p. 49, f.n. 2 *supra*.

OE *tintreg* (*tinterg*), *tintrega* 'torment' has not been explained. The term applies to torment in general, frequently to the soul's torment in the next world. Examples of the latter are: Blickling Hom. 113. 33 *& eac þæs oþres saule of witum generede, & of tintregum alesde* 'and he delivered also the other's soul from punishment and released him from torments'; H.E. V 12 (cf. Miller, op. cit., p. 432. 7) *⁊ wite ðu þæt se legfamblawenda seað ⁊ se fula, þone ðu gesawe, þæt wæs helle tintreges muð* 'And know that the pit which foamed up with flame and was so foul, which you saw, was the mouth of hell's torment'; here *helle tintreges muð* renders Latin *os gehennae;* cf. Bede 4, 24: *de horrore poenae gehennalis: 'be fyrhto ðæs tintreglican wites';* also B.T. sub *tintreg: in gehennam: 'in tintergo'* Mt. Kmbl. Lind. 10, 28. . . .

Central to the concept of punishment in the afterlife is that of the purgatorial fire (the *ignis purgatorius* of Bede and Alcuin) and the Fire of Doom. Fursa in his vision sees four penal fires which join together in one great conflagration (H.E. III 19). This is explained to him by the angel: as everyone burns through unlawful desire, so afterwards, when released from the body he burns through the punishment he has incurred. In the Vision of the Monk of Wenlock (c. 717) the visionary saw pits belching forth flame, on the edges of which human souls in the shape of birds hung for a little and then fell into the depths. According to an OE sermon of about 1009 lighter sins are punished in the 'penal fire' (W. Soames, Doctrine of the Anglo-Saxon Church, p. 360). 'The Anglo-Saxon Church' writes St John D. Seymour (Irish Visions of the Other-World, London 1930, p. 53) 'held the belief that the fire of Doom had purgatorial efficacy. . . . According to a homily quoted by Soames (op. cit., p. 351) *all* men must pass through the Fire of Doom. With this agrees a twelfth century homily, which makes a two-fold division of the human race at the Doom, and says then that all believing men shall be cleansed by the Fire from their sins. . . . On the other hand, Ælfric clearly held that the righteous would not suffer at all, but that only those who were uncleansed should "eat the fire's breath".' Cf. Ælfric, Hom. I 616, of the end of the world: *forðan ðe heofonlic fyr ofergæð ealne middangeard mid anum bryne, and ða deadan arisað of heora byrgenum mid ðam fyre, and ða lybbendan beoð acwealde þurh ðæs fyres hætan, . . . Ne derað þæt fyr nán ðing þam rihtwisum, ðe ǽr fram synnum geclænsode wæron; ac swa hwá swa ungeclænsod bið, he gefret þæs fyres ǽðm* 'for heavenly fire will pass over all the world with one burning, and the dead will arise from their graves with that fire, and the living will be slain by the fire's heat. . . . The fire will in no wise injure the righteous who had before been cleansed from sins; but whoever is uncleansed shall eat the fire's breath'. Cf. also II 588 ff., of men's works: *Godes dæg hí geswutelað, forðan ðe hé bið on fyre æteowod, and þæt fýr afándað hwilc heora ælces weorc bið* 'God's day shall manifest them, because it shall be shown by fire, and the fire shall try of what sort the work of each of them is'; Ælfric distinguishes the 'penal fire' (cf. pp. 590, 592 *on þam witnigendlicum fyre*) from the eternal fire (p. 592 *to þam ecan fyre*) and refers to 'many penal places' where men suffer for their sins before the universal doom.

The motif of penal fire is a commonplace in early Ir. Vision literature, as for instance in FA, the *Vision of Adamnan* (LU 27a–31b; cf. C. S. Boswell, An Irish Precursor of Dante, London 1908; Seymour, op. cit., Chapters I, II). In FA it takes many forms: a river of fire before the second door of Heaven to purge the souls of the righteous, while the wicked are scourged with fiery scourges; also in the description of Heaven a fiery furnace, stream, wall and river to torment the wicked (LU 2089–2123); Hell (LU 2144 ff.) is represented as a fire-scorched land on the further side of which is a fiery glen; persons in chains of fire are fettered to fiery pillars in a sea of fire; others are beaten by demons with fiery clubs while showers of fire rain upon them; some have streams of fire in the hollows of their faces, while others have fiery spikes through their tongues or heads; others are set on islands in the middle of the fiery sea; another throng is clad in red fiery cloaks and wear red glowing chains about their necks; others on fiery flag-stones are tormented by showers of red-hot arrows. Beyond the land of torment is a fiery wall (*múr tened*) which is in the possession of demons till Doomsday. Cf. also the descriptions of Hell in the *Vision of Laisrén*, the *Transitus Mariae*, and *Im. Ua C.* (Seymour, op. cit., Ch. I). The Monk of Wenlock also tells of a wall of fire beyond the Land of Pain; while the *Amra Choluim Chille* composed apparently shortly after AD 597[1] contains the invocation (4) *Dia mor mo anacol de mur teintide, diuderc dér* which may be tentatively translated 'Great God to save me from the fiery wall, the long-lasting pit of tears' (cf. ZCP 28, 243).

The occurrence side by side of the n. a-stem *tintreg* (by metathesis North. *tinterg*) and the masc. n-stem *tinterga* is not explained by the like alternance in personal substantives such as *þéow*/*þéowa*, *mǽg*/*mága*. The variation may be rather due to vacillation in treating borrowed forms. -*trega* appears to be identical with *trega* 'pain, grief, affliction': Goth. *trigō*, O. Sax. *trego*, O. Icel. *tregi*. *Tintrega* then corresponds to *hell-trega* ('Hell-torment' Cd. 4; Th. 5, 18; Gen. 73 (cf. B.T. s.v.)) and *tin-* to *hell-*. *Tin-* is best explained from O. Ir. *tein, teine* 'fire'. The original meaning of *tintrega* is then 'the affliction of fire', with reference to 'penal fire', 'hell's fire', cf. the OE and Irish material cited above.

As *tintrega* appears to represent an adaptation to OE *trega*, it seems likely that *tintreg* from a derivative of Ir. *teine* 'fire' is the prior form. Cf. Early Ir. *teint(r)ech*, gen. *teint(r)ighe*, dat., acc. *teint(r)igh* 'lightning, flashes, sparks': *tinntech taibhsec tromnertmur ag techt a hifern* 'bright (great) and very powerful lightning coming from hell' Études Celt. i 86. 28 (this is coupled in the text with a reference to flames); in Mod. W. Kerry Irish the word means 'great fire, conflagration'. Closely allied to this word is the adj. and subst. *tein(n)tide* (also derived from *teine*) 'fiery; the torrid zone': *múr teintide* 'the fiery wall (of Hell)'

---

[1] This, the oldest Irish poem extant, contains the prosodic feature *Dúnad* (cf. Appendix 2c): § 6 (after the Invocation): § 145 (cf. RC 20 (1899), 30 ff., 132 ff., 248 ff., 400 ff.).

ACC 4, quoted above; *sornd tentide* 'the fiery furnace' LU 2101 (FA 17). In the description of Hell in FA (see above) it is said that red showers of fire (*frassa derga tentide* LU 2185) rain on the tormented ones every day and night, which they must endure for ever.

It appears therefore that in any analysis of OE *tintreg, tintrega* we have to do with Early Ir. *tein, teine* 'fire' or with a derivative of *teine*.

CHAPTER XII

THE ORIGIN OF *CÆDMON'S HYMN*

Bede in H. E. iv. 24 tells us that Cædmon, having by God's grace miraculously acquired the gift of song in a dream, made poetical paraphrases of Scriptural matter previously interpreted to him, verses by which 'the minds of many were often excited to despise the world and to aspire to the heavenly life'. Bede then recounts the circumstances of the dream and gives a Latin paraphrase of the inspired Hymn of Cædmon, the only poem which can with certainty be attributed to this poet. The circumstances of its composition, given in detail, establish that it was composed orally by an unlettered poet in a learned milieu. It is the earliest OE exemplar of the traditional formulaic style and it forms a prelude to the development of OE religious verse. Cf. F. P. Magoun, Bede's Story of Cædman, Speculum 30 (1955), 49–63.

The poem was clearly revered and popular in the OE period as it has survived in no fewer than seventeen MSS. of the H.E.[1] Four of these (M, L, Di, P₁) in the Latin text of the H. E. represent the Northumbrian version of the *Hymn*, M and L dated 737 and 746 respectively being the earliest copies extant. Five MSS give the West Saxon version in the text of the Alfredian translation and eight copies give the West Saxon version in MSS. of the Latin text. The most pervasive criterion for grouping the MSS. is offered in 5b where Bede's *filiis hominum* is rendered in one set by Northumbrian *aelda barnum*, (West Saxon *ylda bearnum*) 'for children of men' and in the other by *eordu* (W. S. *eorðan*) *bearnum* 'for children of earth'. The 'children of men' version is represented by M and L and is followed in six of the eight W.S. copies of the Latin text. The 'children of earth' version is found in the (North.) Dijon (12c.) and Paris (15c.) MSS., in the five Alfredian MSS. of the OE translation, and in two of the W.S. Latin group: the

---

[1] Cf. A. H. Smith, Three Northumbrian Poems, London 1933, pp. 1 ff.; E. Van Kirk Dobbie, The Manuscripts of Cædmon's Hymn and Bede's Death Song, N.Y. 1937; O. S. Anderson, The Leningrad Manuscript of Bede, London 1941; Dobbie, The Anglo-Saxon Minor Poems, London 1942, pp. xciv ff.

12c. Hereford Cathedral and Bodley Laud MSS. The tally then is 8:9 in favour of the 'children of earth' reading.

The Alfredian version renders Bede's *cantare* by *be hearpan singan* and his *surgebat a media cena* by *aras he for scome* 'he arose for shame', thus adding a motive and implying perhaps an independent source of knowledge about Cædmon. Moreover it claims to give *þa fers ond þa word* in their proper order (*ende-byrdnes*) where Bede's Latin paraphrase renders the 'sensus, non autem ordo ipse verborum' a procedure defended by Bede on the grounds that poetry cannot be translated faithfully without losing much of its beauty and loftiness. The Alfredian translator edits Bede's Latin text at this point and it is clear that his version is an authentic representative of Cædmon's original poem. For evidence of the Alfredian Tradition of Cædmon cf. C. L. Wrenn, The Poetry of Cædmon, Procc. of the Brit. Acad. 32, p. 280 ff. (1946). That the five Alfredian copies show the reading *eorðan bearnum* (which goes back to a North. version with *eordu b.*) offers some grounds for believing that this may be the original authentic version. On the other hand this reading is not supported in OE or Germanic, is in fact unexampled outside the *Hymn,* whereas the formula *aelda barnum* occurs frequently in OE and in other Germanic languages (Dobbie, op. cit., p. 48).

The name Cædmon, mod. E. Chadman, Cadman, can be derived from earlier Celtic, cf. Gaul. *Catumandos,* O. Brit. *Catumannos,* O.W. *Cadman,* Mod. W. *Cadfan.* Then too the poet himself was obviously of very humble origin. Hence it is not surprising that efforts have been made to relate the *Hymn* to Celtic tradition. A further factor tending in this direction is the apocalyptic origin of Cædmon's muse. G. Sarrazin compares the Hymn with the Old Ir. *Ninine's Prayer* (Thes. II, p. 322), but the two poems have nothing at all in common save a vague resemblance in theme and form. E. Sievers[1] on the basis of tests in *Schallanalyse* found that the *Hymn* had the type of voice and *Personalkurve* (III) characteristic of the Celts, and that fifty-four lines of the first part of *Genesis* A had them likewise and must be attributed to Cædmon. As the techniques of *Schallanalyse* have been assimilated and developed by few,[2] these statements of Sievers remain cryptic and unproven.

Let us now consider the form of the Hymn as it is found in the earliest Northumbrian Version (M):

[1] *Cædmon und Genesis, Britannica, Festschrift für Max Förster,* Leipzig 1929, p. 72 f.
[2] Cf. Wellek-Warren, op. cit., pp. 163, 296.

Nu scylun hergan hefaenricaes uard
metudæs maecti end his modgidanc
uerc uuldurfadur sue he uundra gihuaes
eci dryctin or astelidæ
5 he aerist scop aelda barnū
heben til hrofe haleg scepen.
tha middungeard moncynnæs uard
eci dryctin æfter tiadæ
firum fold^v frea allmectig
primo cantauit caedmon istud carmen.

'Now should we praise the guardian of heaven's kingdom, the might of the Creator and the thought of his mind, the works of the Father of Glory: how the eternal Lord set a beginning for everything wondrous. The holy Creator first made heaven as a roof for the children of men; then the Guardian of mankind, Eternal Lord, Almighty Ruler, made the earth for men'.

The metre employed is the alliterative long line with free syntactic grouping of these. The verses tend to have a minimum number of syllables and to approach the syllabic norm: 10 of the 18 verses have 4 syllables each, 7 have 5 syllables each and the remaining one has 6. The distribution of types follows a clear symmetrical pattern: the first five verses with five syllables each are followed by the unique 3b with six; the next six verses have predominantly four syllables each punctuated by two with five; the final six verses have four syllables each. The unique 3b with six syllables, merges into the opening group with five if we apply to *gihuaes* the weakening of *ge-* established for Late Old North. The tendency to syllabic structure is characteristic also of Edda poetry in general, where it shows Irish influence at work through the newly-acquired syllabic manner of the skalds (cf. A. Heusler, Die Altgermanische Dichtung, pp. 126, 35).

The language is formulaic and unlike that of prose. It is characterized by compounds and by variation: chiefly of the designation of God, which is varied eight times in nine lines.

Hefaenrice (1b) 'kingdom of Heaven' with parallels in O. Norse and W. Gmc is explained as a loan translation of *regnum coeli*. O. Ir. has the comparable forms *nimiath* 'heaven-land', *nime flatha* 'of Heaven's kingdom', and *flaith nime* 'kingdom of Heaven'. *Hefaenricaes Uard* 'Guardian of Heaven' may be based on a Latin use of *custos* or *defensor* (JEGP 8, pp. 415, 375). Beside it may be placed O. Ir. *coimmdiu na flatha* (Fél. Ep. 415) 'Lord of the realm' and *coimmdiu secht nime* (Fel. Prol. 2) 'Lord of seven heavens', also several other Ir. collocations with variable *rí, ruiri, flaithem, fíadu,* 'king, ruler' + *nime* 'of Heaven'.

Metud (2a) 'Creator' is paralleled in O. Norse and O. Sax. O. Ir. has two formations on the same root (*med-* 'measure'): *Coim(m)diu* 'Lord, God' and *Mider* 'lord of the *síd* (otherworld)'. *Modgidanc* (2b) is found only in OE, but the variant *modgeþoht* occurs in Gen. B (cf. Heliand *môdgithâht*). *Wuldorfæder* (3a) occurs in OE only and may be based on a Lat. collocation such as *pater perennis gloriae* (JEGP 8, 385). *Eci dryhten* (4a, 8a) may reflect Lat. *aeternus dominus, rex sempiternus*. . . . It may correspond to an O. Ir. *bithflaith* recorded in the meaning 'eternal Kingdom' and capable of the meaning 'eternal King'.

Middungeard (7a) reflects an original Gmc compound; *mancynn* (7b) occurs in *Beowulf* and is shared by other West Gmc languages and by Norse; Lat. *genus humanum* seems a less likely source for it (C. T. Carr, Nominal Compounds in Germanic, London 1939, p. 50). *Eallmihtig* (9b) has parallels in West Gmc languages and in O.N. but may be a loan-translation of *omnipotens* (Carr, p. 92). Rankin (JEGP 8, 414) believes that *frea aelmihtig* is a calque on Latin kennings with *dominus, deus* and the like.

It will appear from the foregoing that the influence of Latin compounds and phraseology is paramount for the language of the *Hymn* and that some of its terms may reflect Old Irish usage.

Beside the *Hymn* may be placed the following anonymous Irish poem (stanza) published by G. Murphy, EIL, p. 4, under the title *Lord of Creation* (LC):

Adram in Coimdid	Let us adore the Lord,
cusnaib aicdib amraib,	Maker of wondrous works,
nem gelmár co n-ainglib,	Great bright Heaven with its angels,
ler tonnbán for talmain.	The white-waved sea on earth.

Variae lectiones (from the fifteenth century Book of Ballymote (B) 303 a 5, and the fifteenth century Laud (L) 610 f. 90r, col. 2, line 27 ff.:

a. Adram L., Adraimm B.   b. cusnab aicdib L., cus nahaicdib B.
c. gelmar LB.   d. ler tondban L., leartonn ban B.

The metre is *breccbairdne* ($5^2\ 6^2\ 6^2\ 6^2$) in which the final words of b, d rhyme, and all the final words consonate, cf. G. Murphy, Early Irish Metrics, Dublin 1961, p. 64. Note also the alliteration linking b with a, and d with c; the sequence -(*a*)*ib* in b, c; and the rime between c (*nem gelmár*) and d (*ler tonnbán*).

THE ORIGIN OF *CÆDMON'S HYMN*

The *Hymn* and LC have the following points of similarity: a) An almost identical opening (Let us adore/praise the Lord): LC 1: *Hymn* 1–2; b) An identical sequence of topics: LC 2: *Hymn* 3–4 (the work(s) of creation); LC 3: *Hymn* 5–6 (Heaven); LC 4: *Hymn* 7–9 (world). LC 4 contains a reference to the sea not found in the *Hymn;* against this it may be conceded that *middungeard* 'middle-earth, world, earth' can involve the surrounding sea (ON *úthaf*) which we find in the early ON conception of *miðgarðr*. In any case, the sea is generally included in OE references to the creation with which we deal below.

The *Hymn* is characterized by parallelism and variation absent in LC, which accounts for the difference in treatment and length of the two poems. We have now to consider whether the similarity detailed above may not be due to independent treatment of a common biblical theme. As Klaeber points out (Anglia 35, 113) the *Song of Creation* in Beowulf 90–98 is closely based on *Gen.* I and is very far removed from the treatment of the *Hymn;* but it does include the reference to the sea (cf. 92–93 *eorðan worhte,/wlitebeorhtne wang, swā wæter bebūgeð*). This is also included in the OE *Gen.* passage, lines 112 ff., the first section of which (112–116a) is so close in form to lines 5–9 of the *Hymn* as to suggest a direct connection between them. Sievers (op. cit., pp. 72–73) refers to the possibility of imitation by the *Genesis* poet. Klaeber points out (op. cit., 113) that the references to the creation in OE poetry are of the incidental, passing variety and include the topics heaven, earth and sea, cf. Ps. 145. 6; so for instance *Gen.* 97 ff., *El.* 727 ff., *Jul.* 111 ff., *Andr.* 747 ff. . . . None of these instances shares with the *Hymn* the formal similarity or the thematic sequence as LC does; more importantly, none is a poetic unit in an almost identical spirit as LC is. Again, while Ps. 135. 4–6 is thematically parallel to both poems, the general tone of the sequence (4–9) is that of a litany.

The *Hymn* and LC appear then to be directly related to each other. On the evidence of Bede, Cædmon's *Hymn* was composed between 660 and 680, while its earliest recorded OE versions date from 737 (M) and 746 (L). LC is assigned by G. Murphy to the ninth century (EIL, p. 174). In his Early Irish Metrics (Dublin 1961) p.v, he considers that stanzas (such as LC) common to treatises I and II of his main source (Thurneysen's *Mittelirische Verslehren*, IT iii (1891) 1–182) are 'at least as old as the ninth century', which he obviously takes as a norm. The language of LC is characteristically Old Irish (700–900) and shows no signs of lateness. The absence of nasalization after the neuter

213

s-stem *nem* in line c could be interpreted as an archaic feature: such neuters nasalize by analogy with the o-/n- stem-classes already in Wb. (c. 750), though here the mutation is not consistently shown between consonants, cf. Thurneysen ZCP 5, p. 8; Grammar p. 148. In Ml. it is regularly shown. On the metrical side the rise of the new syllabic metres to which that of L C belongs is placed roughly in the seventh century (Early Irish Metrics, p. 12). To sum up: it would appear possible to assign the extant version of L C to the early eighth century, thus antedating the earliest O E copies of the *Hymn*. The case for an earlier date of composition for L C to antedate an O E version extant before 700 remains open.[1]

The other possibility is that L C derives from the *Hymn*. In favour of this is the fact that most of Bede's works were known in Ireland soon after they appeared (cf. Kenney, Sources, I 230 ff.), and that an O. Ir. epitome of the H.E. is extant. In this case the Latin version of the *Hymn*—or an O E version transmitted in Northumbria or in Ireland—would have given rise to L C. This however runs counter to the main stream of cultural borrowing and religious influence between Ireland and Britain. A more closely relevant point is that L C with its tightly knit structure has much more the tone of an original and spontaneous utterance than the *Hymn*. Besides, it is much more plausible to derive the *Hymn* by elaboration from the Irish stanza than this by contraction from the other.

Professor Wrenn supports the view that the unique *eordu bearnum* reading of the Dijon and Paris MSS. which go back to a North. version, followed by the five Alfredian MSS. (with *eorðan bearnum*), is the original one, (op. cit., p. 283 ff.). Old Ir. offers a model for this, cf. the triadic collocation *na teora muntera .i. munter nime 7 talman 7 ifirn* 'the three households, i.e. the household of heaven and (that) of earth and (that) of hell' Trip. 118. 19; of earth as opposed to heaven cf. Wb. 26d5 *eter muntir nime et talman* 'between the household of heaven and (that) of earth'. *Muinter* 'community' serves here as plural to *fer* 'man' which we find in the corresponding collocations *fer nime* lit. man of heaven 'a religious, cleric, one bound for heaven, an inhabitant of Heaven,' *fer talman* 'man of earth', *fer ifirn* 'man of hell'. (*Imr. Snédg.* § 60 contains the three terms). Closely allied to these are collocations with *mac* 'son', figuratively: 'one involved with': Wb. 33b8 *maic raith* 'sons of grace', *maicc tairngiri* 'sons of (the) promise', *macc lére*

---

[1] Cp. *Ultan's Hymn* (Thes. II 325–6) which is related to ours in subject, tone, and metre (cf. Murphy, op. cit., §§ 59, 61, 34); the edd. place it in the seventh century.

'son of piety', *mac báis* 'son of death' i.e. a wicked man, *mac bethad* 'a son of life' i.e. a religious man. . . .

In her *Poetry and Prophecy* (Cambridge 1942, pp. 4 ff.) Mrs Chadwick points to the currency of poetry of prophetic inspiration in seventh century Ireland and Wales (cf. also Growth of Lit. I 468 ff.) and to the absence of the claim of divine inspiration in OE records after Cædmon. Her suggestion that 'Cædmon was the end of the Celtic rather than the beginning of the Saxon tradition' in this context derives added significance from the occurrence of an O. Ir. poem with unique resemblance to the *Hymn* and for which it may have served as exemplar.

CHAPTER XIII

THE OPENING OF THE
FINNSBURG FRAGMENT

Lines 1–5.   ... *(hor)nas byrnað.'*
(H)næf hleoþrode ða heaþogeong cyning:
'*Ne ðis ne dagað eastan, ne her draca ne fleogeð,*
ne her ðisse healle hornas ne byrnað;
ac her forþ berað, fugelas singað, ...

'. . . Gables are burning!' Then spake Hnæf, the king young in war—
'This is no dawning from the east, nor here does any dragon fly, nor
here do this hall's gables burn, but hither they bear forth (weapons),
the birds (of battle) sing, . . .' (Clark Hall's translation of Klaeber's
text.)

The text suggests the following situation: a watcher comes in and
reports to King Hnæf that he has seen something in the nature of a
gleam, or light. He mentions burning gables (line 1), and in view of
Hnæf's reply(line 4), this seems to be a conjecture on the source of
the light. It appears most likely that in line 3 Hnæf is turning down
other suggestions already made by the watcher.[1] Hnæf then goes on
to point out that the signs in question are those of an approaching
enemy, and he does so in highly poetic language (lines 5–8).

This opening shows two related stylistic features, one dramatic,
and the other rhetorical: the watcher-reporter motif, and the device
of alternative explanations of some unusual phenomenon followed by
the true interpretation. The fact that there *is* a watcher is of course
entirely in context; —that, however, another has to interpret what he
is made to see vaguely shows the intervention of art—or artifice.

Both of these devices, so well blended in *Finnsburg,* may be said to
be a feature of Middle Irish story-telling. Of the watcher-reporter
motif, Thurneysen (Heldensage, 61) says: 'Wie ein Erzähler so dem
anderen seinen Stil ablauscht, so entlehnt er ihm auch seine Motive, so
dass manche stereotyp werden. Ich möchte nur eines hervorheben.

---

[1] Cf. E. van Kirk Dobbie, The Anglo-Saxon Minor Poems, London, 1942, p. xvi.
That these suggestions were in question form is not assured.

In den längeren Sagen fehlt fast nie das Motiv, dass ein Späher oder Bote die nahenden Feinde oder einen heranfahrenden Krieger beschreibt, ohne ihn selber zu kennen. Aus seinem Bericht erkennt dann ein Kundiger, wer der Beschriebene ist, und nennt ihn mit Namen. Wohl am originellsten ist dieser übliche Sagenbestandteil einmal im 'Wegtreiben der Rinder von Cuailnge' (Teil II Kap. 6 § 70) ausgestaltet: der Arzt Fingin erkennt an jeder einzelnen Wunde Cetherns, ob ein Mann oder eine Frau oder mehrere sie ihm beigebracht haben; Cethern beschreibt dann jeweils die, die ihn verwundet haben, und CūChulainn kann sie danach bestimmen und nennen. Solche Schilderungen und Erkennungen schienen so unentbehrlich, dass z. B. beide Fassungen der Bearbeitung des Trojanerkriegs (Dares Phrygius) einen solchen Teil einschieben, obschon er ihrer Quelle fehlt. Aber weit über Irlands Grenzen hinaus hat man gerade an diesen Stücken Gefallen gefunden. Man trifft Nachahmungen in der kymrischen Erzählung von Branwen (The Text of the Mabinogion, ed. Rhys and Evans, S. 35 f., bei Loth, Les Mabinogion I², 137 f.) und in der isländischen Laxdæla Saga, Kap. 63 (in Meissners Übersetzung, Thule, Bd. VI, S. 191 ff.).' Cf. also J. Carney, Studies in Irish Literature and History, Dublin, 1955, 305–321: The 'Watchman Device'.

The *Laxdæla* passage, in which Helgi recognizes the members of a hostile party from his shepherd's description of them, may be compared particularly with *Fled Bricrend* (LU 8585 ff.)[1] A similar situation is found in *Mesca Ulad* (ed. J. Carmichael Watson, Dublin, 1941) lines 527 ff. Here the device is rather highly formalized and the description of the strange warriors long drawn-out. A simpler—though rhetorical—watcher's description is found in *Tochmarc Emere* (LU 10192 ff.), and a brief but colourful one in *Táin Bó Fraích* (edd. M. E. Byrne and M. Dillon, Dublin, 1933), § 4.

The rhetorical device of alternative explanations may be illustrated from the Middle Ir. tale *Togail Bruidne Da Derga,* (ed. E. Knott, Dublin, 1936), paragraphs 54–56, where it occurs twice:

> *In tan ro ngabsat na curaig tír, is and robuí Mac Cécht oc béim tened im Bruidin Dá Derga. La fúaim na sbréde fo-cesa na trí choectu curach co mbátar for formnu na fairrge.*
> *Tá chéin, for Ingcél. Samailte² latsu, a Fir Rogain.*

---

[1] LU = Lebor na Huidre (c. 1100, with later, probably thirteenth century interpolations), edd. R. I. Best & O. Bergin, Dublin, 1929.

[2] *Samailte,* 2. sg. Imperative of *samlaithir* 'compares, likens, . . . assesses . . .' < *samail* 'likeness, similarity . . .', implies identification by comparison, which is the essence

THE EARLY ENGLISH AND CELTIC LYRIC

*Ní fetursa, ol Fer Rogain, manid Luchton Cáinti fail indi innEmain
Machae do-gní in bosorcuine seo oc gait a bíd aire ar éigin, nó gréch ind
Luchduind hi Temair Lúachrae nó béim spréde Meic Cécht oc atúd tened
ría ríg Hérenn airm hi foí . . .*

(55.) *Tos-cuirithir dochum thíri. A ngloim ro lásat na trí. lll. curach oc
tuidecht i tír for-rochrad Bruidean Dá Dergae coná roibe gaí for ailching
inte acht ro láiseat grith co mbátar for lár in tigi uili.*

(56.) *Samailte lat, a Chonaire, cía fúaim so?*

*Ním-thása a samuil, manid talam imid-rae nó manid in Leuidan
timchela in domuin ad-comaicc a erball do thochur in beatha tar a cheann
nó bárc mac Duind Désa ro gab tír . . .*

'As the curraghs landed, Mac Cécht was striking fire in Bruiden Dá
Derga. With the noise of the spark the thrice fifty curraghs were carried
away to the open sea. "Hush!", said Ingcél, "identify that, Fer Rogain".
"I do not know", said Fer Rogain, "unless it is Luchton Cáinti in
Emain Macha striking his hands together because his food is being
taken from him, or the scream of Luchdond in Temair Lóchra,—or
Mac Cécht striking fire for the king of Ireland where he is spending
the night . . ." '

(55.) They put to land (once more). The noise of the thrice fifty
curraghs landing so shook the hall of Da Derga that every spear
clattered down from the rack on to the floor below.

(56.) 'Tell what sound this is, Conaire'.

'I cannot tell, unless it is the earth that has turned round, or the
Leviathan which encircles the earth that has struck with his tail to
overturn the world,—or the boat of the sons of Donn Désa that has
landed'.

The Irish version of the device is characteristically different from the
Finnsburg: it is more subtle and delicate: the third suggestion is
correlative with the other two and contains the solution, while in
Finnsburg three tentative suggestions are squarely rejected and the
solution follows. Unfortunately, we cannot know the form in which
the watcher put his suggestions originally.

Entirely parallel to the *Finnsburg* blending of dramatic and rhetorical
device is the passage in lines 362 ff. of *Mesca Ulad: Is and bar-ecmaing
dóib sin bith ar múr Temra Lúachra in tan sin ic fégad 7 ic forcomét, ic*

of our rhetorical device. Cf. *cuire samla fair* lit. put (a) likeness upon it 'describe it' LU
8587 (*samla*, jā-stem, from *samail*). Clearly, therefore, the device — reminiscent of
Eastern thinking — is at home in Irish.

218

midem 7 ic mórdéscin for cach leth úathu. Is and sin at-bert Crom Deróil,
'Innat-árfaid in ní tárfaid damsa?'
'Cid ní?' ar Crom Darail.
'Atar lim at ruibni rúadgascid 7 ám hám sochaide at-chíu dar leittrib na
hAirlúachra anair'.
'Nírb uráil lim lom cró 7 fola issin mbél tacras sin', ar Crom Darail;
'úair ní slúag ná sochaide sin acht na daire romóra secha táncamar indé'.

'It befell them (the two druids) at that time to be holding watch and
ward ... on the wall of Temair Lóchra. Then said Crom Deróil "Have
you see what I have seen?". "What's that?", asked Crom Darail.
"Methinks I see well-armed hosts . . . coming westward across the
slopes of Airluachra". "I should not think it excessive that there should
be a gush of gore and blood in the mouth that asserts that", said Crom
Darail; "for that is not a company or a host but the great oak-groves
which we passed yesterday".'

The sequel here too is notably like *Finnsburg*. Crom Darail thinks the
chariots are royal dwellings, the shields stone pillars of the dwellings,
the spear-points antlers of deer . . . and the sods from the horses'
hooves birds . . . But Crom Deróil expresses his conviction in two
poems that what he sees is really armed men. The beginning of the
second poem runs: 'O Crom Darail, what do I see through the mist?
On whom is the omen of slaughter in the fight? . . .' The chieftain
CúRoí hears the druids' dispute; and then the sun rises and reveals the
troop of which Crom Deróil had spoken. Similarly in *Finnsburg* (7–9)
the moon lights up the scene and the enemy is revealed. Cf. *nu arisað
weadæda, ðe ðisne folces nið fremman willað* 'now begin evil deeds,
which will further this enmity of the people' (8–9). Farther on in
Mesca Ulad Medb asks Crom Deróil (line 512): *'Canas tánic int
armgrith dar-fánic, inn a haéor anúas no in dar muir aníar no inn a
Hérind anair?'* 'Whence has this clangour of weapons come to us,
down from above, or from the sea to the west, or from the east of
Ireland?' Here again the third suggestion is the appropriate one.

The Ulstermen are entertained and then attacked in a house of oak
(according to the earlier recension) or in an iron house which is set on
fire by their hosts (later recension).[1] However, they rout the enemy
in the ensuing battle and return to Ulster. Cp. with this the outcome
of the *Finnsburg* attack as revealed in *Beowulf* 1071–1159.

An example common to the two chief versions occurs in the *Táin
Bó Cúailnge*, a 7th–11th century production (LU 4488–4501):

[1] Cf. Thurneysen, Heldensage, p. 481.

Trí luirg dī do Chormac oc tochím do Crúachnaib. In cetna lorg broitt brecca i forcipul co filliud impu. Fortíi bértha foraib. léini fo thairinniuth cota ṅglun ⁊ fotalscéith foraib ⁊ manais lethanglas for crúnd midšing i lláim cech fir.

In lorg tánaisi broit dubglasa impuside ⁊ lénti co ndercintliud co horcnib sís ⁊ moṅga tara cenna síar ⁊ lubne gela foraib ⁊ slega cóicrinné inna lamaib. Ni hé Cormac beus or Médb.

Tic in tres lórc dano broitt chorcra ímpu ⁊ lénte culpatacha fo dérggintšlaid co traigthe ⁊ berthai slechtai co guaille ⁊ crómscéith co faebraib condúala ímpu ⁊ turre rígthige i llaim cach fir. is é Cormac inso hifechtsa or Medb. 'Cormac's force marched in three battalions to Cruachain. The first battalion wore speckled cloaks pleated and folded, short hair, and tunics to the knee. They had long shields, and each man had a broad, grey, slender-shafted spear in his hand.

The second battalion wore dark-grey cloaks, and red-embroidered tunics reaching to their calves, and (longer) hair which flowed backwards. They wore bright shields, and had five-pronged spears in their hands. 'It still is not Cormac', said Medb.

Then the third battalion appeared in purple cloaks and hooded, red-embroidered tunics reaching to the feet. Their hair reached to the shoulder. They had bent shields with embroidered edges, and each man had a 'pillar of a palace' (i.e. 'a splendid spear') in his hand. 'This time it is Cormac', said Medb.'

The magnificent appearance of Cormac—who is known to the watcher, Queen Medb, but not to her companions—is conveyed suspensefully as being associable only with superlatives, and so with the third group. This scene, perhaps an early example, is finely conceived and executed and shows a very skilful use of the *watcher* and *alternatives* devices. These are found combined too in comparable passages in the *Vita Kentegerni*, in Eilhart von Oberge's version of *Tristan and Isolde*, and in a passage written by Notker in St. Gall towards the end of the ninth century (cf. Carney, op. cit., 308 f.).

The Ingcél of *Togail Bruidne Da Derga*, § 54 (supra), is almost certainly to be linked with the Hinieldus of Alcuin's letter (797) to Bishop Speratus of Lindisfarne, and to the Ingeld of *Beowulf* (2024 ff.) and of *Widsið* (48). The form *Ingcél* seems to be British, corresponding to Irish *Éiccel*.[1] In comparing the tale of Ingeld with the lay of Finn and Hengest in Beowulf, Prof. Wrenn (Beowulf, Introd. p. 74) writes 'Ingeld's renewed war with the Danes who are his guests at the

Cf. E. Knott, op. cit., Note 404.

marriage-feast parallels the attack made by Finn's men on Hnæf's followers in a hall where they too were guests'.—It parallels also the Briton Ingcél's slaughter of his own kinsfolk at a reception given by a local king, which in turn motivates the main action of the Irish tale: the slaughter of King Conaire in the hall of Da Derga by his own kinsmen assisted by Ingcél. It is doubtful whether the *Finnsburg* hall, like Heorot (cf. *Beowulf,* 81–85) was set on fire. In the Irish tale the hall was set on fire three times but each time the flames were extinguished. The popularity of the Ingeld story in the Anglo-Irish milieu of Northumbria attested by Alcuin's rebuke provides the key to one source of these correspondences.

The Irish tales *Mesca Ulad* and *Togail Bruidne Da Derga,* which we have cited in the first instance for their stylistic devices reminiscent of the opening of *Finnsburg,* but which are based too on a similar theme, derive from very old native traditions and may contain a nucleus of historical fact.[1] The language of *Mesca Ulad* belongs to the Old Irish period (before 900) though modernized in transmission,[2] while the transmitted version of *Togail Bruidne Da Derga* was compiled in the eleventh century from two versions of a floating tradition which were written down probably in the ninth century;[3] some of its forms are of the early eighth century.

The subject matter of *Finnsburg* is also very old, but Hickes's version of the lost MS. shows the language of about the middle of the eleventh century.[4] In view of this, and of the *Táin Bó Cúailnge* parallel, a stylistic influence from Irish story-telling seems likely. The Ingcél of *Togail Bruidne Da Derga,* meanwhile, points to a literary intercourse in which the Irish acquired new matter in return for the manner borrowed from them.[5]

---

[1] Cf. Watson, op. cit., p. xxxvi; Thurneysen, op. cit., p. 621; T. F. O'Rahilly, Early Irish History and Mythology, Dublin, 1946, p. 129.

[2] Cf. ed., p. xxxiiiff.

[3] Cf. ed., p. xi; Thurneysen, op. cit., p. 627.

[4] Cf. C. L. Wrenn, Beowulf, 1958, p. 229; Fr. Klaeber, Beowulf, 1950, p. 238.

[5] In a detailed comparison of the structure (and presentation) of *Beowulf* and of *Táin Bó Fraích* – including the coastguard episode (*Beowulf* 229ff.), which he compares with TBF § 4 – Carney (op. cit., 114 ff.) suggests that the early Irish tale was 'a small-scale model for *Beowulf*' (p. 121). The encounter between hero and legendary water monster is, however, an old and a widespread theme, of which TBF and the death tales of the two Ferguses (F. mac Roig and F. mac Léti) seem to be expanded versions (cf. ZCP 14, 304). *Echtra (Aided) Fergusa maic Léti,* known in the seventh century, offers in the two early recensions (of c.AD 700, and of the eleventh century respectively) a more striking parallel to Beowulf's encounters with the monsters than does TBF.

NOTES ON THE IRISH POEMS

I. *Uga Corbmaic Meic Cuilendain*

Metre: Duan Chenelach (Ir. Texte iii 144).[1] The final words of 5c and 10c do not consonate. There are 15 cases of *aicill* wanting in first couplets, 9 cases in second couplets and one defective *aicill, toir: mor* in 11c, d. The absent *aicill* is often compensated: by an internal rime as in the second couplet of stt. 17, 15, 20, 21; by profuse alliteration as in 14c, d; and by alliteration coupled with repetition as in stt. 2, 3. Stt. 22–23, 25–26, however, have each a first couplet in which the absent *aicill* is not compensated.

The poem seems to be late Old Ir. The meaning of *tarcuib* 24c is old, its form less so, cf. Contrr. sub *do·rogaib* 'transgresses'. The Old Ir. infixed pronouns are on the whole well preserved (5c *innamtairber* < *indam-*, 22c...); the old nom. *dál* in 19b is guaranteed by the rime with *slán*, 19d. Nasalization is shown after A. sg. and N. n. in 3c (*n-arm*), 6a, 19a (*ndian*), 14a (*ndur*)... O. Ir. final -o is retained in *maro* (5d, 7c, 26b), *bratho* 11b; elsewhere it interchanges with -a: 1c *mara mur*/7c *maro mur, rechta* 27b. Final -a for -ae in *cuingena* 9c, *sorcha* 19b, and for -ai in *bochta* 2a, *saorsa* 12a, are also O. Ir. In *aonta* 16c we have -a for old -u. The old superlative *moam* occurs in 22a.

Pretonic vowels sometimes have their O. Ir. forms. Cf. interrogative *in*, 1a, 2a, 5a, 6a, 7ac, 8c; *im* 9a, b; but *an* 8a, 9c. Forms of the art. vary too: *in*, 16d, 19a, 20c, d but *an* 18c, 22a, 27d. The prep. *i*^{n} occurs also in the form *a*^{n} (cp. 15b, 28d, 29b with 26d, 29c).

Later forms guaranteed by the metre are monosyllabic *ol* 3a; *coir* 5a, here riming with *moir*; in 27d riming with *toir*. Line 19a has metrically correct (denominative) *coicertuis* for O. Ir. *conacertuis* with its hypermetric syllable. But as early as Wb. 31b25 we find prototonic pass. pl. *coisctir*, beside deuterotonic sg. *consecht(h)ar*. In 6c we encounter the later 1. sg. fut. ending in -*at: in ferfat*. This type is rather common in *Saltair na Rann* (S.R.) but does not seem to occur in the *Vita Tripartita*. *Toigeb* of 8a (cf. Thurneysen, Gr., p. 526) is matched in the *Vita*. Here it rimes with *oicen* of 8b which appears in a late dress. The non-palatal *r* of *rag* in 8c and the palatal final -*b* of *tarcuib* 24c and *farguib* 24d are also paralleled in the *Vita*. Inorganic *f* of *romficfa* 11b and *domficibsa* 27c has parallels in the late Glosses. *Druing* of 3a seems to be an Acc. sg. form of the later fem. a-stem for the N. sg, which is paralleled

[1] Cf. Murphy's *rannaigecht dialtach cetharchubaid* (Early Ir. Metrics, p. 52): Ir. Texte iii 143.

APPENDIX I

in the *Vita* and common in S.R. The old neuter *lin* 'number' shows a change of gender in 26a, c as also in the *Vita*. *Frie* and *ria* occur in 5d, 19c and 24b for O. Ir. *fri*, *re*; *ar* in 15c, 18b, beside O. Ir. *for* in 1c, 7b, 8d, 24b, d. *Roell* of 18b is probably a M. Ir. form of *do·ella*. *Brogad* of 1c probably stands for original *mrogad* to alliterate with *mara* and *mur*. Kuno Meyer interpreted *maro ruaidh* of 5d as referring to the Red Sea, which as it is supported by the rime and occurs in a clearly original part of the poem would be a strong evidence of later composition: O. Ir. had *Muir Robur*; S.R. has *Muir Romor* and *Muir Romuir Ruad*; later this is superseded by *Muir Ruadh*. A reference to the Red Sea seems out of place in the context, so that this evidence falls away.

II. Colum Cille (L), Cormac mac Cuillionáin (N . . .) cecinit: *Mithidh damh-sa taireradh . . .*

Our second Ir. poem, associated with Cormac, as with the expatriate figure par excellence Colum Cille, is contained in Laud Misc. 615, p. 108, which seems to offer the oldest and most satisfying version; also in the Four Masters where it is entered under the year 926 and attributed to one Celedabhail, son of Scannal on departing on his pilgrimage to Rome from the abbacy of Bangor; in the (fifteenth century) Book of Lismore 95d16; and in 3 O'Longan MSS. of the eighteenth and nineteenth centuries in the R.I.A.: 23 N 3, F VI 1, and 23 H 24. The latter are incomplete, somewhat corrupt and belong to the same version. They have a certain amount in common with the Lism. version but are not copies of it.

This poem is written in the metre aí fhreisligi: heptasyllabic lines with rime between the trisyllabic finals of a, c and between the disyllabic finals of b, d. Imperfect rime is often found with this metre. *Taireradh* (L.) of 1a can represent O. Ir. *tairired* from *tair-shired*, or exceptionally *tairirith* with neutral final consonant in place of the old u-stem *taiririuth*. In this case the rime with *ailithir* is still imperfect on account of the quality of the final consonant.

The rimes are often perfect, however, as in 1b, d and throughout stanzas 2, 3 and 4: the finals of 2a, c *dualach : sualach* are trisyllabic. The finals of 3a, c can represent older *indládud*, probably 'pampering' (Ériu 19, 119): O. Ir. *imrádud* 'contemplating'. 3b, d rime in the O. Ir. forms *caire : Maire*; 4a, c represent the O. Ir. rimes *cairigiud : taiririuth*—FM has the latter form (footnote 11). The final -*i* in the riming finals of 5b, d represent O. Ir. final -*e*. The final word of 6a, *tarbhata*, (:*turbaid*) may represent *terbaidi*, compare Wb. 14d13 n.pl. *tirbithi* 'troubles' and S.R. 8319 acc.pl. *terbaide*. In this case it rimes passably with *ernaigthi* of 6c, allowing for the consonant cluster in this word. *Tiglaithi* of 7a and *idnaidi* of 7c show a rime between final -*i* and -*e*, which is a tenth century feature, *Comaísi* and *robhaísi* (9a, c) likewise.

Unstressed O. Ir. final -*a* appears in *mara* 1d, *colla* 3b, *flatha* 5d, *brátha* 7b. Final -*e* of *gnúise* in 7d represents O. Ir. final -*i*. O. Ir. -*ae* appears as -*a* in *cora*, 3d; O. Ir. -*u* as -*a* in *derna* 2b.

Other late forms are *colla* 3b, n.sg. *crí* 4b, *faichill* 7a, *theasta* with lenition 8b, *bud* without *ro* in an independent clause 8d, *do bud* 9d. Here F M and Lism. have modal *ba*(*mithigh*), a usage found as early as the Wb. glosses.

ON CELTIC-ENGLISH RELATIONS

(*a*) In an article on '*The Irish Substantival System*' in ZCP 28 (1960), 19–50, it was pointed out that the use of the verbal noun to represent a finite verb in the preterite, characteristic of Celtic, is found in Layamon's *Brut*. As this has a bearing on the case for Layamon's connections with Wales[1] and the wider Celtic background urged most recently by H. Pilch in his *Layamons 'Brut'* (Heidelberg 1960), and as it may have been overlooked, we reproduce the relevant section in slightly contracted form (ZCP 28, 29–30): 'A striking use of the Ir. verbal noun, namely, to represent a finite verb in the preterite is favoured by Irish annalists for narrative purposes, as I point out in my Preliminary Report, Lochlann I, p. 93 (Example: *Hua Brain Laighen do eg in bliadhain si* 'Ua B. of Leinster died this year') . . . In this respect Ir. is surpassed by Welsh, cf. I. Williams, Pedeir Keinc Y Mabinogi, Caerdydd, 1951, p. 1 (Pwyll) *A chanu y gorn a dechreu dygyuor yr hela, a cherdet yn ol y cwn, ac ymgolli a 'y gydymdeithon* 'and he sounded his horn and began to muster the hunt, and followed after the dogs and lost his companions'. Here the four E. finite verbs are rendered in W. by four verbal nouns. Of considerable interest in view of his Welsh connections is the fact that Layamon has this usage also, cf. Dickins and Wilson, *Early Middle English Texts*, Cambridge, 1951, p. 26:

> *Heuen here-marken, halden to-gadere,*
> *Luken sweord longe, leiden o þe helmen;*
> *Fur ut sprengen, speren brastlien . . .*

Elevated *their* standards; advanced together; drew *their* long swords, [and] smote on the helms; [*so that the*] fire out sprang; spears splintered; (F. Madden, Laʒamons Brut, London 1847, Vol. III, p. 141, verses 28546–28551).

Editors disagree about the verbal forms. O. F. Emerson, Middle English Reader, London, 1938, considers *heuen, sprengen, brastlien* to be presents, *luken* to be preterite and ignores *halden*. Dickins and Wilson agree about *luken* and they too ignore *halden*; they take *heuen* to be preterite and give *sprengen* a special entry as such also. *Brastlien* has a special entry as present plural and a meaning 'may clash'. *Fur* is entered with the meaning 'sparks'.

---

[1] Cf. R. S. Loomis, Arthurian Literature in the Middle Ages (Oxford 1959), Chap. 10: *Layamon's Brut.*, p. 105: 'Ironically, too, it (i.e. Layamon's poem) uses the language, the poetic form, and the style of the (English) people it disparages.'

Summing up, one must support Madden's view that *sprengen* and *brastlien* are infinitives. There are indeed a few cases (cited by Madden) of *heuen* or *hefuen* and somewhat more of *halden* (in our meaning) as pret. plurals in the Brut, but it is most likely that in our passage they are infinitives. *Luken* may be a pret. plural pairing off with *leiden*, or it may be an infinitive. The really significant point—coming into focus just here—is that pret. plural and infinitive can be functionally, as well as formally, identical.'

(*b*) In the course of an article entitled *Beowulf Cruces* (KZ 77 (1961), 140–159) the problematic *ealuscerwen* (Beowulf 769) is discussed in the context of *bitter mead*, and a solution put forward. A further important Welsh illustration of the theme is found in the *Hirlas Owain* of Prince Owain Cyfeiliog, who retired after a long rule over his kingdom of Powys to a Cistercian monastery where he died in 1197. *Hirlas* means 'long (and) blue' and refers to the buffalo-horn used for drinking mead at banquets. The poem, though comparatively late, harks back to the old poetry, particularly to the *Gododdin*, in vocabulary and phrases such as *they paid for their mead*. The scene is Owain's court at nightfall, where his battle-weary warriors have gathered round the banquet table by the 'light of tapers'. In a curt, sudden opening reminiscent of the old style, Owain 'calls on the cup-bearer, who is pouring out the drink, to pour drink for the heroes of the day, each in his turn. . . . Then he says a word in praise of the warrior's valour in the battle, and playfully threatens the cup-bearer if he does not give him the honour he deserves. . . . Then he remembers suddenly that not everybody in whose honour he bids mead be poured is still alive:

> Ochan Grist! mor wyf drist o'r anaelau,
> O goll Moreiddig, mawr ei eisiau.
> 'O Christ how sad I am for the sorrow
> Of Moreiddig's loss, so sorely needed.'

(cf. Parry-Bell, A History of Welsh Literature, Oxford 1955, pp. 63 ff.). For 'the wretched drink of death's deep cup' cf. *Guthlac* B, 982–991; for 'flame proffered for drink'[1] *Guthlac* A 623 f. For the symbolic ale (cup, goblet, drinking-horn) of sovereignty (KZ 77, p. 159, f.n. 2) and the investing goddess cf. further T. F. O'Rahilly, Ériu 14, p. 14 ff.; D. A. Binchy, Ériu 18, 134 f.; also SCano, Introd., xxvi.

(*c*) In *A Celtic-English Prosodic Feature* (ZCP 29 (1962), 91–99) the occurrence in Early English of the pervasive Celtic feature of closing a poem by reproducing or re-echoing its opening is noted and related to other Celtic connections in the Late Middle English period. It is found in the earliest Irish poetry, including *retoiric*. This kind of recapitulation recalls a

---

[1] MS 624b *lege biscencte:* emended by some edd. to *bisencte* (cf. Krapp-Dobbie, 265).

similar phenomenon in Early Greek literature known as *Ringkomposition*[1] (cf. W. A. A. Van Otterlo, *Untersuchungen über Begriff, Anwendung und Entstehung der Griechischen Ringkomposition*, Mededeelingen der Ned. Akad. v. Wet., Afd. Letterkunde, N. R. Deel 7, no. 3, Amsterdam 1944, pp. 131–176). By this is meant primarily the technique of 'framing' a section of a work by repeating in the final sentence of the section the theme which was stated in the opening words. This is one of the literary devices characteristic of the λέξις εἰρομένη (paratactic style) and its function is to knit into a formal pattern the sequence of disparate parts. To a discussion of paratactic style belongs also the technique of *Rahmenerzählung* as we see it in the History of Herodotus, where digressions are made to serve a central *leitmotiv* from which they spring and to which they return. A more developed and more complicated recapitulatory device than *Ringkomposition* is that known as *Ritornellkomposition* 'theme repetition' which seeks to sustain the main theme through a sequence of related parts, as in Iliad Verses 251–365 (op. cit., p. 162). Incidental to his discussion of this is Van Otterlo's point that verses 230 and 250 correspond, and this passage he describes as 'having a circular shape' (*ringförmig*) (op. cit., p. 161; Mnemosyne, 3. Series, 12 (1945), p. 193).

For the origin of our feature, then, in Early Celtic and English, Hebrew and Greek models (cf. Ml. gloss 26 b 10) are available in the first instance, while for Mod. English divers sources are possible. Its discussion belongs to a wide range of recapitulatory features covering many art-forms (e.g. rondeu (redoublé), rondel ... lyric ... novel ... heterogeneous types such as *Finnegans Wake*), and it may apply to content as well as to form. Its *function* will vary between certain limits from work to work and from epoch to epoch; so that the question of *distribution* in the narrower field with which we have been primarily concerned is but one of the many facets from which our feature can be studied. Where it is elevated to the status of poetic norm as in Early Ir., and to a less extent in Early Welsh, its significance for the individual poem is bound to diminish accordingly; in Mod. English on the other hand it is of sporadic occurrence, and here its function in the individual poem is a study which could yield interesting results.

[1] I am grateful to Dr Johannes Bechert of Munich for many references.

OLD IRISH POEMS ON THE TRANSITORINESS OF ROYAL GLORY

(Cf. p. 22 *supra*)

In her ed. of the *Seafarer*, pp. 15–20, I. L. Gordon points out that the elegiac contemplation of the empty hall in Beowulf 2247–66, 2444–62, and in the later lyrics has become stylized into conventional motifs; and she cites examples from the literature of Gaul in the fifth and sixth centuries. 'In some instances the poet may be describing a ruin at first hand, but the vogue of elegiac contemplation of ruins is likely to have literary authority. Moreover, the ruin theme in the Old Welsh elegies is always a part of the theme of exile, as it usually is in the Latin poems.' (p. 20).

The exile context is absent in three Old Irish poems on the transitoriness of royal glory. The first of these is unique of its kind: its subject, the Fort of Rathangan in Co. Kildare, is made the vehicle of a plaint on its former lords, the kings of the Ui Berraidi of Leccach, whom it has survived. Normalized edd. by K. Meyer (Bruch. 59) and G. Murphy (EIL xvi) from Rawl. B 502, 122 b 48, and LL, 314 b 29, q.v.:

Ind ráith i comair in dairḟedo,	The fort over against the oak-wood,
ba Bṛuidgi, ba Cathail,	it was Bruidge's, it was Cathal's,
ba hÁedo, ba hAilello,	it was Aed's, it was Ailill's,
ba Conaing, ba Cuilíni,	it was Conaing's, it was Cuilíne's,
ocus ba Máele Dúin.	and it was Maeldúin's.
Ind ráith d'éis cach ríg ar úair,	The fort remains after each king in turn,
ocus int ṡlúaig foait i n-úir.	and the hosts sleep in the ground.[1]

The poem stands mid-way between the old native tradition and the later syllabic verse. It is dominated by parallelism which unites corresponding members in a varied and pleasing rhythmical pattern, binding them by repetition rather than by alliteration; internal alliteration is confined to c, d. The finals of e–g, a–c are linked by rime, and that of f with the following

---

[1] Cf. *Cáine dind dem i foat ollomain*:/ *Alenn chruind, Crúachu, Temuir thōibglan* 'Fairest of hills is the shelter in which the warriors sleep: round Alenn, Cruachu, bright-sided Tara' (sixth or early seventh century, according to K. Meyer: Ält. Ir. Dicht. II 4, 20, Hail Brigit 8–9). Cf. also *is ūar in adba hi faat* 'cold is the dwelling in which they sleep', Otia Merseiana I 125. The metaphor also appears in the earliest Welsh poetry: cf. I. Williams, Canu Taliesin 12. 13–14 *kyscit lloegyr llydan nifer/a leuuer yn eu llygeit* 'sleeps now the wide host of the English with the light in their eyes' i.e. open-eyed in death.

line (*úair: slúaig*). This rime points to a date later than c. 750; (it is not found in LL, which reads: (g) na rig ronfoat inúir). An earlier rime *ar óir: int šlóig* is intrinsically possible, but only the collocation *ar úair* seems to be on record. This is consistent with the language of Wb. (c. 750, *úar* beside *hór* 'Lat. hora'), and an earlier date cannot be excluded. To the hosts sleeping in the ground (of g) compare Beowulf 2457–8(*The Father's Lament*) 'the riders sleep, the warriors in their graves', 2256–7 (*Lament of The Last Survivor*) 'the polishers sleep/who should prepare the war-helmet', *Wanderer* 76 ff. '. . . many a wall stands wind-beaten . . ./The guest-halls crumble; the masters lie/bereft of joy; the warrior-band has all fallen,/once so stately at the rampart . . ./Thus did the Creator of men lay waste this abode,/until, deprived of the noise of its inhabitants,/the ancient buildings of the giants stood empty . . .; *Ruin* 6 ff. 'The clutch of the grave,/the strong grip of the earth holds the master-builders,/who have lain in corruption until a hundred generations/of peoples have passed away. Often has this wall,/grey with lichen and mottled with red, endured one sovereignty after another . . .'

In two Old Irish poems of the syllabic tradition the transitoriness of royal glory is set off against the abiding fame of the saints whose monastic settlements have replaced the citadels of pagan prowess. The homiletic treatment of former glory is parallel to that of *Seafarer* 80 ff., and of *Wanderer* 60 ff., 73 ff., 88 ff., where the halls, walls, and ancient buildings find mention.

The poems in question are: the Prologue to the Martyrology of Oengus 'the Culdee' (*c.* AD 800; verses 1–340), especially the section 165–216 which includes a treatment of the theme in terms of Irish onomastics; and *Hail Brigit*, ed. K. Meyer, 1912, from about the same period, which as Meyer points out, looks like an amplification of the Prologue 189–192 (*infra*).

We select the following stanzas for illustration: *Hail Brigit* (LL 49 b 9 ff.; 26 stanzas; cp. Meyer's ed.):

I

Sit thou safely enthroned, triumphant Brigit,
upon the side of Liffey[1] far as the strand of the
    ebbing sea!
Thou art the sovereign lady with banded hosts[2]
that presides over the children of Catháir the Great.

2 (c, d)

. . . though glittering Liffey is thine today,
it has been the land of others in their turn.

---

[1] i.e. the Plain of the Liffey, which includes the Curragh and Kildare town.
[2] i.e. the monks and nuns of Kildare.

3

When from its side . . .
I gaze upon the fair Curragh,
the lot that has fallen to every king
causes awe at each wreck.

4

Loegaire was king as far as the sea,—
Ailill Áne, a mighty fate:
The Curragh with its glitter remains—
none of the kings remains that lived thereon.

7

Far-famed Alenn! delightful residence!
many a prince is under its sward:
it was greater than can be fathomed
when Crimthann the Victorious was seen in its
    bosom.

8

The shout of triumph heard there after each victory
around a shock of swords, a mettlesome mass;
the strength of its warrior-bands against the dark-
    blue battle-array;
the sound of its horns above hundreds of heads.

9

The tuneful ring of its even-coloured bent anvils,
the sound of songs heard there from the tongues of
    bards;
the ardour of its men at the glorious contest;
the beauty of its women at the stately gathering.

10

Drinking of mead there in every homestead;
its noble steeds, many tribes;
the jingle of chains unto kings of men
under blades of five-pronged bloody spears.

11

The sweet strains heard there at every hour;
its wine-barque upon the purple surge;
its shower of silver of great splendour;
its torques of gold from the lands of the Gaul.

14

Worship of auguries is not worth listening to,
nor of omens and charms that death may distort;
all is vain when it is probed,
since Alenn is a deserted doon.

15

Bright is the smile that smiles on you
from the plains of Corc's land;
of each generation which it reared in turn
Liffey of Lorc has made ashes.

17

Catháir the Great—he was the choicest of shapes
ruled Erin of many aspects:
though you cry upon him at his rath,
his prowess of many weapons has vanished.

20

The spoils of Feradach—a goodly diadem—
around whom crested bands would move;
his blue-speckled helmet, his shining mantle,—
many a king he overthrew.

25

Oh Brigit whose land I behold,
on which each one in turn has moved about,
thy fame has outshone the fame
of the king—thou art over them all.

To the whole theme compare from the *Father's Lament* (*Beowulf* 2444 ff.): 'Sorrowful he sees in his son's dwelling/the deserted wine hall, the wind-swept resting place/bereft of joy,—the riders sleep,/the warriors in their graves; there is no music of the harp,/mirth in the dwelling, as there was of yore.'; and the sequel (2460 ff.): 'He goes then to his sleeping-place, sings a song of sorrow,/the lone one for the lost one . . ./Then with that sorrow in his heart, which befell him all too sorely,/he forsook human joy, chose God's light;/left to his sons, as does a blessed man,/land and towns, when he departed from life'.

Parallel passages in *Wanderer* and *Seafarer* have been alluded to above. Cp. also the epilogue plaint in *Elene*. The description of former regal splendour in *Hail Brigit*, stanzas 7–11, 20, recalls those of the *Lament of the Last Survivor* and *Ruin* 21 ff., where the homiletic intent is absent:

Beowulf 2247 'Now, earth, do thou hold, now that heroes might not, the wealth of noblemen . . . Death in war,/a fearful slaughter, took off each of the men/of my people who gave up this life;/they had seen joy in the hall . . . the polishers sleep/who should prepare the war-helmet; and the coat of mail, likewise, which in battle endured/the stroke of swords mid the crashing of shields,/follows the warrior to decay . . . There is no joy of the harp,/delight of the glee-beam, nor does the good hawk/sweep through the hall, nor the swift steed/stamp in the court. Baleful death has caused/to pass many generations of men'.

Ruin 21 ff. 'There were bright buildings . . . a great martial noise,/many a banqueting-hall full of revelry/—until Fate the mighty changed everything./Men fell dead all round . . . /Death destroyed all the valiant ones./ Their bastions became deserted,/the city decayed . . . /Therefore these courts are desolate . . . where once many a warrior,/joyous and bright with gold, splendidly arrayed,/proud and flushed with wine, shone in his armour,/looked upon treasure, upon silver, upon precious stones,/upon wealth, upon possessions, upon jewellery,/and upon this bright city with its wide dominion. . . .'

The Prologue of Oengus's Martyrology shows a further progression in the homiletic use of the ruin theme,—but a diminution in poetic quality. The Irish onomastic references in 165–216 and elsewhere belong to the general mode of associating name with place, especially place of residence or burial, and homiletic generalizations of the prevailing type are found here too. The following selection of stanzas may serve to show how the section in question fits into its environment:

61–64

(The great kings of the pagans wail ever in burning:
the hosts of Jesus without a fall, they are joyous after triumph.

65–68

The sinners with the abundance of their cruelty, by whom they
have been slain,
their splendour has perished, their strongholds are desolate.

81–84

They are grand before multitudes, Christ's kingfolk after their
wounds:
the kings of the world, after (having had their) desires, have quite
passed away.

113–116

Nero, not known is his grave: 'tis just, he was not godly:
the world with a multitude of people magnifies Peter's little tomb.

125–128

Though proud was Pilate's queen of her dwelling of down,
her splendour has vanished since she went into a place of mould.

145–148

The might of the world is a lie to every one whose abode it is.
This is all the might: great love for Mary's Son.

157–160

The wretched world wherein we are, transitory is its kingdom:
the King that ruleth angels is lord of every land.)

165–168

Tara's mighty burgh perished at the death of her princes:
with a multitude of venerable champions the great Ard Machae
(Armagh) abides.

173–176

The Faith has grown; it will abide till Doomsday:
guilty pagans who are carried off, their raths are not dwelt in.

185–188

Ye have nothing that is dearer than the love of God, if ye can
achieve it,
adoration of the Cloudy King: 'tis thence ye will not be mournful.

189–192 (similarly 193–200)

Aillen's proud burgh has perished with its warlike host:
great is victorious Brigit; fair is her multitudinous city.

205–208

The old cities of the pagans, wherein ownership has been acquired
by long use,
they are waste without worship, like Lugaid's House-site.

209–212

The cells that have been taken by pairs and by trios,
they are monasteries with assemblies, with hundreds, with
thousands.

213–216

Heathendom has been destroyed, though fair it was and widespread:
the kingdom of God the Father has filled heaven, earth and sea.

221–224

(Donnchad the wrathful, the ruddy, the choice, or victorious Bran
of the Barrow,
visiting their tombs takes not from me the anguish of weakness.

233–236
The famous kings have been stifled, the Domnalls have been
  plagued:
The Ciaráns have been crowned, the Cronáns have been mag-
  nified.

245–248
Though haughty are earthly kings in robes that are brightest,
they will perish after abundance, each goes before another.

249–252
The fair King with piety, Jesus over a wave of flood
—He was happily born of Mary—abides after them all.)

The later Metrical Dindshenchas ('lore of famous places', ed. E. Gwynn)
commemorates famous localities and the traditional figures associated with
them. Cf. Heldensage, 36 ff.; also the poem on the death-places and graves
of the heroes, RC 23, 304, discussed Heldensage 20 f.; to which compare
T. F. O'Rahilly, Early Irish History & Mythology, p. 213, f.n.2, D. A.
Binchy, Ériu 16 (1952), p. 33, and G. Murphy, ibid., 151 ff.

ADDENDA

1. Many important facets of the present study are illuminated by *biblical precedent*. God's counsel to Abraham, which appears in Ch. 1 above as the text for Irish *peregrinatio*, is but one example in *Genesis* and *Exodus* of the theme of wandering and sojourning divinely motivated (cf. *Gen.* 4; 21; 31; 46; *Ex.* 3. 7; 3. 18; 18). The Book of Daniel, exile from Judah, provides a most significant precedent to the story of Suibhne Geilt (Ch. XI above) in the vicissitude of Nebuchadnezzar:[1] 'He was driven from among men, and ate grass like an ox, and his body was wet with the dew of heaven till his hair grew as long as eagles' feathers, and his nails were like birds' claws' (*Dan.* 4. 33). In his vision Nebuchadnezzar was symbolized by a gigantic tree hewn down, and his distortion continued through 'seven times' till he had learned that the Most High rules the kingdom of men . . . *Dan.* 4. 34 runs: 'At the end of the days I, Nebuchadnezzar, lifted my eyes to heaven, and my reason returned to me, and I blessed the Most High . . . and for the glory of my kingdom, my majesty and splendour returned to me . . . and I was established in my kingdom . . .' So after seven years the wandering tree-dweller Suibhne was taken to his kingdom, and 'his sense and memory came to him, likewise his own shape and guise. They took his bonds off him, and his kingship was likened to him'. Later, he relapsed.

For the emphasis on *wisdom* and the *wise man* in O E and Icelandic literature, discussed above (Chs. 5, 8) cf. *Gen.* 41. 39; *Obad.* 8; *Jer.* 49. 7; 18. 18; *Prov.* 1. 1–6; 22. 17; 24. 23; *Job* 12. 12; 1 *Kings* 4. 29–34; *Eccles.* 1. 12–17. *Prov.* 1 has the form of a father speaking to his son, which reappears in 22–23. *Eccles.* contains gnomic criteria familiar to us from Ch. V above: 3 lists the times *fitting* for various activities, 7 things *better* (*good*). The *Riming Poem* has been referred to *Job* 29–30; it might also be referred to *Eccles.* 2 which concentrates on the vanity of human endeavour. For the influence of the penitential Psalms cf. Ch. 9.

Among *formal* features discussed in this work and found in the Old Testament may be mentioned: (*a*) The interchange of first and third persons in the lyrics (Ch. VIII B): cp. the words of Nebuchadnezzar in the first person above (*Dan.* 4. 34); cp. also *Eccles.* 1. 2 to 1. 12 (1. 16, 2. 1); (*b*) Parallelism (Chs. V, XII) is illustrated in the Psalms, and in the songs and prose of *Gen.* (e.g. 27. 39–40, 43–45); (*c*) Doxology (Ch. V) as at the end of Books 1–4 of the Psalms; (*d*) The beginning-end nexus (Appendix II c) as in *Psalms* 8, 103–106, 113, 117, 135–6, 146–150 (Masoretic), *Ex.* 6. 6–8.

[1] The voice from Heaven heralding Nebuchadnezzar's fall and distortion is a precedent for the case of the *geilt* in Ireland and Wales (p. 202 above). Note that this whole biblical parallel reinforces the etymology of *geilt* proposed in Ch. XI.

2. To Appendix II: A piquant example of Celtic-English innovation is independent *Oðþæt* lit. 'until that' (capitalized and introducing new fitts in *Beowulf* 1740, 2039, *Genesis* 1248; capitalized also in *Gen.* 715, 2750): independent O.Ir. *Co^n* (<*co* 'to, till' + *sa^n*, acc.sg.n. of the article; hence exactly parallel in formation to *oðþæt*; subordinating *co^n* has the meanings 'until', 'so that' in common with subordinating *oðþæt*, but also the further meaning 'and'): independent Early W. *(H)yny* (<O.W. *hit ni*, recorded as subordinating conjunction in O.W., cf. ZCP 8, 408); *hit* (*hyd*) 'length of time', *ni* (*ny*) 'not'; *(h)yny* lit. 'while not' > 'until'.

Two O.Ir. verbs, *ro·cluinethar* 'hears' and *ad·cí* 'sees' mark the narrative preterite by prefixing the (independent) conjunction *co^n*, as in *Co·cúalae* 'he heard', *Co·n-accae* 'he saw' (Thurn. Gr. § 536). For early exx of subordinating *co^n* cf. the archaic text *Baile Chuind*, assigned by G. Murphy to the seventh century (*Ériu* 16 (1952), p. 145 ff.). Independent *Co^n* occurs in the very early incomplete version of *Im. Brain* in MS H 4.22 (1363), cf. ZCP 18, p. 410, § 2; also in *Im. Brain* § 62. It is well established by the eighth century: cf. *Aisl. Óeng.* § 1 for three instances of *Co n-accae*, also *TBF* 208, 377. In these two texts the negative corresponding to *Co^n*: *Nicon* (*ni* + *co^n*) is also found. This has yielded the common Mod. Sc.G. negative *cha*. For exx of Early W. independent *(H)yny* cf. D. Simon Evans, A Gr. of Middle Welsh, Dublin, 1964, p. 245.

The usage, a full discussion of which we must hold over, develops in each language via the subordinating connective and bears witness to the spread of the subordinating motif in these languages. Hence Klaeber, ed.[3] of *Beowulf*, Introd., pp. lvii, ci, is on the right track for O E *Oðþæt*; otherwise von Schubert, Kommentar to ed.[16], p. 16, who follows E. Glogauer (Neue Anglistische Arbeiten 6, § 20: *Oðþæt* an adv. = *þá* 'then'). O E *Oðþæt*, Ir. *Co^n*, W. *(H)yny* are pointers to dynamic moments (developments) in narrative which they serve to underline rhetorically—with such minor distinctions of meaning, emphasis or nuance as will appear. To call, e.g. independent *Co^n* 'meaningless' is to refer to the lexicon what chiefly concerns syntax and style.

3. Sources of *Dream of the Rood*: Chapter IX of the *Gospel of Peter* which describes the Resurrection and tells of the Cross speaking seems to have been overlooked in this connection. The Cross has an independence and individuality of its own: (IX. 39–42) '. . . they (the soldiers) saw again three men come out of the sepulchre, and two of them sustaining the other (*lit.* the one), and a cross following after them. And of the two *they saw* that their heads reached unto heaven, but of him that was led by them that it overpassed the heavens. And they heard a voice out of the heavens saying: Hast thou (*or* Thou hast) preached unto them that sleep? And an answer was heard from the Cross, *saying*: Yea.' (M. R. James, *The Apocryphal New Testament*, Oxford 1963, pp. 92–3). The reference to preaching to the sleepers is significant for *Dream of the Rood*.

236

ADDENDA

4. A crux: *Ruin* 30–31a   *ond þæs teaforgeapa tigelum sceadeð*

                          hrostbeages [h]rof.

Translate: 'and this red curved roof parts from the tiles of its circular wooden framework'. *Teaforgeapa*, as Leslie, op. cit. 73–4, has suggested, is an adj. qualifying *[h]rof.* For an analogous construction cf. Riddle 14, ll. 8–9 *hwilum mægða sum minne gefylleð/bosm beaghroden* 'sometimes a woman, ring-adorned, fills my bosom'.

5. Pp. 55 ff.: *Uga Corbmaic:* Mr. E. G. Quin has kindly communicated some comments on the printed version. He suggests that MS *roghso* of 1a might perhaps be *metri gratia* for *raghsa*. *Mo brogad* in 1c would then be a cognate acc.: 'Shall I go . . . my journey' or the like; cf. Contribb. sub *téit* II; for *rogaid* 'chooses' cf. LL 216 b 33. In 3a he tentatively suggests reading *mesctar druing* (by which bands are intoxicated' (emendation), and, attractively, in 3b *cin teglach torm* 'without din of households'. 13c *Él* is still a crux; the contraction has a mark of length (hence hardly *do leith tempuil*). In 20c perhaps 'who betrayed herself'? 21c *naill*, dat. sg., is curious. In 24c perhaps read *o tuarcaib for doman dreich* 'since he appeared in the world'?; cp. Contribb. sub *drech*, (a). 25c, perhaps 'after the hour of (mid)night'? 28c, perhaps *leg. nimfargba* 'for the sake of your passion . . . when I join . . . do not leave me . . .'?; cf. EIL, No. 15, st. 3d.

6. P. 67, *Kintevin*, l. 7: *muc* (*mwg*). This word is the etymological equivalent of the rare Ir. *múch* 'smoke', beside the more common *múich* (*muich, muích*) 'gloom, dejection, sadness'. Of the latter an excellent 'Columban' example in a parallel context occurs on p. 32 above. As the meaning 'smoke' here is really out of place and as we already have the context marked by two terms signifying 'grief' (*llauuridet* and *anhunet*) we infer that *muc* completes the triad in the meaning 'dejection'. Support for this is also found in the abstract meanings of the word in Cornish and Breton, cf. Corn. *mōk* 'smoke . . .; stifling', Middle Bret. *moug* 'suffocation, extinction . . .'; further, Ped. Gr. I 122.

7. P. 85, l. 36 of Welsh poem: for MS *a lluidet* we read and render *alluidet*.

INDEX

INDEX